The
NeXT
Book

The
NeXT
Book

Bruce F. Webster

Addison-Wesley Publishing Company, Inc.
Reading, Massachusetts • Menlo Park, California • New York
Don Mills, Ontario • Wokingham, England • Amsterdam • Bonn
Sydney • Singapore • Tokyo • Madrid • San Juan

Many of the designations used by manufacturers and sellers to distinguish their products are claimed as trademarks. Where those designations appear in this book and Addison-Wesley was aware of a trademark claim, the designations have been printed in initial capital letters (e.g., MegaPixel Display).

Library of Congress Cataloging-in-Publication Data

Webster, Bruce F.
    The NeXT Book

    Includes index.
    1. NeXT (Computer) I. Title
QA76.8.N49W43 1989   004.165   89-6833
ISBN 0-201-15851-X

Sponsoring editor: Carole McClendon
Cover design by Copenhaver Cumpston
Text design by Leslie Bartlett
Set in 10-point Trump Mediæval by Leslie Bartlett

ABCDEFGHIJ-KR-89
First printing, July 1989

To Mom and Dad,
who always believed in me

CONTENTS

ACKNOWLEDGMENTS

Long lists of acknowledgments have become a cliché, but only when you've written a book do you realize how many people (besides the author) help to make that book a reality. At Addison-Wesley, I need to thank Steve Stansel, who contacted me initially about the book and was very supportive during the long wait for a machine; Rachel Guichard, ever cheerful, who handled a lot of the procedural details; Abby Genuth, who set up marketing and promotion; Perry McIntosh, who worked under some tremendous time pressures to turn what I gave her into a finished book; Joanne Clapp, who oversaw the revisions made for Release 0.9; and most of all, Carole McClendon, who performed just about every editorial task on this book except for actually writing the prose—and even there, she gave me excellent direction and feedback. Without her, this book just wouldn't exist.

There are lots of people to thank at NeXT, including: Bruce Blumburg, who suggested my name when the idea for this book first came up, answered lots of technical questions, and taught me most of what I know about programming on the NeXT; Jeff Bork (now at Informix), who patiently fielded my repeated and continuous requests for a machine, and who, with Dan'l Lewin and John Ison, provided internal support at NeXT for the book's concept; Bob Fraik, who actually handed over my first NeXT system and gave me technical support over the phone; Ali Ozer, Phil Heller, John "Baker" Corey, and Allan Markham, who (along with Bruce Blumburg) did a great job at the NeXT Developers Conference; Lovette Coleman, Janet Coursey, Alex Fitz, Eddie Lee, Patty Leeper, Phyllis Quinn, Cheri Murray, Susan Kare and Joe Hutsko, who all made me feel welcome; John Anderson, Bill Tschumy, Keith Ohlfs and Trey Matteson, who wrote the software (WriteNow, Scene, Preview) used to create this book; and the rest of the people at NeXT who made their product, and therefore this book, a reality, including—but definitely not limited to—Rich Page, Bud Tribble, Leo Hourvitz, Jean-Marie Hullot, Bill Parkhurst, Mike Demoney, Julius Smith, Avie Tevanian, Lee Boynton, Brian Yamomoto, Caroline Rose, Richard Crandall, and, of course, Steve Jobs.

Finally, I want to thank my wife, Sandra, who not only proofread and gave me valuable feedback on all the chapters, but who rode the roller coaster with me and saw this through to the end.

PREFACE
TAKING THE NEXT STEP

Puns and wordplay surround NeXT, Incorporated, and the products they've created. They come not only from within the company but also, because of the large amount of editorial coverage, from writers such as myself always looking for clever phrases. So the title above may look like yet another attempt at cuteness; as such, it would probably deserve hearty reprobation.

It's not cleverness, though, but rather a commemoration of a man I never met: the late Dr. Thomas McGetchin, a planetary scientist and one-time director of the Lunar and Planetary Institute in Houston, Texas. In a journal he kept while dying of cancer, McGetchin talked about what he felt was important in living. To him, the challenge in life was taking the next step—moving into new territory, pushing out—though, he noted, it's always hard to do so. It's always easier to stay with what's comfortable, what's familiar, what works for us now.

His words come to mind because I think that the people at NeXT are attempting to do just that: to take the next step—or, at least, *a* next step—in the development of personal computers. While much of their technology is an adaptation of or improvement on what's found elsewhere, it has been brought together in some honestly new ways. Ideas that have been bandied about in the industry for years have come to rest in a small black cube. And those elements criticized the most are those that most represent a departure from established norms.

In short, the NeXT computer system, taken as a whole, is not just a stepwise refinement of currently available personal computers and workstations. In a market where another company can put a somewhat faster processor into an existing computer and call it a major new product, NeXT's accomplishments have real significance. True, NeXT may never seriously threaten the pocketbooks of established, successful companies such as Apple, Digital Equipment Corporation (DEC), Hewlett-Packard, Sun, and Apollo. But there are a lot of bruised egos: NeXT is perceived to have captured the lead in innovation, and these other firms find themselves running to catch up.

The chance to see some of that innovation up close is what led me to accept the offer to write this book. I first saw a prototype of the NeXT system in March 1988, at which time I learned the basic details about the hardware and software configuration. I wanted to start the book then, but many changes were going on, and features were being added or discarded, especially in the software. I decided not to do much work on the book until I could actually sit down and work for an extended period on a released system. Neither I nor Addison-Wesley anticipated how long that would actually take, and there were a few nerve-wracking months in mid- to late 1988 during which we wondered if and when the book would get written.

Patience, however, was finally rewarded by a phone call in mid-December from Jeff Bork, my liaison at NeXT, who said he had a system for me. A few days later, on December 14, 1988, I drove over to the NeXT offices in Palo Alto. Bob Fraik sat down with me, gave me a brief overview of how to boot up and power down the system, and sent me off with two large boxes, one with the cube, the other with the display. (I came back and picked up a laser printer the following week.) I don't know if I was the first private individual to bring a functioning NeXT system home, but I doubt there were more than a few.

The first draft of this book was written entirely on that same NeXT system (serial number AAK00000200), using a beta version of WriteNow running under Release 0.8 of the NeXT system software. As chapters were finished, they were turned over to Carole Alden at Addison-Wesley for review; I would then make appropriate changes. After a few iterations, polished drafts were printed on the NeXT Laser Printer and sent to the production department at Addison-Wesley for typesetting and layout. All the chapters were also transferred over to a Macintosh and converted into Microsoft Word format so that the manuscript wouldn't have to be keyed in. With the book nearly finished, Carole and I made the decision to hold off long enough to incorporate all the changes found in the Release 0.9 software; for the sake of time, most revisions were done on hard copy or in Microsoft Word format. Time constraints, as well as the unfinished nature of NeXT system and application software, prevented us from producing camera-ready copy directly on the NeXT—but we plan to use the NeXT system to create future books.

The purpose of this book, then, is not to hype a given product or a particular company. It is to explain the technology and concepts that have been brought together to form the NeXT computer. The wide spectrum of NeXT users—ranging from hardcore UNIX hackers to corporate executives to computer novices with humanities backgrounds—has made it a challenge to present information detailed enough for the former and basic enough for the latter. When in doubt, I've aimed more toward the computer novice; after all, NeXT is publishing technical manuals, and it would be foolish to attempt to reproduce more than a fraction of that information here.

All information in this book is based on Release 0.9 of the NeXT computer system and software. By the time you read this, Release 1.0 should be out, with some new features and a number of improvements. A number of people at NeXT have been kind enough to check this manuscript for technical accuracy; all errors remain my responsibility.

While it's taken far longer than I thought it would, writing this book has been fun. I hope you enjoy reading it as much as I did writing it.

Bruce F. Webster
Soquel, California

May 1989

INTRODUCTION
A GUIDE TO THE NeXT SYSTEM

The book you hold was written for anyone interested in learning more about the NeXT computer. It assumes a minimum of "computer literacy;" most terms used are defined in place, as well as in the glossary at the back of the book. There are a few parts, such as Chapter 5, that will be of interest mostly to someone with a technical background, but those are the exceptions, rather than the rule. The goal of this book is to help you feel able to discuss the NeXT system and its components intelligently, as well as to instruct you on how to use the NeXT system, if you have access to one.

The book is divided into three major sections. Part I, The Hardware, covers the actual physical computer equipment that makes up a NeXT computer system. The section starts with the cube itself, then goes on to discuss the motherboard, where all the computing actually takes place. The MegaPixel Display is discussed in some detail, along with the keyboard and mouse, and information about the NeXT system's sound capabilities is given. The NeXT Laser Printer is then covered. The last chapter in that section presents detailed information, about pinouts and signal definitions for all the connectors found in the back of the NeXT system.

Part II, The Software, discusses the computer programs that make the NeXT system work. First, you'll learn about the numerous applications bundled with the NeXT system, such as WriteNow, Mathematica, Digital Librarian, and the NeXT SQL Database Server. After that is an explanation of the NeXT user interface. This includes coverage of NextStep, which consists of Workspace Manager, Interface Builder, the Application Kit, and Window Server; Display PostScript, which performs all drawing on the screen and to the printer, is also covered. Finally, Mach, the UNIX-compatible operating system used on the NeXT system, is discussed.

Part III, Using the System, is a hands-on guide to using the NeXT system. First, you'll be introduced to the user interface, Workspace Manager, and taught how to use its various features. Next, you'll get instructions on how to use some of the bundled applications to accomplish actual tasks, such as creating and printing a document. After that comes an introduction to the UNIX shell, the command-line interface that lets you directly interact with the Mach operating system. Finally, you'll get step-by-step instructions on creating a simple program using Interface Builder and Objective C.

At the end of the book are a few appendices, the glossary, and the index. Appendix A discusses some of the third-party hardware and software products that were under development (or, in a few cases, shipping) when this book went to press. Appendix B explains how to perform certain system tasks under Release 0.9.

Each part starts with the upper, visible layers of the system and then gets into more and more detail as you go through it. You can read to the level of detail at which you feel comfortable, then leave the more complex material until you are ready. The chapters themselves present the information with occasional editorializing; the opinions expressed, of course, are the responsibility of the author and no one else.

The
NeXT
Book

The NeXT Hardware Architecture

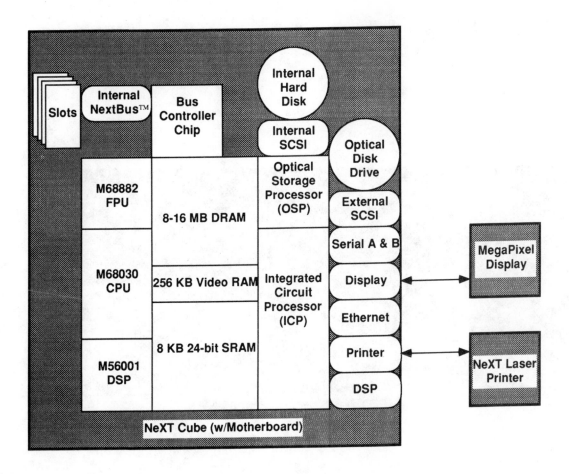

Part I
The Hardware

We've all heard how the progress of technology over the last few decades has shrunk room-size computers down to a size that a single human can use on a desktop. And yet that information seems oddly fresh when looking at the NeXT computer. The NeXT system used to write this book has a 660-megabyte (MB) hard disk, a 256-megabyte optical disk drive, and 16 megabytes of memory—more on-line mass storage and memory crammed in a 1-foot cube than was found on entire university campuses ten to fifteen years ago. In fact, "crammed" isn't even an appropriate word, since all the memory, video hardware, and computer logic fits onto a single board occupying one of four available slots in the cube.

The NeXT system consists of three major components: the NeXT computer, (the cube), the MegaPixel Display, and the NeXT Laser Printer. The computer, consisting of the cube itself and the motherboard inside, does all the work, stores all the data, generates all the output. The display interacts with the user, accepting input from keyboard, mouse, and microphone, and talking back with images and sound. The printer produces tangible results, writing documents with light and ink. Information flows back and forth between the three components, transformed between various formats. The aim: to let you accomplish your goals faster, easier, better.

1
The Cube

The main computer unit is a black cube, a design that was one of Steve Jobs's earliest concepts. The NeXT logo, created by Paul Rand, reflects that concept, and the computer, designed by Hartmut Esslinger at Frog Design, embodies it. In an industry where most computers look like variations on a single theme, the visual impact of NeXT is dramatic.

Five of the cube's six sides are a single piece of cast magnesium; the back side is also magnesium and attaches to the rest via four Torx screws. The resulting enclosure is light, durable, and resistant to the radio frequency (RF) leakage that plagues manufacturers of high-speed micros and workstations.

The cube is only 12 inches along each edge, with four small rubber feet adding 1/2 inch to its height. It's meant to be unobtrusive, sitting under a table, beside a desk, or on a bookshelf. Some clearance is required in the back, where the various connectors are, as well as in the front, where the slot for the optical disk drive is.

The NeXT system continues the trend of the last decade away from switches and lights on computers. There are no switches or knobs anywhere on the system—power, brightness, volume, and system reset are all controlled from the keyboard—and no lights, anywhere.

The outside of the cube is covered with a black, water-based paint. This paint can be scratched, so avoid scraping or gouging the surface with any sharp points or edges. To clean the cube, use a water-based soap cleaner (such as Formula 409); cleaners with ammonia, alcohol, or abrasives can soften or peel the paint. This holds true for the rest of the NeXT system—display, keyboard, mouse and printer.

Looking at the front of the cube in Figure 1.1, you can see where the mass storage devices—hard disk and optical disk drives—are located. The cube has room for two such 5.25-inch drives. Note that there are slots for removable media, such as the read/write optical disks. The small holes above the right end of each slot are for emergency removal of optical disks.

Figure 1.1. The front of the NeXT cube

The power socket is in the back of the cube, as you can see in Figure 1.2. You can also see the openings for the four slots located within the NeXT cube. The **motherboard**—an 11-by-11-inch circuit board that contains all the computer's logic and memory—fits into one of the slots, leaving the other three empty.

CONNECTORS

The computer communicates with all outside devices, including the MegaPixel Display and the laser printer, through a series of connectors. These connectors are part of the motherboard

Figure 1.2. The back of the NeXT cube

and stick out of the back of the cube. You can see them in Figure 1.2, going from the top to the bottom of one of the slots. Here's a description of each one, organized by how the ports are actually labeled. Exact pinouts and signals for each connector are given in Chapter 5, Internals and Externals.

DISPLAY

While the computer can do lots of work, it needs some way to communicate with you, the user. So one of the most important connectors is the video monitor interface, which connects the computer with the MegaPixel Display using a 3-meter (9.8-foot) video cable. The actual display information is generated within the cube, on the motherboard, and then sent to the display through this cable, much as a VCR sends picture information to a TV set. Sound information, in digitized form, is also sent to the display through this port. And, in a departure from most computer systems, the power that the display needs comes through this port, from the cube's power supply; the display itself doesn't have a power cord or outlet.

Information comes into this port as well. Anytime you press a key, click a button, or move the mouse, you send data from the display to the computer over the same cable. This includes a special signal to detect when you press the Power key on the keyboard. Likewise, when you use the microphone port in the back of the display, any sound coming in is digitized—converted from an analog (electrical level) signal to digital form (bits and bytes)—and sent to the computer.

E-NET

Computers—and humans—work best when they can share information with one another. Recognizing this, NeXT has built into its computer all the hardware and software necessary to run on Ethernet. Ethernet is a widely-used, high-speed networking system that allows computers and users to share data and access one another's files. If you want to hook your system up to an Ethernet network, you just attach the network cable to the E-Net port and then ask the systems administrator to do whatever system configuration is required.

PRINTER

Since the most common use of computers is for word processing, desktop publishing, and document layout, the ability to produce high-quality output is important, if not critical. The standard (and, at this writing, only) printer that NeXT offers with their system is the NeXT Laser Printer, capable of 400-dot-per-inch resolution. The laser printer port connects the computer with the printer, using a 3-meter (9.8-foot) cable. Much as it does with the display, the computer generates the image to be printed, then sends it at a high rate of speed to the printer through this port. It also tells the printer—which has its own power cord but no power switch—to turn itself on when you power up the computer. The printer, in turn, sends status information back through the cable and port, telling the computer when it's out of paper, when there's a paper jam, and so on.

SCSI

The computer industry has been moving toward a series of hardware standards to make it easier for manufacturers to design equipment for different machines. One such standard is the Small Computer Standard Interface (SCSI, pronounced "scuzzy"). This defines a set of signals and protocols to allow computers to "talk" to devices such as hard disks, digitizers, and scanners. If your computer has a SCSI port on it, you can hook up any hard disk, etc., that uses a SCSI connector. With this approach, you can "daisy chain" up to seven such devices, connecting them all to your computer through one SCSI port.

The external SCSI port on the NeXT computer provides that interface for you. The connector and pin assignments are identical to the SCSI ports found on Apple Macintosh Plus, Macintosh SE, and Macintosh II computers, so that you can use the same cables as you would with a Macintosh. However, special software modules (known as **device drivers**) are required for the NeXT computer to recognize and communicate with any SCSI device you might use; be sure those are present before connecting the SCSI device to your computer.

SERIAL A AND SERIAL B

The simplest and most common way for computers to communicate with other devices (modems, printers, terminals, and other computers) is through a serial port, so called because information is sent and received in serial fashion, one bit at a time. The NeXT computer offers two such ports, serial A and serial B. Both are based on the RS-422 standard and are capable of transferring data at a rate of over 50 kilobaud (5,000 bytes per second).

Both ports use a DIN-8 round connector, the same as is used on the Apple Macintosh Plus, Macintosh SE, and Macintosh II connectors. The actual pinouts on serial port A are identical to the pinouts used on a Macintosh, so you can use the same cables. Serial port B differs slightly, changing the signal on one pin from a handshaking line to a +5 V power source. This allows you to connect devices that need to take their power from the computer, but it requires cables specific to NeXT.

DSP

Every NeXT computer has built into it a special chip, a **digital signal processor**, or DSP. This chip, a Motorola DSP56001, can produce synthesized sounds and music, perform array processing, and (as the name implies) process information as it comes in. Because of its versatility, it has its own private serial connector, the digital signal processor port.

Through this port, the DSP can communicate with an external serial device, such as facsimile (fax) or high-speed modem hardware, or equipment for sampling sounds and digitizing them (that is, converting them to binary values that can be stored in memory or on the disk).

INSIDE THE CUBE

Up until now, you've seen the cube only from the outside. Figure 1.3 shows you how it looks on the inside. There are four basic elements inside the cube: the power supply, the fan, the slots, and the mass storage devices. The first three will be covered briefly, after which you'll learn about mass storage in detail.

FIGURE 1.3. Inside the NeXT cube

THE POWER SUPPLY

The 300-watt power supply sits at the bottom of the cube, going from back to front. This device can adapt to a wide range of voltages (90 to 270 volts AC) and frequencies (47 to 63 HZ, single phase). When you plug the NeXT system into a power outlet, the power supply takes whatever power levels it gets and conditions them to the correct internal levels. It provides 25 watts to each of the four internal slots, with the balance of the power going to mass storage devices (such as the optical disk and any hard disk drives) and the MegaPixel Display. The flexibility of the power supply allows you to use the NeXT system in most industrialized countries without special adapters or transformers.

THE FAN

The fan is located in the back, above the power supply. Its job is to keep the interior from getting too hot; integrated circuits can put out a surprising amount of heat. It blows the air straight out the back, so you shouldn't have the cube pushed back flush against some surface; the cables in the back will probably keep you from doing that anyway. Likewise, the intake vent for the fan is located on the bottom of the cube, so you should not set the cube directly on thick carpet or other plush materials that might block that vent. Instead, put something flat and sturdy underneath, such as a thin sheet of wood, metal, or plastic, or a large book. Naturally, if the cube is already sitting on a hard, flat surface (tile floor, desk, table), you don't need to worry about this.

THE SLOTS

Four slots are provided, with Euro-DIN 96 connectors for each. One slot is used by the NeXT motherboard, but the other three are available for adding hardware devices, such as color graphics systems and extra processor boards. These slots communicate with each other via a **bus** (set of signal wires) that allows for the interchange of data and instructions. This bus, called NextBus, is based on the NuBus architecture developed by Texas Instruments, but has some significant differences. First, it runs at a faster clock rate—25 MHz (megahertz), that is 25 million cycles per second, instead of the standard 10 MHz—which speeds up any communications between cards. Second, it uses CMOS instead of bipolar logic. For hardware companies and developers interested in designing their own cards, NeXT is offering a single chip that will handle all interfacing with the bus. Bus pinouts and signals are given in Chapter 5.

MASS STORAGE DEVICES

Most computers—with the exception of certain diskless workstations—have some form of mass storage, that is, a place to store applications, documents, pictures, and other files when not in use or while the computer is turned off. With personal computers, that storage is most often in the form of floppy disks and hard disks. Floppy disks are removable and typically hold from 360 kilobytes to 1.4 megabytes per diskette, depending upon the disk drive in the computer and the diskette itself. Hard drives are usually nonremovable (and so are sometimes called "fixed drives") and typically hold from 20 to 300 megabytes, with 40- and 80-megabyte sizes being most popular right now in personal computers. Hard disk drives are typically much faster at reading and writing information than floppy disk drives, while floppy drives have the advantage of "unlimited" storage; if one diskette fills up, you can pull it out and start using another.

Both floppy and hard disk drives come in two sizes: 3.5-inch and 5.25-inch. The 3.5-inch floppies, pioneered by the Macintosh and used in the IBM PS/2, Atari ST, and Commodore Amiga computers, have become popular because they are encased in rigid plastic and are better protected from dust and other materials. The 3.5-inch hard drives are favored for their small size, while the 5.25-inch hard drives generally have a larger capacity.

Both floppy and hard drives use standard magnetic recording technology: a read/write head moving very close to a rapidly spinning disk of magnetic material. This renders the disks vulnerable in several ways. First, the heads are so close to the disk itself, especially on a hard drive, that particulate matter such as dust and smoke can actually get caught between the two and cause physical damage to the disk. Second, a sudden shock or blow to the computer while operating can cause a "head crash," bringing the head in physical contact with the disk and again causing damage and/or loss of data. Third, floppy disks can have their data modified or damaged by magnetic fields, such as those generated by telephones, memo-holding magnets (often found on refrigerators or filing cabinets), and electric motors.

THE OPTICAL DISK DRIVE

The basic mass storage device in the NeXT computer is an optical disk—not really a floppy, and not really a hard disk, but combining the features of both while using a different technology for reading and writing information. Figure 1.4 shows an optical disk, which looks like a compact disc inside a plastic case. Like a floppy drive, it's removable; like a hard disk, it holds a lot of information.

Unlike either, the NeXT optical disk drive uses magneto-optical technology—a combination of lasers and magnetic heads—to read and write information. Here's how it works: the writing area on the disk itself consists of a rare-earth transition-metal alloy, sandwiched between a covering of transparent plastic and aluminum. Figure 1.5 shows a diagram of the optical disk surface. When the drive wants to write information to the disk, it shines a tiny laser beam on the spot in question, heating the alloy to a certain temperature, known as its "Curie point." At this point, the crystals in the alloy at that spot can be aligned in one of two directions (corresponding to bit values of 0 or 1) by applying a magnetic field. When the laser ceases to shine on that spot, the crystal cools, and the alignment is fixed.

To read information, the drive again shines the laser on the disk, but at a lower power level and with the magnetic field turned off. The light goes through the crystals, reflects off the aluminum, and shines back onto a tiny sensor. This sensor can

Figure 1.4. An optical disk, capable of holding 256 megabytes

tell from the changes in the light beam which way the crystals are aligned, thus determining whether the corresponding bit is a 0 or a 1. The lower temperature and the lack of a magnetic field prevent accidental writing to the disk.

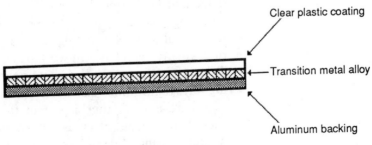

Figure 1.5. The layers in an optical disk

While this process may sound somewhat awkward or clumsy, the reverse is actually true. The beam can be fixed with such precision that the drive can write over 1 billion separate bits (256 megabytes) on one side of a single 5.25-inch disk. Since the actual writing area on the disk is only about 18 square inches, that works out to a density of over 55 million bits (about 7 million bytes) per square inch.

What's more, most of the causes of lost or damaged data don't exist with an optical disk. The disk is not vulnerable to magnetic fields, since the information can only be changed when the crystals are heated to a certain temperature. There are no "flying heads," so head crashes can't happen. And particulate matter can't jam things up because the optical disk is stored in a plastic case similar to those found on 3.5-inch floppy disks; that and the plastic layer on top of the disk itself protect the crystalline layer from dirt, grease, or other materials.

There is a price to pay for the safety and convenience, namely a small reduction in speed. The access time on the optical disk drive—the amount of time it takes the drive to get itself set up to start reading a given block of information—is currently around 90 milliseconds, or just under a 1/10th of a second. By comparison, many hard disk drives have access times ranging from 10 to 50 milliseconds, and even a lot of floppy disks have times well under 70 milliseconds. Slowing the optical drive even more is the need for up to three passes when writing to the disk: one pass to erase the destination section, one to write the information, and one to verify what was written.

Still, the **transfer rate**—the speed at which data can actually be moved between disk and memory—is just over 1 megabyte per second, comparable to or better than most hard disk systems, and far better than most floppy disk drives. Also, the operating system is set up to "pre-erase" available portions of the optical disk, eliminating the first pass in writing information. Finally, NeXT is still working on ways to improve optical disk performance, both by lowering the access time and by finding ways to minimize disk access.

There is one other aspect of the optical disk drive you should know about: it's noisy, about on the level of some of the noisier 5.25-inch floppy disk drives found on MS-DOS systems.

This doesn't affect performance, but there are people who are bothered by such things. It might also be important if the computer itself were located in a room where ambient noise had to be kept to a minimum.

The optical disk drive hooks up to the NeXT motherboard through a custom connector; the actual pinouts and signals are considered proprietary knowledge by NeXT. The drive is controlled by the Optical Storage Processor (OSP), a special chip that will be discussed in more detail in the next chapter.

HARD DISKS

If you want more storage, you have two choices: you can add another optical disk drive, or you can add a hard disk. NeXT currently offers two internal 5.25-inch hard disk drives, one holding 330 megabytes, the other holding 660 megabytes. Either one can be added to a regular NeXT system, giving you either 586 or 916 megabytes of on-line storage (the hard disk plus the 256-megabyte optical drive). These hard disks work just the same as hard disks found on most personal computers, such as IBM PCs and Macintoshes. They use Winchester technology, so called because the first such drive, produced by IBM years ago for mainframe computers, had a model number (3030) coinciding with the famous Winchester 30-30 rifle. These disks hook up to the NeXT motherboard via an internal SCSI connector, much like the internal hard disks found in the Macintosh II; the pinouts and signals for this connector can be found in Chapter 5. Likewise, a standard SCSI controller chip handles communications between the motherboard and the hard drive, as well as with any SCSI devices hooked up to the external SCSI port.

Using a hard disk really can make a difference, in both speed and (for those concerned about such things) in noise. The hard disk/optical disk combination works well, because it allows you to easily store or back up files onto your optical disk, while keeping the operating system files and applications on the hard disk. In much the same way, it makes it easier for a number of people to share a single NeXT system, since each user can keep all of his or her files on a separate optical disk.

As stated above, the optical disk drive has an access time of 90 milliseconds, and a transfer rate of just over 1 MB per second. By contrast, the 330-megabyte hard disk drive has an access time of 14 milliseconds, while the 660-megabyte drive has one of 18 milliseconds. Both have **burst transfer rates**—that is, transfer rates that they can sustain for a brief period of time—of 4.8 megabytes per second, and sustained transfer rates of 1.4 megabytes per second.

COMMENTARY

In a day when most personal computers are large beige or gray boxes, either lying flat or tilted up on one side, the NeXT cube stands out. It may well be the most distinctive computer design since the original Macintosh. Behind the snazzy design lies some thoughtful functionality, though. The heavy-duty power supply and limited number of slots should help NeXT avoid the problems suffered by IBM, Compaq, Apple, and others as users started cramming various cards into the machine. The large form factor of the expansion cards—11 by 11 inches—opens the door for some significant add-on products, including high-end graphics workstations. And the decision to go with 5.25-inch (rather than 3.5-inch) mass storage and SCSI connectors allows NeXT and NeXT owners to tap into the high end of the mass storage market.

The optical disk drive was somewhat controversial when the NeXT system was originally announced. The question of performance was raised, but that's more an issue of perception than anything else. The relatively slow access time does make it hard for the optical disk drive to stack up to the current generation of hard disks. But there are still a few hard disk drives on the market that have equivalent access times and much slower transfer rates.

A more substantive issue is that of software distribution for third-party software firms. Most software companies are oriented toward mass distribution via floppies; they may be put off by the lack of an inexpensive distribution medium. Some solutions have been proposed, such as site licensing and distribution of locked or crippled copies on a single optical disk that NeXT would distribute to every owner, but it's not clear how well those schemes will work. Most likely, the flexible and innovative companies will end up making most of the money.

Even with these issues, NeXT has probably established the optical disk as a viable, acceptable storage medium in the computer industry, and other companies have been quick to announce optional optical drives. Because it bridges the growing gap between high-capacity hard disk drives and low-capacity floppy disk drives, the read/write optical disk drive may well become a common medium for primary, secondary, or backup storage on personal workstations within a few years.

2
The Motherboard

The NeXT computer—the cube itself—looks impressive when you think about how much computing power fits into a cubic foot of space. When you open it up, though, you find that the actual computer logic fits on a single 11-by-11-inch circuit board, holding a total of 45 integrated circuits. And the layout looks clean and elegant, as you can see from the photo on the opposite page.

The motherboard fits into one of the four slots in the cube. It plugs into a Euro-DIN 96 connector that links it with the other three slots and provides power from the power supply as well. The board is manufactured in NeXT's production plant in Fremont, California. The assembly line for the board itself is 100 percent automated, with several key pieces of robotic imaging and assembly equipment designed and built by engineers at NeXT, Inc.

As mentioned in Chapter 1, this board does all the work in the NeXT computer system. Specifically, it handles the following tasks:

- All memory (plugged into the 16 memory slots on the board)

- All computation (via three processors)

- Control of both the hard drive and the optical disk drive

- All video signal generation

- All printer bit-image generation

- All input and output (via the various ports)

Let's look at these various capabilities of the motherboard and how they are implemented.

MEMORY

A computer does its work by following instructions that tell it how to process information: numbers, words, and images. It needs someplace to hold both the information and the instructions while it's working. That "someplace" is called memory. **Memory** is where the computer stores, changes, and manipulates data. It's where computer programs—applications—must be loaded before they can be executed. Let's talk a bit how memory, and information in general, is organized.

HOW INFORMATION IS ORGANIZED

The basic unit of information is a **bit** (short for **b**inary d**igit**). A bit always has one of two values: 0 or 1. That's not a lot of information by itself, but a group of bits can represent a larger range of values. The most common grouping is a **byte,** which is 8 bits long. If you listed all possible bit combinations in a byte, you'd find that they range from 00000000 to 11111111, and that there are 256 (2^8) different combinations in all. These combinations of bits, when interpreted as **binary** (base-2) numbers, correspond to the **decimal** (base-10) numbers 0 to 255, and are usually treated as such. This binary orientation explains why values describing computer hardware tend to be powers of two (2, 4, 8, 16, 32, 64, 128, 256, and so on).

When talking about large numbers of bytes, some common groupings are used. The first is a **kilobyte** (KB). As the name indicates, this is about 1,000 bytes; the exact figure is 1,024 (2^{10}) bytes. The next level is a **megabyte** (MB), or about a million bytes (2^{20} or 1,048,576 bytes). This is the most common unit used on the NeXT system; for example, the optical disk drive holds about 256 megabytes of information. A higher measure, which is becoming more common, is the **gigabyte** (GB). As you might guess, this is just over a billion bytes (2^{30} or 1,073,741,824 bytes); a NeXT system with a 660-megabyte hard disk and a 256-megabyte optical drive has almost a gigabyte of on-line storage. There is a higher grouping, the **terabyte** (TB), which is over a trillion bytes (2^{40} or 1,099,511,627,776 bytes).

TYPES OF MEMORY

Random-access memory (RAM) has a name rooted more in computer history than in present-day technology, coming from a time when computer memory sometimes consisted of a rotating cylinder or a moving wire. As used today, the term RAM refers to computer chips that can store information so long as power is supplied to them. The contents of these chips can be read, updated, and overwritten. However, if the power goes off, the information is lost.

Read-only memory (ROM) consists of memory chips that have instructions and/or data permanently encoded in them. You can't write over or erase the contents, hence the name. Unlike most RAM, ROM doesn't lose its information when you turn off the power. It's often used to hold the instructions a computer executes when you first turn the power on.

Electronically erasable programmable read-only memory (EEPROM) is a special type of ROM that can be modified by the computer. The changes made are then preserved, even when the power is off.

MEMORY ON THE NeXT SYSTEM

The NeXT system requires—and gives you—a lot of memory. The basic system comes with 8 megabytes of main memory. The actual memory consists of eight 1-megabyte **SIMMs** (Surface-mount In-line Memory Modules). Each SIMM is about 4 inches long and 1 inch high, and has eight 1-megabit memory chips on it.

The motherboard actually has slots for up to 16 SIMMs and will accept configurations of 8, 12, and 16 megabytes. According to NeXT, the same sockets should be able to accept SIMMs using 4-megabit chips, allowing you to eventually expand up to 64 megabytes on a single motherboard.

In addition to main memory, the NeXT motherboard has two other sections of memory. First, there's a 256-kilobyte section of video memory, containing the actual bit image that is displayed on the MegaPixel Display. Second, there's 32 kilobytes of fast static RAM used by the Motorola DSP56001, with a small (4KB) section used by the Optical Storage Processor. Both of these sections have a dedicated channel processor for DMA (Direct Memory Access) transfers to and from main memory.

Finally, the NeXT motherboard has 128 kilobytes of ROM and 64 kilobytes of EEPROM. The ROM contains memory and system diagnostics, as well as the **bootstrap code**, that is, the set of instructions that loads the operating system into memory from the optical disk, hard disk, or over the Ethernet network. The EEPROM contains certain system settings, which can be examined and modified; these settings are preserved even when the power is turned off.

PROCESSORS

A processor is an integrated circuit—a computer chip—that reads or receives instructions, and then executes them, moving or manipulating data in the process. Most personal computers and workstations are designed around a single processor, the **central processing unit,** or CPU. The CPU runs the entire system, executing all program instructions, moving all data, modifying any information or screen displays. Since the CPU does all the work, it can become a bottleneck—that is, the limiting factor in how fast the computer performs tasks.

The NeXT motherboard has not one, but three major processors on it, as well as a dozen specialized ones. These are designed to work together to distribute the workload, so that the CPU doesn't become as much of a bottleneck as it is in other systems.

THE CENTRAL PROCESSING UNIT (CPU)

While there are a variety of CPU chips on the market, two "families" tend to dominate. One, designed and manufactured by Intel Corporation, includes the 8080, 8088, 8086, 80186, 80286, and 80386 chips, with the 80486 already in the works. This is the family used in the IBM PC and PS/2 computers, as well as most other MS-DOS (IBM PC-compatible) systems, such as Compaq and Zenith. This series is most noted (and sometimes cursed) for its segmented architecture and specialized registers.

The other family, designed and built by Motorola, includes the 68000, 68008, 68010, 68020, and 68030 chips—and, yes, there's a 68040 being designed. They contrast with most of the Intel family in having a "flat" (nonsegmented) address space and a lot of general registers, though the Intel 80386 has moved in much the same direction. The Motorola family is used in

Figure 2.1. The Motorola 68030 processor

Macintosh, Atari ST, and Amiga personal computers, as well as in many Sun, Apollo, and Hewlett-Packard workstations.

As it turns out, Motorola is also the family used in the NeXT computer. Specifically, the NeXT CPU is a Motorola 68030 chip, like the one shown in Figure 2.1, running at a clock rate of 25 MHz. It has a 32-bit address bus, and a 32-bit data bus. It features a built-in paged memory management unit, and it has both data and instruction caches. And if you don't understand what all that means or why it's important, just keep reading.

How Processors Work

Think of a processor as a machine that performs various tasks as you turn a crank. Each task takes so many turns of the crank, some more, some less. The faster your turn the crank, though, the faster each task gets done. In the same way, each

Processor	Typical system	Clock rate
6502	Apple II	1 MHz
8088	IBM PC	4.77 MHz
	Compaq	
80286	IBM AT	10 MHz
	Compaq 286	
80386	IBM PS/2-70	25 MHz
	Compaq 386	
68000	Mac Plus	8 MHz
	Atari ST	
	Amiga 500	
68020	Mac II	16 MHz
	Amiga 2500	
68030	Mac SE/030	16 MHz
	Mac IIx	
	Mac IIcx	
68030	NeXT	25 MHz

Figure 2.2. CPU clock rates for systems using various processors

processor instruction takes a certain number of cycles; some as few as one or two cycles, others as many as a hundred. The **clock rate** of the processor—how many cycles take place each second—determines the actual amount of time it takes to perform a given instruction. The NeXT's 68030 runs at 25 MHz. Thus, if a given instruction takes 10 cycles to execute, then the NeXT's CPU can execute about 2.5 million of those instructions each second. Figure 2.2 shows you how the NeXT CPU's clock rate compares with that of other systems' CPUs.

A processor can address a certain amount of computer memory based on how many **address lines** it has. A particular memory location is selected by adjusting the voltage level on each address line. The voltage levels are interpreted as being either 0 or 1, so the entire address is a collection of 0s and 1s—in short, a binary number. As mentioned earlier, this is why so many values used in computers are based around powers of two. The collection of address lines is sometimes called the **address bus.**

The M68030 has 32 address lines, giving it an address space of 2^{32} bytes, or 4 gigabytes (4096 megabytes). This means that you'll probably run out of memory long before you run out of address space. In fact, you'd probably run out of physical space, not to mention money; even at a conservative $2000 per 8

Processor	Address space
6502	64 KB
8088	1 MB
80286	1 MB
80386	4 GB
68000	16 MB
68020	4 GB
68030	4 GB

Figure 2.3. Maximum address space for various processors

megabytes of RAM, you'd need over a million dollars to buy that much memory. Figure 2.3 shows the address space for most common processors.

Yet another measure of a processor's power is how much data it can move around at once. It moves data over a set of data lines which, like the address lines, each transmit either 0 or 1, that is, a single bit. A processor with 8 data lines can move 8 bits (1 byte) at a time, and so on. Thus, the more data lines a processor has, the faster it can fetch instructions and data from memory or write values back out to memory. The data lines collectively are known as the **data bus**.

The M68030 has a 32-bit data bus, which means that it can read or write up to 4 bytes at a time. Furthermore, unlike some processors, this bus isn't multiplexed with the address bus. With a **multiplexed bus**, the same set of lines are used for addresses and data; another signal line is used to tell how they're being used at any given moment. This approach makes for slower reads and writes, since the CPU has to switch constantly between the two modes. With a **nonmultiplexed bus** (such as the 68030's), completely separate sets of lines are used for address and data, increasing performance and making things less complicated. Figure 2.4 shows the data bus sizes for most common processors.

Processor	Data bus
6502	8 bits
8088	8 bits
80286	16 bits
80386	32 bits
68000	8 bits
68020	16 bits
68030	32 bits

Figure 2.4. Data bus sizes for various processors

Data and Instruction Caches

With a large address bus, any processor still spends a fair amount of its time fetching data and instructions from memory. Even if it read a memory location just a few instructions back, it has to go through the same steps to read it again. And when it's fetching an instruction, it has to do a certain amount of decoding before deciding what it needs to fetch next. The result is that the whole business of fetching can become a bottleneck, limiting the overall performance of the CPU.

The M68030 offers two solutions to that bottleneck. First, it automatically implements a certain amount of instruction **pipelining**. This means that while it's decoding one instruction, it goes ahead and fetches the next one (or more of the current one) and starts decoding it as well. The pipeline can handle from one to three instructions simultaneously, depending upon the size of the instructions involved.

The second solution involves a small chunk of memory known as a **cache**. This cache isn't in the computer's memory; it's built into the processor chip itself. Each time the processor fetches something from memory, it leaves a copy of it, along with its address, in the cache. That way, when the processor needs to read a given address, it first checks the cache. If that address and its contents are in the cache, then the processor reads from the cache, avoiding the time involved in doing a fetch from memory.

The M68030 has two caches, one for data and one for instructions. Both are organized into 16 entries; each entry consists of a 4-byte address and 16 bytes of information, corresponding to the contents of the 16 bytes found at that address in memory. The appropriate cache is updated each time a fetch is done from memory.

A question arises, though: what if you write a new value out to a memory address whose value is currently in the cache? Unless the cache is updated somehow, the old value will be read from the cache the next time the CPU wants to fetch the value at that address. The solution is a **write-through** data cache, which means that whenever the processor writes data out to a given address in memory it also updates the cache. The M68030 actually has two modes here. In one, it updates the cache only if the destination address is also in the cache; in the other, it updates the cache regardless, adding a new entry if the address isn't found among the existing entries.

An important note for assembly language hackers: this write-through ability applies only to the data cache, not to the instruction cache. In other words, if you write **self-modifying code**—small sets of instructions that write over themselves, changing themselves to new instructions—your programs may not work if the instruction cache is enabled. If you must use such techniques, you'll have to disable the instruction cache first.

Managing Memory

The NeXT computer runs Mach, a multitasking, virtual-memory operating system. **Multitasking** means that you can have multiple applications (or **tasks**) running at the same time. Each task thinks that it has all the computer's resources to itself and doesn't worry about where it's actually located in memory or what other tasks might be doing. **Virtual memory** means that each task thinks that it has all the memory it needs, even if that's more than the physical memory—the actual RAM—within the computer.

To help support this kind of operating system, a computer needs to provide some sort of **memory management unit**, or MMU. An MMU makes the currently executing task "think" that it has the entire address space of the computer. It makes the task think that its code and data are located at certain fixed addresses, even though the task may actually be located anywhere in memory and may even be relocated during execution. All the addresses the task uses, for both code and data, are located in **logical memory**, that is, the memory space the task thinks it has. As the task executes, the CPU reads and writes using addresses in the task's logical memory space; the MMU then intercepts those operations, translating the addresses to the corresponding locations in physical memory. Use of an MMU not only makes it easier to implement a multitasking operating system, it also provides protection for each task by not allowing other tasks to write into its physical memory space.

Adding virtual memory to this makes things even more complex. When a program is launched, its **memory space**—the range of addresses being used for code and data—is divided up into **pages**, equally sized chunks of memory. Some of the pages are kept in memory, and the rest are written out to a portion of the disk (usually called the "swapping file"). As the program runs, it may try to execute instructions or access data residing in pages that are not currently in memory. This causes a **page fault**, which is a signal to the operating system that it needs to suspend the program, load that page or pages into memory, and then let the program continue. If necessary, other pages belonging to that (or another) program are **swapped out** to disk, that is, written to the swapping file, in order to make room for the page(s) coming in. The program itself usually isn't aware of all this moving around, or of being suspended; the work is all handled transparently by the operating system and the computer hardware.

As you might guess, the M68030 has a paged memory management unit (PMMU) built right into it. This PMMU manages logical-to-physical address translations for all the tasks currently running, including the operating system itself. As a task requests memory, the PMMU allocates it from the physical memory available. The "paged" aspect, as mentioned, means that memory is allocated or deallocated in fixed sizes, ranging from 256 bytes to 32 kilobytes; on the NeXT system, the page size is 1024 bytes (1 kilobyte). The PMMU also helps in the virtual memory implementation on the NeXT computer, though most of the work there is done by the Mach kernel (see Chapter 8 for more details on Mach).

THE FLOATING POINT UNIT (FPU)

CPUs are generally pretty good at performing basic arithmetic operations on **integer** numbers. You probably knew integers as "whole numbers" back in high school: numbers like 42, -7832, 0, 887132, and so on. These numbers are easily represented in binary form, and calculations such as addition, subtraction, multiplication, and division are simple to implement; in fact, most CPUs offer these operations as single instructions.

However, CPUs slow down a lot when they have to work with real, or **floating-point,** numbers. These are any numbers with a fractional part, such as 3.387 and −0.00017325, or with an exponent, such as 8.3523×10^{321}. Not only do they require a more complex binary format, but the CPU has to do a lot more work to perform basic arithmetic on them. More advanced operations, such as trigonometric functions or raising numbers to a certain power, bog things down even more.

The solution is a **floating point unit,** or FPU. This is a chip that has special hardware for doing complex mathematics, such as floating-point operations, and transcendental and trigono-metric functions. In many cases, the FPU can carry out these operations over a hundred times faster than the CPU, dramati-cally improving performance in programs involving lots of cal-culations. The FPU used in a given system is almost always from the same firm that made the CPU, since the two have to work together; you'll usually find an Intel 8087 or 80287 FPU in an IBM PC or compatible, while the high-end Macintosh mod-els come equipped with a Motorola 68881 or 68882 FPU.

The NeXT FPU, which comes with every motherboard, is a Motorola 68882 chip, running at 25 MHz, the same clock rate as the CPU. This chip, shown in Figure 2.5, performs high-speed floating-point operations using an 80-bit extended format, with a 64-bit mantissa and a 15-bit signed exponent). This means that it has enough precision to represent numbers with about nineteen significant decimal digits, while exponents can range roughly from $10^{-9,864}$ to $10^{+9,863}$. If this all seems a bit imprecise, it's because the number is coded in binary format, and binary numbers don't convert "evenly" into decimal places; for example, the actual exponent range is $2^{-32,768}$ to $2^{+32,767}$.

The Motorola 68882 supports other formats: single-preci-sion (32 bits) and double-precision (64 bits) reals; byte (8 bits), word (16 bits), and longword (32 bits) integers; and a packed dec-imal string (96 bits) real, which uses binary-coded demical (BCD) values to avoid the roundoffs and errors that occur in binary-decimal conversions. In all cases, though, these values are converted to the 80-bit extended real format prior to being operated on, then are converted back when the M68882 is done.

Figure 2.5. The Motorola 68882 FPU

The Motorola 68882 carries out the operations that you'd expect: multiplication, division, modulo, addition, subtraction, negation. A number of other arithmetic operations return such things as the absolute value of a number, its integer portion, its exponent, and its mantissa. Power functions include 10^x, 2^x, ex, (e^x)-1, $\log_{10}(x)$, $\log_2(x)$, $\log_e(x)$, $\log_e(x+1)$, sqrt(x). Trigonometric functions include sin, cos, tan, arcsin, arccos, arctan, as well as some of the hyperbolic functions (sinh, cosh, tanh, arctanh).

For the most part, you don't have to worry about any of this. The Objective C compiler, as well as most of the bundled applications that use floating-point values (such as Mathematica), make use of the Motorola 68882 when appropriate. And since every NeXT system has the Motorola 68882 built in, developers and programmers can always count on it being there, to tremendously speed up any floating-point calculations

there, to tremendously speed up any floating-point calculations that might be required.

THE DIGITAL SIGNAL PROCESSOR (DSP)

The CPU is essential to any computer, and FPUs have become common accessories, or even standard in some systems (such as the Macintosh II and the NeXT system). However, there is yet another class of operations that computers are often called on to perform, especially in research or laboratory environments, namely array and signal processing. Array processing involves performing operations on lists (arrays) of numbers, such as multiplying all the numbers in a list by a specific amount, or adding an offset to all the numbers. Signal processing is mainly just a specific application of array processing, analyzing data that has been sampled by some means (microphone, radar, camera) and then digitized. An FPU can help out here, particularly if floating-point calculations are involved, but performance is still limited.

In a radical departure from conventional design, NeXT equipped each motherboard with a **digital signal processor**, or DSP: the Motorola DSP56001, running at 25 MHz. No other personal computer or workstation has even a socket for a DSP, much less comes equipped with one as a standard feature; you can buy expansion boards for some of these systems that include DSP chips, but these boards usually cost a few thousand dollars, and none of the standard software for those systems takes advantage of the DSP.

As you might guess, a DSP is designed to perform array and signal processing. Specifically, it's geared toward performing multiplication and division on long lists of numbers, looking up values in a table, and combining two lists of numbers together by multiplying corresponding elements together and summing all the products. Tasks in which a DSP outperforms a conventional CPU include fast Fourier transforms (FFTs), waveform synthesis (music and sound), and matrix operations (two-dimensional graphics).

The Motorola DSP56001, shown in Figure 2.6, is a fully-programmable DSP with its own 8 kilobytes of high-speed static RAM. It can load both data and code into that memory, then execute it, sending the results out either to main memory or through its own serial port (the DSP port). Likewise, it can receive code and data from both main memory and the DSP. Data transfers to and from the 8 kilobytes of static RAM are done by custom I/O (input/output, or channel) processors, thus freeing both the CPU and the DSP from handling that chore.

The most common and possibly most important use of the DSP in the NeXT machine is not for analyzing signals, but for synthesizing them, producing music and sound. As it turns out, the DSP is ideal for setting up and accessing waveform tables that can, for example, model various instruments. Information about the notes to be played comes in from main memory; the DSP does the processing and produces 16-bit digitized stereo sound at a sampling rate of 22.05 KHz, that is, 22,050 samples per second. This is transferred back to main memory by one I/O processor, then sent to the MegaPixel Display (via the display

Figure 2.6. The Motorola DSP56001

port) by another one. There, the digitized sound is run through a 16-bit digital-to-analog (D-to-A) converter that produces full stereo sound, which is then played out through the internal speaker, the stereo headphone jack, or the dual line-out jacks.

While most other computers can do some form of sound or music synthesis, they typically put a lot of the work load on the CPU. With the NeXT system, the DSP often does most, if not all, of the work. The DSPMusic demo that comes with the 0.8 software demonstrates this capability: it performs real-time music synthesis with almost no degradation to overall system performance.

Developmental use of the DSP is supported in two major ways. First, the Music Kit provides a series of objects and methods for music generation within programs. Second, programmers will be able to create their own DSP assembly language routines, called "DSPwraps," load them into the DSP memory, and then call them from their C programs. Planned and potential uses of the DSP include high-quality sampling through the DSP port, speech recognition, high-speed coordinate transformations for two-dimensional graphics, and implementing a 9600-baud modem in software (with a small amount of external hardware required, again attached to the DSP port). The most interesting uses, though, probably haven't been thought of yet.

THE INTEGRATED CHANNEL PROCESSOR (ICP)

As mentioned before, the CPU is often the bottleneck in a typical computer system, limiting overall performance. Why? Because the CPU is usually responsible for moving all information, every single byte, from one location to another. In most personal computers, the CPU draws each and every dot on the screen, writes every character out to the printer, reads every byte from the disk drive into memory. Mainframes and minicomputers, by contrast, use small, specialized I/O processors to perform such data transfers. When the CPU needs to move a block of data, it sends the appropriate information to the correct channel processor, which then handles the actual transfer, signaling the CPU when it's done. Since this makes it appear as though the peripherals (displays, printers, disk drives, serial ports) have direct access to the main memory, these processors are referred to as **direct memory access (DMA)** channels.

The NeXT design team used this approach to avoid the CPU bottleneck that plagues most personal computers and many workstations. To this end, they built 12 channel processors into one of the Very Large Scale Integration (VLSI) chips on the motherboard. This chip is known as the **Integrated Channel Processor (ICP)**. It sets up and handles DMA channels for all the major peripherals in the NeXT system.

Each channel processor has a small, private memory area—called a **buffer**—that's 128 bytes in size. When it transfers data in or out of memory, it fills the buffer completely, using a high-speed "burst" mode, before passing the data along. This minimizes its access of memory, avoiding contention with other devices that are working with memory as well.

The 12 channel processors are assigned to the various ports and devices in the system:

- Ethernet: two processors (one for sending, one for receiving)

- SCSI port: one processor (reading, writing)

- Optical disk: one processor (reading, writing)

- Serial ports: one processor shared by both ports (reading, writing)

- Sound: two I/O processors (sending to display or receiving from it)

- Printer: one I/O processor (sending bit-images to laser printer)

- Video: one I/O processor (writing into video display memory)

- DSP: one I/O processor (transfers between main and DSP memory)

In addition to those listed above, there are two channel processors which can be used for moving chunks of data from one location in main memory to another, and which could also be used for data transfers over the bus.

THE OPTICAL STORAGE PROCESSOR (OSP)

The other large chip on the NeXT motherboard is the **Optical Storage Processor,** or **OSP.** This chip implements the entire disk controller for the optical disk drive(s) and, like the IPC, was designed and developed entirely at NeXT. It processes all requests by the CPU to read from or write to the optical disk. To ensure the accuracy of the data being transferred, it performs a sophisticated error-correction algorithm, known as the "Reed-Solomon algorithm," while the transfer is in progress. It has two internal buffers (private memory areas, each 128 bytes long) and uses **double-buffering** to perform the error correction; that is, it transfers corrected data out of one buffer (via the DMA channel) while reading data into the other buffer and then correcting it.

The OSP also implements the SCSI controller used for both the internal and external SCSI connectors. This controller can transfer data at a burst rate of 4.8 megabytes per second and a sustained rate of 1.2 megabytes per second. It provides the interface and controller for the internal hard disk, if any, as well as for any external SCSI devices.

VIDEO

The memory and other chips used to generate the video signal for the MegaPixel Display are located on the motherboard itself. As mentioned above, a 256-kilobyte video buffer holds the actual bit image. This memory uses a straightforward mapping scheme to represent each pixel on the display: the two high-order bits of the first byte represent the pixel in the upper-left corner of the display, the next two bits represent the pixel to its right, and so on. Each row takes up 280 bytes; multiplying that by 832 rows yields a total memory requirement of 232,960 bytes, or about 228 kilobytes. One of the ICPs is dedicated to transferring bit-images from main memory into the video RAM.

The video circuitry scans the video buffer and produces three signals used to create the picture: the video signal itself, a horizontal synchronization signal, and a vertical synchronization signal. These signals go out over the cable at a bandwidth frequency of 100 MHz. The result on the MegaPixel Display is a high-resolution 1120-by-832-pixel display showing four levels of gray (black, dark gray, light gray, and white).

COMMENTARY

The NeXT motherboard is an impressive piece of hardware design. A large amount of functionality is placed on a single board: three major processors, two large custom VLSI chips, bus interface, complete video circuitry, and RAM—up to 16 megabytes of user RAM—serial ports, SCSI ports, complete Ethernet hardware, and so on. Doing it all in 45 chips and with a layout that looks clean even to the untrained eye adds to the impression.

The choice by NeXT to go with the Motorola family of processors was no surprise, especially given the Apple background of the founders and many of the employees. There are ongoing heated discussions about the relative merits of Intel versus Motorola, none of which will be rehashed here. But the most telling observation is that about the only products in which you'll find Intel processors are computers designed to be IBM-compatible. Most other firms (Apple, Apollo, Atari, Commodore, Hewlett-Packard, NeXT, Sun, etc.) use either Motorola processors or custom, in-house designs, with a few older, low-end systems, such as the Apple II, using the 6502 family.

The surprise was the Motorola DSP56001. Having it as a standard feature of every system means that developers can count on it being there. The obvious applications, such as music and sound, will certainly be exploited. But since developers have a knack for using hardware in ways no one ever thought of, there will undoubtedly be some not-so-obvious uses of the DSP.

To sum up, the motherboard is NeXT's real strength in competing with other firms. The combination of features, clean design, and automated production gives the motherboard an excellent price/performance ratio. The modular approach—pull one board, put in another—protects the user against obsolescence. And the distributed approach, with multiple processors handling specialized tasks, gives the system room to grow without quickly hitting a bottleneck. The success of NeXT will largely be due to the time and effort spent on the motherboard.

3

The Display

The cube sits by itself, out of sight or as part of the background. It's not what you look at, not what you use, not what you interact with when you're working. That's an entirely different object: the MegaPixel Display. While the cube is solid, monolithic, dark, and quiet, the display is sleek, spread out, bright, and sonic. It catches your attention with contrasts of darkness and light. In fact, one photographer who came in to shoot photos of the NeXT system focused entirely on the display and didn't realize initially that the computer was that black cube under the table.

The MegaPixel Display is made up of three components: the display unit itself, the keyboard, and the mouse. The display presents information to you, while the keyboard and the mouse let you communicate with the computer. The MegaPixel Display also handles all sound input and output for the NeXT system. Let's look at these aspects in detail.

THE DISPLAY

The display houses a high-resolution 17-inch grayscale monitor, with a 68.3 Hz (Hertz, or one cycle per second) refresh rate and a crisp, sharp image, free from flicker or visual distortions.

The display tube is enclosed in a black plastic casing, which in turn sits on a cast metal support. The casing and support meet in a tilt joint, allowing you to adjust the tilt of the screen through about a 30-degree range. The height of the support is fixed, but you can use the rubber rollers at its bottom to swivel it to one side or the other. Figure 3.1 shows some of the different angles possible for the display. If you want to get the keyboard out of the way, you can place it back in the crook of the support.

THE SCREEN

The screen has a resolution of 1120 pixels across by 832 lines down; not quite a million pixels, but close. With a pixel density of 94 dots per inch, it produces images that are about 78 percent of the size they'll be on printed documents. It supports four shades of gray per pixel: white, light gray, dark gray, and black.

Figure 3.1. The side of the MegaPixel Display

Dithering effects are used to produce additional shades, though with less precision in resolution. Even four gray shades lets you see a lot of detail missing in plain monochrome.

The video image displayed is actually generated on the motherboard in the 256 kilobytes of video RAM; the signal is sent to the display via the video cable, being refreshed 68 times per second (68 Hz). In turn, that image in video RAM is being created and updated by Display PostScript and the Window Server. Because Display PostScript is used to create both video images and printer output, there is a much stronger correlation than on many systems between what appears on the screen and what appears on paper; in this case, the only major difference is size.

CONNECTORS

At the back of the display, shown in Figure 3.2, are several connectors. The main one accepts one end of the video cable, the
other end is plugged into the display port on the motherboard
back. This cable carries power, video, and sound to the display;
in turn, it carries digitized sound, keyboard, and mouse information back to the motherboard. The keyboard plugs in with a
curled cord. Also on the motherboard back are sound inputs and
outputs: a microphone input, which accepts a mini-jack; gold-
plated left- and right-channel line-outs (RCA-standard); and a
stereo headphone output (mini-jack).

Figure 3.2. The back of the MegaPixel Display

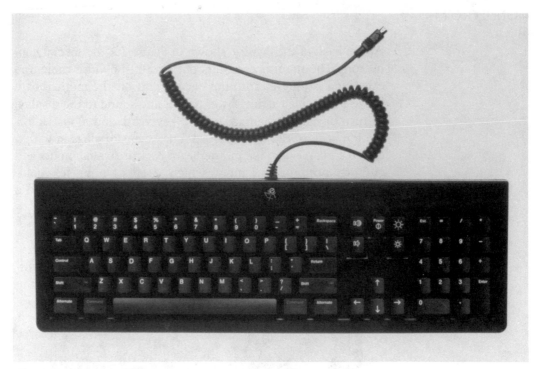

Figure 3.3. The NeXT Keyboard

THE KEYBOARD

The keyboard, shown in Figure 3.3, communicates with the computer through the display. The keyboard plugs into the display, and the display sends the data to the computer through the video cable. All data flow goes in one direction; the computer doesn't send information back to the keyboard.

The keyboard has 83 keys, divided up into four groups: the keyboard proper, the system control keys, the arrow keys, and the numeric keypad.

THE KEYBOARD PROPER

The keyboard proper provides a full set of printable ASCII (or American Standard Code for Information Interchange) characters, with the exception of tilde (~) and accent grave (`), which are located over in the numeric keypad. It offers Tab, Control, Delete, Return, and Esc, as well as left and right Shift, Alternate, and Command keys. Most of the keys act just as they would on a typewriter, sending the indicated letters, digits, and symbols to the computer.

Auto-Repeating

When you press a regular key on the keyboard, the corresponding letter, digit, or symbol is typed. If you hold that key down beyond a certain time, it will start typing that character repeatedly. This feature is known as **auto-repeat** and lets you type a string of characters without having to press the same key over and over again.

You can adjust the auto-repeat feature using the Preferences application, a program supplied with the NeXT system that lets you customize various settings. Figure 3.4 shows the keyboard display in the Preferences window. The top row of buttons (labeled "Key Repeat") lets you select how fast the key is repeated; the second row (labeled "Initial Key Repeat") lets you select how long you must hold a key down before it starts

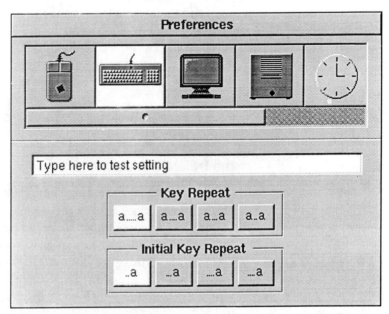

Figure 3.4. The keyboard display in the Preferences application

repeating. The Preferences application is discussed in greater detail in Chapter 10.

The Control Key

The Control key is one found on most microcomputers, as well as on most computer terminals. It is used to generate special control codes, having ASCII values of 0 through 31. It's not used by most NeXT applications running under the standard NeXT user interface (Workspace Manager). However, if you use the Shell or Terminal applications, you'll find that the Mach shell and many of the UNIX applications respond to control codes.

To generate a particular control code, type the appropriate letter while holding down the Control key. For example, you generate Control-C (sometimes written "Ctrl-C" or "^C") by holding down the Control key and typing the letter "C." It doesn't matter if you type in upper- or lowercase; Control-Shift-C is the same as Control-C.

The Tab Key

As on a typewriter, this key sends a "tab" character to the computer (ASCII code 9 = Ctrl-I). How the tab is interpreted depends upon the application that's asked to handle it. A word processor such as WriteNow will treat it as a tab and format the document you're editing correspondingly. Other applications might treat it differently or ignore it altogether. The Tab key generates ASCII code 9 (Control-I). Shift-Tab generates a "back tab" character (ASCII 25, or Control-Y), which some applications will interpret as a request to move to the previous tab stop or text field.

The Delete Key

This is used as a "correcting" key. If you are currently entering or modifying text, pressing this key causes the character to the left of the insertion cursor to be deleted. This is often the last character you typed, so it's an easy way to correct mistakes as you type text into the computer. The Delete key generates ASCII code 127. Pressing Shift-Delete will generate a backspace (ASCII 8) character, which you can also generate by typing Control-H.

The Return Key

As on a typewriter, the Return key is often used to signal the end of a line of text, causing any additional text to start on the next line. Quite frequently, though, it's used to mark the end of data input or to accept a particular choice presented to you. For example, you will see buttons with a left-pointing arrow on them; this means that you can select them by pressing Return, just as if you had clicked on the button. In word processors, such as WriteNow, pressing Return signals the end of a paragraph. The Return key generates ASCII code 13 (Control-M).

The Enter Key

The Enter key is used by some applications to signal entry of data. For example, Mathematica will start a new line if you press Return, but it doesn't process what you've typed until you press Enter. The Enter key generates ASCII code 3 (Control-C); this code can also be generated by pressing Command-Return.

The Esc Key

Like the Control key, the Esc (for "escape") key has a long tradition in computers. Most standard NeXT applications won't make use of it, though some UNIX utilities will. The Esc key sends ASCII code 31 (Control-[) to the computer.

The Shift Keys

As you can guess, holding either Shift key down while typing a letter causes the uppercase version of the letter to be sent to the computer. For the keys showing two symbols on them (such as $ and 4), holding the Shift key down while pressing the key causes the upper symbol to be sent.

You can enter alpha lock mode by holding the Command key down and pressing either Shift key. A green light on both Shift keys will come on, and any letters typed will always be sent as uppercase. The two-symbol keys are unaffected; pressing the $/4 key would still type a 4, and you'd have to hold a Shift key down to get the $ symbol. You can get out of alpha lock mode by repeating the process (Command-Shift).

The Alternate Keys

The Alternate keys are used to produce characters and punctuation not found in the normal ASCII character set. You use either Alternate key much like a Shift key; that is, you hold it down while typing another character. For example, the character æ is produced by typing g while holding down either Alternate key. Likewise, Alternate-Shift-G produces Æ.

The Command Key

The Command key is used to produce keyboard equivalents of menu items. For example, to select the Cut command from most Edit menus, you press Command-x, while the Paste command is Command-v. Note that case is significant: Command-x is different from Command-Shift-X.

The Command key serves other purposes as well. Generating alpha lock mode has already been mentioned. Command-Return is the same as pressing the Enter key on the numeric keypad.

The Command key also performs a few special system functions. If you hold down the left Command key, then press the upper-left key of the numeric keypad, you will force an exit out of NextStep into the NeXT ROM monitor. If you hold down the left Alternate and Command keys, then press the upper-right key of the numeric keypad, you'll force a system reset and reboot.

THE SYSTEM CONTROL KEYS

The System Control keys represent the only "switches" and "knobs" that you'll find on the NeXT system. The Power key is used to turn the system on and off. You press this to power up the system, as described in Chapter 9, Working with NeXT. When you're completely done using the system, and after you've logged out, you can power down by pressing this key again.

The Brightness keys are the two keys to the right of the Power key; they control the brightness of the screen. The upper key increases the brightness by a measured amount each time you press it; likewise, the lower key dims the screen until it is completely dark. Holding either key down will cause it to auto-repeat until the screen reaches its maximum or minimum brightness. You can also adjust the brightness using Preferences. Figure 3.5 shows the display settings in the Preferences window.

Note that Preferences lets you set an automatic dimming delay from 5 to 60 minutes. This means that if you don't move the mouse or press a key for that period of time, the screen is automatically dimmed. The previous brightness is restored as soon as you move the mouse or press a key.

The Volume keys are to the left of the Power key; they control the volume of the sound produced by the display. This applies both to the speaker inside the display and to any headphones plugged into the mini-jack in the back. It does not, however, affect the sound level through the dual stereo line-outs. As with the Brightness keys, the upper key increase the sound volume while the lower key decreases it; auto-repeat

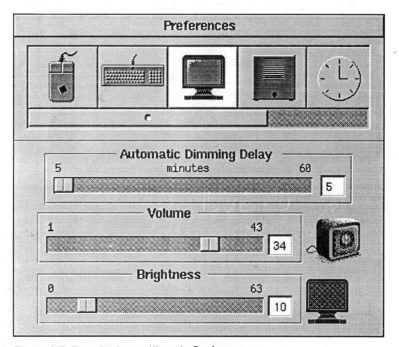

Figure 3.5. The display settings in Preferences

works with both keys. Pressing the lower key while holding either Command key down turns the sound off completely; the same action restores the sound to its previous level. Note that you can also set the volume using Preferences.

THE ARROW KEYS

Below the Power, Brightness, and Volume keys are the four arrow keys. These keys may be, but are not necessarily, supported by applications running on the NeXT system. The up, left, down, and right arrow keys generate ASCII codes 173, 172, 174, and 175, respectively.

THE NUMERIC KEYPAD

At the far right of the keyboard is the numeric keypad. It gives you all 10 digits, all four arithmetic operators (+,−, *, /), the equals sign, and the Enter key. It also gives you the tilde and accent grave keys, as mentioned before. These keys are there for your convenience; they mostly duplicate characters found on the regular keyboard.

THE MOUSE

The NeXT mouse, shown in Figure 3.6, is a standard optical-shaft mouse. This means that when you move it, the rubber ball inside rubs against two wheels; optical sensors detect how fast and how far the mouse is moving along both horizontal and vertical axes. The mouse comes with a 36-inch cable that attaches to the top edge of the keyboard, right next to where the keyboard cable comes in from the display; mouse signals are then passed on through the keyboard cable to the display, and on down through the video cable to the motherboard. The mouse also has two Teflon pads on the bottom to aid movement across surfaces.

    As you move the mouse, it causes the cursor to move across the screen. When you press either button, the location of the cursor is noted, and the message that you've clicked the

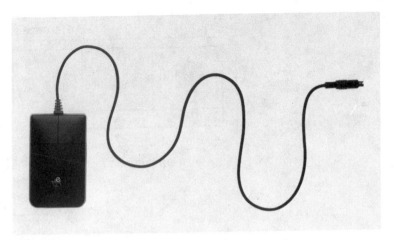

Figure 3.6. The NeXT mouse

mouse (a "mouse down" event) is sent to the appropriate program, which handles it accordingly. This is how you do a lot of your work, choosing menu items, pushing buttons, selecting text, and launching applications from their icons.

The Preferences application lets you differentiate between the two buttons, as shown in Figure 3.7. Each application usually has a main menu associated with it; this menu normally appears in the upper left corner of the display, though you can drag it to any location on the screen. Even so, it can be a distraction to locate it with the mouse and select the proper command. The good news is, you don't have to. When the Select Menu Button option is selected, pressing the right button causes a copy of the main menu of the current application to "pop up" right under the cursor. While holding the button down, you can select any command in the menu or in any of its submenus. When you release the mouse button, that command is executed, and the copy of the menu disappears.

For those of you who would prefer to swap buttons—that is, have the right button act normally and the left button cause a menu to pop up—Preferences allows you to make a switch. Just select the "Left Handed" box, and the mouse buttons will be set as described.

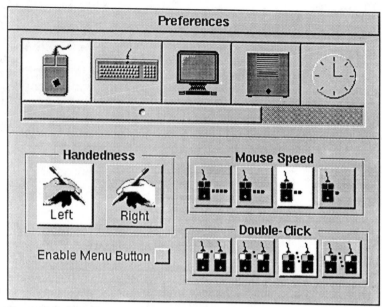

Figure 3.7. The mouse settings in Preferences

SOUND

All sound input, output, and generation is handled through the MegaPixel Display. Any sound information produced by programs running on the motherboard is sent in digitized form (as a string of bits) to the display by way of the video cable. Inside the display, a 16-bit, 2-channel D-to-A converter turns those bits into actual stereo sound. The D-to-A chip can accept sound data coming at a sampling rate of 22.05 or 44.1 kilohertz (KHz), that is, 22,050 or 44,100 16-bit values per second. The faster rate is identical to that used for compact discs, and the sound produced is likewise very crisp and clear.

An internal speaker mixes the stereo output from the D-to-A chip into a single source and plays it; volume is controlled via the volume keys on the keyboard. However, if you have Walkman-style stereo headphones plugged into the display, the sound to the speaker is cut off completely, and is heard only through the headphones.

You can also route sound through your stereo or other mixing system using standard RCA-jack audio cables. Separate left and right channel outputs are provided in the back; the signal coming out is at a low wattage and so will require an amplifier to drive most speakers.

Besides all the sounds coming out, the display handles sounds going in. You can plug a microphone (using a mini-jack) into the back of the display and then digitize sounds and speech for use in applications. (If your microphone has a large standard jack, you can buy an adaptor at any electronics or audio store.) The display has an 8 KHz CODEC chip that performs 8-bit A-to-D conversions, changing the incoming sound to digital values, which are then sent to the cube through the video cable. The sound quality isn't the greatest in the world, but it's adequate—comparable to phone quality—and it's there in every system. Several applications, including Mail, Interface Builder, and Scope, take advantage of it.

Developmental support of sound is given through the Sound Kit, a set of objects and methods designed to make sampling and playing sounds relatively easy. In addition, a number of UNIX-style utilities allow manipulation of sampled sound files. The system software has full editing capability for sampled sounds, including cutting and pasting.

COMMENTARY

When the NeXT system was introduced, Steve Jobs repeatedly stated how important it was that the NeXT system have a large screen display in the minimum configuration, even to the point of foregoing color initially, to be able to support a large screen as the standard. Problems elsewhere in the industry tend to support his assertion. Most software for IBM compatibles has to aim either at an 80-column by 25-line text-only display, or at one of a number of incompatible graphics systems (CGA, EGA, VGA, etc.). Much of the software for the Macintosh is still oriented to the original monochrome Macintosh display, 512 pixels across by 342 lines.

Going with 2-bits-per-pixel grayscale was a good compromise. The four shades allow for a sense of depth and detail in images, especially when dithering is applied. Also, all software developers are required to deal with multiple bits per pixel at the start, rather than running into the problem later on, as most Macintosh developers did. Four bits per pixel, 16 shades of gray, would have been nicer, but it would also have required twice as much video RAM and would have slowed down graphics processing.

The keyboard and mouse are good enough not to call attention to themselves, though the keys on the keyboard rattle just a bit. The idea of controlling the entire system through the keyboard isn't completely original, though few computers carry it to the extent of eliminating all other switches and knobs. Thanks to that and the three-meter video cable, you can put the cube some distance away from the display, under a desk or table, or on a shelf.

The extensive sound support, on the other hand, is original, unprecedented, and—like the DSP discussed in the previous chapter—something that developers will exploit because they know it's there. This is especially true of the built-in digitizing hardware, allowing for voice input and user sampling of sounds. The only question here is one of quality: the 8 KHz sampling rate, with 8 bits of precision, is adequate, but a faster rate and/or greater precision would have opened the door to a lot of sound and music applications that will now have to wait for third-party hardware and/or software, probably using the DSP.

4
The Printer

The ultimate goal of any computer, any program, is some form of output. And while the MegaPixel Display produces wonderful output, it's not enough. Sooner or later, you want hard copy, something you can hold or mail or file away or publish. NeXT's goal was to have the output quality match the display quality, so they decided to use a laser printer as the standard hard-copy output device.

The NeXT Laser Printer is small, simple, compact, and relatively cheap. It offers two resolutions: 300 dots per inch (standard on most laser printers) and 400 dots per inch (not available on most laser printers). It prints on most things that you would want to run through it: paper, letterhead, transparencies, labels, envelopes, and so on. There are no lights or switches on the laser printer; it is completely controlled from the NeXT cube. The printer is turned on by the cube when needed and turned off by the cube when done; error messages, such as "out of paper," appear in a small dialog window that appears on the screen.

The printer itself is about 14 inches wide, 17 inches deep, and 7 inches high (36 centimeters x 43 centimeters x 18 centimeters). It has two connectors in the back; one is for power. The printer doesn't take power from the cube (like the display does). The printer requires a power source giving 5.6 amps at 110-120 volts and a frequency of 50 to 60 Hz. (A switch under the cover lets you set the printer to accept voltages in the 220-to-240 volt range.) The other connector is for the printer cable from the cube. This cable brings a power-up signal from the cube, as well as two data lines and a clocking signal to aid in high-speed transfers. Another data line goes back to the cube, carrying status information, such as "printer ready" and "out of paper."

The paper cartridge fits into the right side, requiring about a foot of clearance to get it in and out, but only sticking out about 9 inches when actually in place. Besides holding about 250 sheets of paper (either standard letter size or A4), it also has a single-sheet feeder that will adjust in width from letter size (8.5 inches) down to 3.75 inches; A4 and B5 widths are marked for your convenience.

A tray to catch sheets as they come out can be attached to the left side, adding another 9 inches to the overall width. (The total width, with cartridge and tray, is 32 inches.) You can, of course, leave the tray off and let the sheets drop to the counter-top or into a bin or tray of your own devising.

The path the paper follows is also short and simple, moving less than 2 feet from the paper cartridge to the output tray. This greatly reduces the possibility of a paper jam and allows greater flexibility in what kind of paper you pass through the printer.

POSTSCRIPT OUTPUT

When you print something, the NeXT system follows most of the same steps as it does when you display something on the screen. It uses the same software—the Display PostScript inter-preter—to prepare the bit-image. The major differences are the resolution—300 or 400 dots per inch, versus 94 dots per inch on the screen—and the scaling, since screen images are 78 percent of "real" size.

Most laser printers are really just specialized computers. They have powerful processors, such as the Motorola 68000 or 68020. They have lots of memory, both RAM and ROM. If they are PostScript-compatible printers, they accept a mixture of PostScript commands and bit-images from your computer, cre-ate a final bit-image in the printer's memory, and then print it out on paper.

The reason the NeXT Laser Printer is small and inexpen-sive is that, unlike most laser printers, it has little computer logic or memory inside of it. Instead, all the bit-image process-ing is done by a task running on the NeXT system itself. When the bit-image for a given page is ready, it is sent to the printer, helped along by a special channel processor that frees the NeXT's CPU from doing all the transfer work. The result is that the bitmap can be sent to the printer at a transfer rate of up to 5 megabits (5 million bits) per second. This process is illustrated in Figure 4.1. (See Chapter 2 for more discussion on channel processors.)

There is a slight penalty to this approach, namely that your NeXT system has to spend some of its CPU time creating the bitmapped image. However, the actual impact is limited, espe-cially since NeXT's multitasking operating system allows you

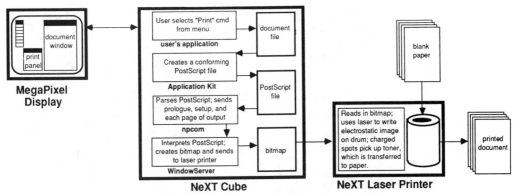

Figure 4.1. Printing a document page

to carry on other tasks while the document is being printed; once you initiate the print job, you can go on with your work. If you want, you can set up several print jobs, then perform other tasks while the documents are printed, one by one. In fact, this is the most efficient way to use the printer, because, once it gets started, it can print about eight pages a minute. The initial delay—the time from the moment you request that a document be printed until the moment the first page comes out—is typically around 20 seconds.

THE STANDARD PRINT PANEL

The NeXT system software provides a standard **print panel** used by most applications when you select the "Print" command in that application's main menu. That panel, shown in Figure 4.2, indicates the name, type, and status of the printer being used. For example, in this case the printer's name is "np," its type is a NeXT 400 dpi Laser Printer, and its status is idle (that is, nothing is currently printing). The Choose button brings up a window that lets you select which printer you wish to use; this window is shown in Figure 4.4 and will be discussed later in the chapter.

Below that section are some fields that you can modify by moving the cursor over them, clicking the mouse button once, and then typing in the desired value. The Copies field lets you determine how many copies of your document should be printed. For example, if you have a 10-page report, and you request

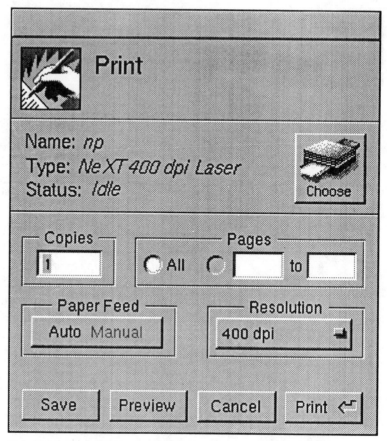

Figure 4.2. The standard print panel used by most NeXT applications

20 copies, you'll end up with 200 printed pages, already collated and ready to be bound or stapled. In such a case, it probably makes more sense to print just one copy and then have it reproduced elsewhere, but you do have this option. The Pages field lets you select whether to print all the pages in a document, or just a selected range. To choose the latter, enter the starting and ending pages of the range desired into the left and right boxes. If you want multiple copies of the same page, enter that page number into both boxes.

Below those fields are two more controls. The Paper Feed button lets you select between automatic and manual paper feed. The mode currently selected is written in black (in this case, Auto), while the alternate mode is written in gray. Clicking on the button switches to the other mode. In automatic mode, the printer uses the paper already loaded into its paper cartridge. In manual mode, the printer expects you to single feed paper through the paper guide on the top of the paper cartridge.

The Resolution button is actually a pop-up list (so indicated by the small "handle" near its right edge). When you click on this button and hold the mouse button down, a list of choices appears, much like a menu. You can then move the cursor up and down the list, highlighting the different resolutions that the current printer offers; for example, the NeXT 400 dpi Laser Printer offers two settings, 300 dpi and 400 dpi. When the desired resolution is highlighted, just release the mouse button, and that resolution will then be selected and displayed in the print panel.

At the bottom are four buttons allowing you to decide what to do with the print request. The Save button brings up a directory panel that lets you save out (in text or WriteNow format) the PostScript commands required to print the document; the print panel will then go away. You can then open up this file, using Edit or WriteNow, to see exactly what commands are used in generating your printed output. This file is at least as large as your original document, since it contains all the text in your document along with all the PostScript commands.

The Preview button launches a utility called Preview, which displays your document as it will appear when printed. Generally, this will look pretty much like your application's document window, though it will be free of any special controls or markings (rulers, grid lines, etc.) that the application might use. Preview will also let you zoom in and out on the document and perform other manipulations on it. Note that you can run Preview separately from other applications; in fact, it will be launched automatically when you double-click on an file with a .ps or .eps extension (PostScript and Encapsulated PostScript, respectively). Selecting the Preview button causes the print panel to go away.

The Cancel button does just what you'd think it does: it cancels the job request. Likewise, the Print button causes the document to be submitted as a print job. Note that the Print button can also be selected by pressing the Return key; this is what the little left-pointing arrow in the Print button means. Also, be aware that the print panel is modal; in other words, once you bring up the print panel in an application, you can't do anything else in that application until you select one of these four buttons, and selecting any of the four buttons makes the print panel disappear.

THE PRINTER APPLICATION

Since printing can go on independent of a given application, NeXT provides a separate program—called Printer—that allows you to monitor and control the printing process. Let's look at some of the functions it provides.

THE PRINT QUEUE

The NeXT system handles your print requests as fast as it can, but it may have several requests waiting to be processed. You can think of the requests as standing in line, first come, first served. This standing-in-line analogy is commonly used in com-

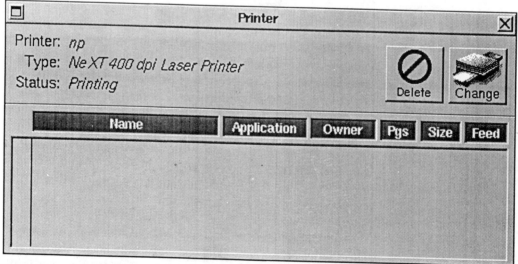

Figure 4.3. The main window of the Printer application, used to list any pending print requests

puter software; the resulting list of tasks or documents is referred to by the term "queue." Thus, this series of print requests forms what is known as the **print queue**.

The Printer application shows you the status of the print queue for a given printer, using the window seen in Figure 4.3. Each print request occupies a single line and gives the document name, the application, the owner, the number of pages in the request, the PostScript file size (in bytes), and the type of paper feed (automatic or manual). You can delete individual print requests by clicking on the corresponding line (so that it's highlighted), and then clicking on the Delete button in the upper right portion of the window. If you need to delete all jobs in the queue, you can do so by selecting the Reset Queue command in the Utilities submenu. You can also suspend printing by selecting the Disable Queue command in that same submenu, at which point all printing ceases, and the menu item changes its name to Enable Queue. To resume printing, just click on the Enable Queue command.

CHOOSING A PRINTER FOR OUTPUT

Both the print panel and the main window of the Printer application let you select between different printers, using the panel shown in Figure 4.4. This is because you can access multiple printers from a single machine. The NeXT system software supports not only the NeXT 400 dpi Laser Printer, but also most PostScript printers, including the Apple LaserWriter II and LaserWriter NXT, and the Linotronic 300 with Raster Image Processor (RIP). These printers connect to your system using one of the Macintosh-compatible serial ports in the back, allowing you to have both a NeXT Laser Printer and a third-party printer hooked up to the same cube.

The NeXT system software also supports printing over a network. This means that if you have several NeXT cubes hooked together using the built-in Ethernet connectors, each cube can access any printers hooked up to any of the other cubes. This allows several NeXT systems to share one or more printers, eliminating the need (and expense) of having a printer for each system.

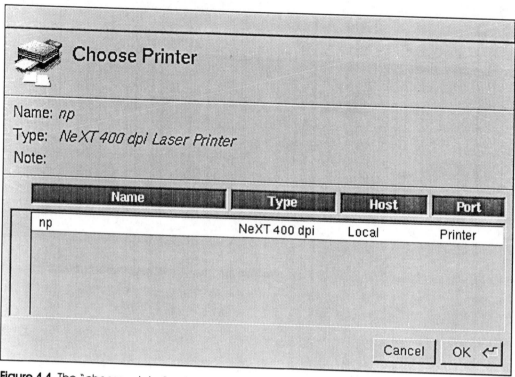

Figure 4.4. The "choose printer" panel for selecting which printer to use

TESTING THE PRINTER

The Printer application also has a built-in utility for testing the printer. Clicking on the Test item in the Printer main menu brings up the panel shown in Figure 4.5. The "switch" on the left side lets you manually turn the printer on and off. The Test Pages section prints one of four test patterns, each consisting of a block of lines, either horizontal or vertical, at the indicated resolution.

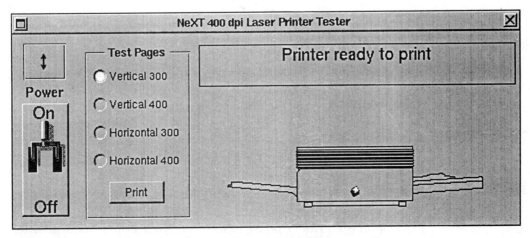

Figure 4.5. The "printer test" panel, used for testing the NeXT Laser Printer

PRINTER ALERTS

While the NeXT Laser Printer is simple and relatively fool-proof, problems, such as running out of paper, running low on toner, and having a paper jam, can occur when you are printing. When a printer alert occurs, you are notified via the MegaPixel Display by an alert panel, a voice message, or both. An alert panel (such as the one shown in Figure 4.6) remains on the screen until you click the OK button; if the error is not fixed, the panel will appear again during your next effort to print. Note that you will get this message even if the printer you are using is hooked up to another system on the network.

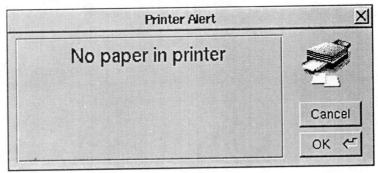

Figure 4.6. A typical "printer alert" panel

To select between voice and panel display, use the System Alert settings in the Preferences application. These settings, shown in Figure 4.7, let you select voice messages, dialog panels, or both. Selected settings are highlighted; for example, Figure 4.7 shows that only panels are to be used. To change a selection, just click on the appropriate button. Note that these settings apply to all system alerts, not just those involving printers.

The most common error is "out of paper," though you'll start to get the "low on toner" message more frequently when the toner gets low. Paper jams are relatively rare. For example, in five months of usage and having printed out hundreds of pages of chapter drafts, the NeXT Laser Printer used to write this book had one paper jam, which was fixed in a matter of seconds.

For details on handling system alerts, including adjusting toner levels, clearing paper jams, and cleaning the printer, see the *NeXT User's Reference Manual*.

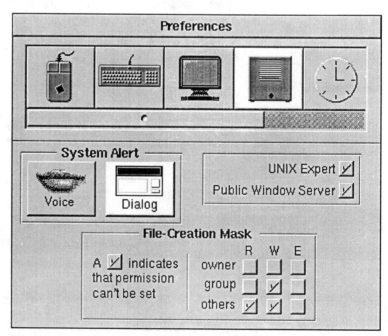

Figure 4.7. The system settings in the Preferences application

ADDING OR CHANGING PAPER

As mentioned, running out of paper is common, especially if you're printing large documents or if several systems are sharing a single printer. Also, you may want to use different paper sizes or colors. The NeXT Laser Printer is also capable of printing on envelopes, as well as on transparencies and mailing labels that are designed for laser printers.

To add paper to the printer, or to change the paper that's there, pull the paper cartridge out of the NeXT Laser Printer. If that side of the printer is close to the wall, be sure that you've got 4" to 6" clearance so that you can get the paper cartridge out. Remove the plastic cover by lifting it straight up. If there's paper in there that you need or want to remove, then do so.

Now put the desired paper (envelopes, etc.) into the cartridge tray. If necessary, adjust the paper guides on the side and back to fit snugly around the paper. If you are using A4 paper, slide the switch at the front of the cartridge to A4; for all other paper sizes (including letter, legal, and envelope), set the switch to LTR. Replace the plastic cover and re-insert the cartridge into the printer; you'll need to give it an extra little push to get it to seat properly.

MANUAL FEEDING

There are times when you just want to feed a few sheets or envelopes through without changing the paper in the cartridge. To do that, use the manual feed guides on the plastic cover. These slide in and out to adjust to the width of the paper being fed in, from 8.5" (letter size) down to 3.5". Adjust them appropriately, then slide in your first piece of paper as far as it will go. You should hear a click as you slide it in; the paper should go in a little more, then stop.

When you bring up the print panel in your application, click on the Paper Feed button so that manual feeding is selected, then click on the Print button. The first sheet of paper (which you should already have inserted) will be pulled in and used. If the document is more than one page long, you will then get the alert box shown in Figure 4.8. Insert another sheet of

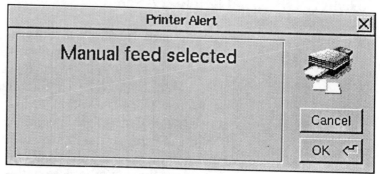

Figure 4.8. The "manual feeding alert" panel

paper as you did the first; after a few moments, the printer will recognize that it's there and will print the next page. This process will continue until the print job is finished.

COMMENTARY

As they did with other aspects of the NeXT system, the designers at NeXT, Inc., decided to set a high minimum standard of print quality. While it is possible to hook up a dot-matrix or ink-jet printer to the NeXT serial port, the system software and bundled applications don't currently support such output. Instead, the only supported printers are all laser printers. This, of course, raises the cost of a system substantially, especially for a stand-alone workstation. On the other hand, it guarantees software developers that their applications can count on at least 300 dpi laser output, avoiding worries about image degradation due to low-density or imprecise print technology. And it anticipates the current trend in the marketplace, in which laser printers have replaced (in both usage and price) the letter-quality impact printers of a few years ago, while adding speed, quality, and graphics integration.

There are two strategies for absorbing the cost of a laser printer for your NeXT system. One is to use an existing PostScript laser printer, if you have one. For example, if your department or office already has an Apple LaserWriter II or LaserWriter NXT, you can hook it up to your NeXT system without any more expense than the necessary cable (which you may already have). The second strategy is to share a printer between several NeXT systems. As mentioned, this requires hooking the systems up using Ethernet connectors and cabling, but that's a relatively minor expense given the added capabilities for electronic mail, file transfers, and shared peripherals.

Is laser-quality output worth it? In most cases, yes. Not only does it lend a high degree of professionalism to letters and reports, it also allows you to produce camera-ready copy for printing. And, of course, you can merge text with high-quality graphics. Given the strengths of the NeXT system for document preparation and desktop publishing, and especially given the use of Display PostScript for both screen and printer imaging, you should consider a laser printer a necessary component—not just an option—of any NeXT-based work environment.

5
Internals and Externals

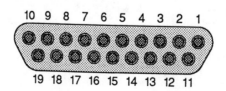

Here's hard information for you techies who aren't satisfied until you know the pinouts and signals for every port; chances are, you turned to this chapter first. The internal ports are given first, followed by the external ports. The external ports are listed by their official names, followed by the label that each is given on the back of the computer (in parentheses).

INTERNAL NeXTBUS CONNECTOR

Each slot on the internal NextBus connector uses a Euro-DIN 96 connector, with pinouts following the NuBus standard developed by Texas Instruments. The Macintosh II uses an almost-identical pinout for its NuBus slots.

You really shouldn't need to know that much about the pinout here. NeXT is making available to third-party developers a single VLSI chip that will perform all interfacing with the bus.

The connector has three rows of 32 pins. Each row is lettered (A,B,C), while each pin in the row is numbered (1 to 32). Figure 5.1 shows how the connector is set up.

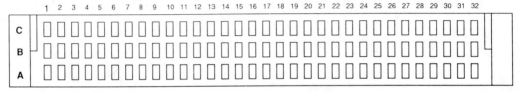

Figure 5.1. Pinout diagram of NuBus connector

Here are the signals for each pin:

Pin	Row A	Row B	Row C
1	−12v	−12v	RESET
2	GND	GND	GND
3	SPV	GND	+5v
4	SP	+5v	+5v
5	TM1	+5v	TM0
6	AD1	+5v	AD0
7	AD3	+5v	AD2
8	AD5	−5.2v	AD4
9	AD7	−5.2v	AD6
10	AD9	−5.2v	AD8
11	AD11	−5.2v	AD10
12	AD13	GND	AD12
13	AD15	GND	AD14
14	AD17	GND	AD16
15	AD19	GND	AD18
16	AD21	GND	AD20

Pin	Row A	Row B	Row C
17	AD23	GND	AD22
18	AD25	GND	AD24
19	AD27	GND	AD26
20	AD29	GND	AD28
21	AD31	GND	AD30
22	GND	GND	GND
23	GND	GND	PFW
24	ARB1	$-5.2v$	ARB0
25	ARB3	$-5.2v$	ARB2
26	1D1	$-5.2v$	ID0
27	ID3	$-5.2v$	ID2
28	ACK	+5v	START
29	+5v	+5v	+5v
30	RQST	GND	+5
31	NMRQ	GND	GND
32	+12v	+12v	CLK

Here's what each signal means:

RESET	Bus reset
SPV	System parity valid
SP	System parity
TM0,TM1	Transfer mode lines
AD0..AD31	Address/data lines
ARB0..ARB3	Arbitration
ID0..ID3	Slot identification
ACK	Acknowledge
START	Start of transfer
RQST	Request
NMQR	Nonmaster request
CLK	Bus clock
+5v, $-12v$, $-5.2v$	Power
GND	Ground

INTERNAL SCSI CONNECTOR

The internal SCSI connector hooks up to the internal hard disk drives (or any other internal SCSI devices you might have installed). It is a keyed, 50-pin flat cable connector, numbered as shown in Figure 5.2.

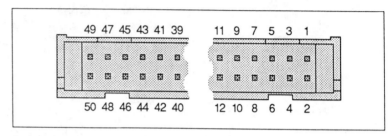

Figure 5.2. Diagram of internal SCSI connector

Here are the signals associated with each pin:

1	GND	18	DP	35	GND
2	D0	19	GND	36	BUSY
3	GND	20	GND	37	GND
4	D1	21	GND	38	ACK
5	GND	22	GND	39	GND
6	D2	23	GND	40	RST
7	GND	24	GND	41	GND
8	D3	25	NC	42	MSG
9	GND	26	NC	43	GND
10	D4	27	GND	44	SEL
11	GND	28	GND	45	GND
12	D5	29	GND	46	C/D
13	GND	30	GND	47	GND
14	D6	31	GND	48	REQ
15	GND	32	ATN	49	GND
16	D7	33	GND	50	I/O
17	GND	34	GND		

Here's what each signal means:

REQ	Request for data transfer handshake
MSG	Message phase
I/O	Direction of data movement
RST	Bus reset
ACK	Acknowledge (in handshake)
BUSY	Bus is busy
D0..D7	Data lines
DP	Data parity bit
C/D	Control/data indicator
ATN	Attention
SEL	Select (target or initiator)
NC	Not connected
GND	Ground

EXTERNAL SCSI CONNECTOR (SCSI)

The external SCSI connector—identical to that found on the various Macintosh models (the Plus, SE, and II)—lets you hook up external SCSI devices (hard disks, scanners, etc.). Of course, you still have to have the software for the drivers. It uses a female DB-25 connector, numbered as shown in Figure 5.3.

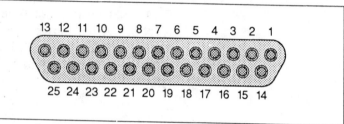

Figure 5.3. Diagram of external SCSI connector

Here are the signals associated with each pin:

1	REQ	14	GND
2	MSG	15	C/D
3	I/O	16	GND
4	RST	17	ATN
5	ACK	18	GND
6	BUSY	19	SEL
7	GND	20	DP
8	D0	21	D1
9	GND	22	D2
10	D3	23	D4
11	D5	24	GND
12	D6	25	TERM POWER
13	D7		

Here's what each signal means:

REQ	Request for data transfer handshake
MSG	Message phase
I/O	Direction of data movement
RST	Bus reset
ACK	Acknowledge (in handshake)
BUSY	Bus is busy
D0..D7	Data lines
DP	Data parity bit
C/D	Control/data indicator
ATN	Attention
SEL	Select (target or initiator)
NC	Not connected
TERM POWER	+5v power (for SCSI terminator, not for device)
GND	Ground

ETHERNET CONNECTOR (E-NET)

This Ethernet connector is a standard one, accepting Ethernet cabling. All hardware for running Ethernet is built into the NeXT motherboard. The necessary connectors and cabling can be purchased from NeXT and NeXT retailers (such as Businessland), as well as from a number of other sources. Software support for Ethernet is provided by the NeXT system software; this includes automatic configuration for small (less than 10) networks of NeXT cubes, and a utility (NetInfo) for more complex or non-homogenous configurations.

VIDEO MONITOR INTERFACE (DISPLAY)

The video monitor interface connects the video circuitry on the motherboard to the MegaPixel Display. It uses a female DB-19 connector, numbered as shown in Figure 5.4.

Here are the signals associated with each pin:

1	+12v		11	+12v
2	− 12v		12	− 12v
3	MON CLK		13	GND
4	MON DATA OUT		14	GND
5	MON DATA IN		15	GND
6	MON PWR SWITCH		16	GND
7	NC		17	GND
8	VSYNC		18	GND
9	HSYNC		19	GND
10	VIDEO			

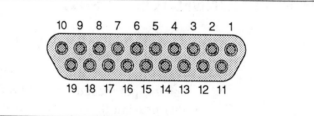

Figure 5.4. Pinout of display connector

Here's what each signal means:

+12v, − 12v	Power for monitor
MON CLK	Clock signal
MON DATA OUT	Sound data to display
MON DATA IN	Keyboard, mouse, and sound data in
MON PWR SWITCH	Power switch on keyboard
VSYNC	Vertical sync signal
HSYNC	Horizontal sync signal
VIDEO	Video signal
NC	Not connected
GND	Ground

LASER PRINTER PORT (PRINTER)

The NeXT Laser Printer connects with the NeXT mother-board through this port, a female DB-9 connector. Its pins are numbered as shown in Figure 5.5.

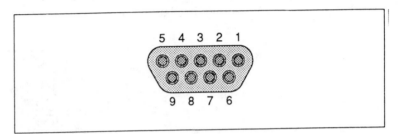

Figure 5.5. Pinout of printer connector

Here are the signals associated with each pin:

1	LP CLK	6	GND	
2	LP DATA IN	7	GND	
3	LP DATA OUT 1	8	GND	
4	LP DATA OUT 2	9	NC	
5	LP PWR ENABLE			

Here's what each signal means:

LP CLK	Timing signal from mother-board
LP DATA IN	Status information from printer
LP DATA OUT 1	Data to printer
LP DATA OUT 2	Data to printer
LP PWR ENABLE	Power-up signal
NC	Not connected
GND	Ground

SERIAL PORT A (SERIAL A)

The NeXT motherboard has two RS-422 serial ports, with slightly different pinouts. Both ports, though, use a round DIN-8 connector, identical to those found on various Macintosh models (the Plus, SE, and II). The pins are numbered as shown in Figure 5.6.

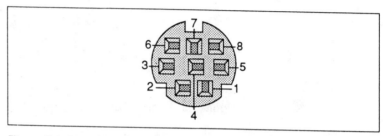

Figure 5.6. Diagram of serial port A

Here are the signals associated with each pin:

1	DTR	5	RXD –
2	CTS	6	TXD+
3	TXD –	7	DCD/RTXC
4	GND	8	RXD+

The pinouts are identical with both serial ports found on the Macintosh SE and Macintosh II (pin 7 on the Macintosh Plus is not connected). Here's what each signal means:

DTR	Data terminal ready
CTS	Clear to send
TXD –	Transmit data –
RXD –	Receive data –
TXD+	Transmit data +
RXD+	Receive data +
DCD/RTXC	Data carrier detect or Receive/transmit clock
GND	Ground

SERIAL PORT B (SERIAL B)

This is similar, but not identical, to Serial Port A, the difference being that pin 7 provides power (+5v) instead of a general-purpose input channel. The pin numbering is identical:

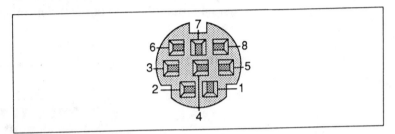

Figure 5.7. Diagram of display connector

Here are the signals associated with each pin:

1	DTR	5	RXD –
2	CTS	6	TXD+
3	TXD-	7	+5v
4	GND	8	RXD+

Here's what each signal means:

DTR	Data terminal ready
CTS	Clear to send
TXD –	Transmit data –
RXD –	Receive data –
TXD+	Transmit data +
RXD+	Receive data +
+5v	Power for device
GND	Ground

DIGITAL SIGNAL PROCESSOR PORT (DSP)

The Motorola DSP56001 has its own port with which it can communicate directly. This actually provides two serial ports, one synchronous, the other asynchronous. See Chapter 7 of the DSP56001 User's Manual for more details. This port uses a female DB-15 connector, numbered as shown in Figure 5.8.

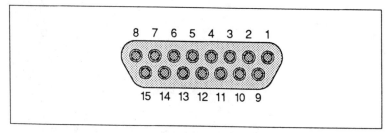

Figure 5.8. Diagram of DSP connector

Here are the signals associated with each pin:

1	SCK	9	GND
2	SRD	10	GND
3	STD	11	GND
4	SCLK	12	SC2
5	RXD	13	SC1
6	TXD	14	RESERVED
7	+12v	15	GND
8	− 12v		

Here's what each signal means:

SCK	Serial clock signal (synchronous)
SRD	Serial receive data (synchronous)
STD	Serial transmit data (synchronous)
SCLK	Serial clock signal (asynchronous)
RXD	Receive data (asynchronous)
TXD	Transmit data (asynchronous)
SC1, SC2	Serial control pins
+12v, − 12v	Power for external use
GND	Ground

MODEM AND TERMINAL CABLING

Both serial ports (A and B) are capable of being hooked up to a modem, to a terminal, or to another computer. Figure 5.9 shows the cabling diagram for a modem cable, while Figure 5.10 shows the diagram for a null-modem cable (for a terminal or a direct connection to another computer).

Note that in many cases, commercially available cables will suffice, even those designed for other systems (such as the Macintosh). However, be sure to test the cables to ensure that they work properly, especially if you plan to have users dialing into your NeXT system through a modem.

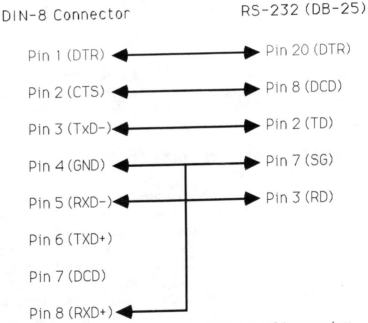

Figure 5.9. Cable for connecting Serial Port A or B to a modem

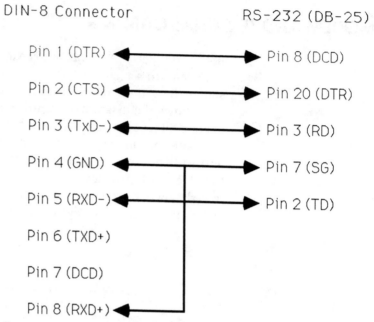

Figure 5.10. Null modem cable for connecting Serial Port A or B to a terminal or another computer

CHARACTER AND KEYBOARD CODES

When you press (or release) a key on the NeXT keyboard, a unique **key code** is sent to the NeXT system (via the MegaPixel Display). The system then decodes the current set of depressed keys and generates the appropriate **character code**, which it passes on to the appropriate application.

Figure 5.11 shows the key codes for each key on the NeXT keyboard. The codes are given as hexadecimal (base-16) values, since the notation is more compact and also gives a better idea of the patterns on the keyboard. Note that there are no key-codes for the system control keys (Power, Brightness, Volume); these directly affect the hardware and are not processed like the others.

The character codes used by the NeXT system have no relationship to the key codes. Their purpose is to represent (in memory and on disk) the letters, digits, puncuation and symbols within documents and other data files. They are based on

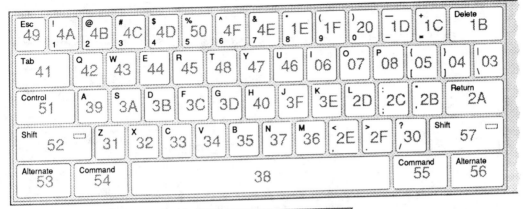

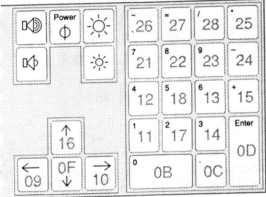

Figure 5.11. Key code values (in hexadecimal) for the NeXT keyboard

an extended version of the ASCII character set. ASCII uses a seven-bit code, giving a range of 0..127. These values are used as follows:

Decimal	Hex	Usage
0..31,127	00..1F,7F	control codes; only a handful are still used
32..63	20..3F	digits and punctuation
64..95	40..5F	uppercase letters and more punctuation
96..126	60..7F	lowercase letters and yet more punctuation

The regular fonts on the NeXT system (Times, Helvetica, Courier) implement the standard ASCII character set. However, by using the eighth bit in each byte, they can represent another 128 characters, with codes ranging from 128 to 255. Figure 5.12

hex	0	1	2	3	4	5	6	7	8	9	A	B	C	D	E	F
0x	NUL	SOH	STX	ETX	EOT	ENQ	ACK	BEL	BS	HT	LF	VT	FF	CR	SO	SI
1x	DLE	DC1	DC2	DC3	DC4	NAK	SYN	ETB	CAN	EM	SUB	ESC	FS	GS	RS	US
2x	space	!	"	#	$	%	&	'	(	)	*	+	,	-	.	/
3x	0	1	2	3	4	5	6	7	8	9	:	;	<	=	>	?
4x	@	A	B	C	D	E	F	G	H	I	J	K	L	M	N	O
5x	P	Q	R	S	T	U	V	W	X	Y	Z	[	\	]	^	_
6x	`	a	b	c	d	e	f	g	h	i	j	k	l	m	n	o
7x	p	q	r	s	t	u	v	w	x	y	z	{	|	}	~	DEL
8x	figsp	emsp	ensp	thinsp												
9x																
Ax		¡	¢	£	⁄	¥	ƒ	§	¤	'	"	«	‹	›	fi	fl
Bx		–	†	‡	·		¶	•		‚	„	"	»	…	‰	
Cx		`	´	^	~	¯	˘	˙	¨		˚	¸		˝	˛	ˇ
Dx	—															
Ex		Æ		ª					Ł	Ø	Œ	º				
Fx		æ				ı			ł	ø	œ	ß				

ASCII control character

not assigned

Figure 5.12. Character codes used by the NeXT system fonts

hex	0	1	2	3	4	5	6	7	8	9	A	B	C	D	E	F
0x	NUL	SOH	STX	ETX	EOT	ENQ	ACK	BEL	BS	HT	LF	VT	FF	CR	SO	SI
1x	DLE	DC1	DC2	DC3	DC4	NAK	SYN	ETB	CAN	EM	SUB	ESC	FS	GS	RS	US
2x	space	!	∀	#	∃	%	&	∋	(	)	*	+	,	-	.	/
3x	0	1	2	3	4	5	6	7	8	9	:	;	<	=	>	?
4x	≅	Α	Β	Χ	Δ	Ε	Φ	Γ	Η	Ι	ϑ	Κ	Λ	Μ	Ν	Ο
5x	Π	Θ	Ρ	Σ	Τ	Υ	ς	Ω	Ξ	Ψ	Ζ	[	∴	]	⊥	_
6x	‾	α	β	χ	δ	ε	φ	γ	η	ι	φ	κ	λ	μ	ν	ο
7x	π	θ	ρ	σ	τ	υ	ϖ	ω	ξ	ψ	ζ	{	|	}	~	DEL
8x	figsp	emsp	ensp	thinsp												
9x																
Ax		ϒ	′	≤	⁄	∞	ƒ	♣	♦	♥	♠	↔	←	↑	→	↓
Bx	°	±	″	≥	×	∝	∂	•	÷	≠	≡	≈	…	|	—	↵
Cx	ℵ	ℑ	ℜ	℘	⊗	⊕	∅	∩	∪	⊃	⊇	⊄	⊂	⊆	∈	∉
Dx	∠	∇	®	©	™	∏	√	·	¬	∧	∨	⇔	⇐	⇑	⇒	⇓
Ex	◊	〈	®	©	™	∑	⎛	⎜	⎝	⎡	⎢	⎣	⎧	⎨	⎩	⎪
Fx		〉	∫	⌠	⎮	⌡	⎞	⎟	⎠	⎤	⎥	⎦	⎫	⎬	⎭	⎪

ASCII control character

not assigned

Figure 5.13. Character codes for the Symbol font on the NeXT system

shows how these fonts encode their characters. This diagram gives a two-digit hexadecimal value for each cell, with each column representing a 1's digit, and each row a 16's digit; so, for example, the letter "A" has a character code of 41₁₆, which is 65₁₀.

Note that the control codes occupy the first two rows (hex values 00 through 1F), and that the extended characters are in the range 80 through FF (again, hexadecimal). Less than half of these codes are currently in use; they are designed primarily for use with foreign languages.

Even with these special characters, there are many other symbols that you may need to use within a document. Because of this, NeXT also provides the Symbol font, whose characters are shown in Figure 5.13. The codes 20 through 7E correspond closely to the standard ASCII set, but with Greek letters (both upper- and lowercase) replacing the English letters. A few punctuation symbols are changed as well. The extended codes are heavily used, offering a variety of mathematical and logical symbols, as well as some more commonly used special symbols (such as © and ™).

TECHNICAL SPECIFICATIONS

The following product specifications are taken from NeXT documentation and are subject to revision.

The NeXT MOTHERBOARD

Processors

Central processing unit: Motorola MC68030, running at 25 MHz

- 16 general-purpose address and data registers
- 2 stack pointers and 10 control registers
- Non-multiplexed 32-bit address and data buses
- 4 gigabyte (GB) flat address space
- 256-byte data and instruction caches; data cache is write-through
- Automatic instruction pipelining
- Built-in paged memory management unit (PMMU)

Floating point unit: Motorola MC68882, running at 25 MHz
  8 80-bit floating point registers (64-bit mantissa, 15-bit exponent)
  Conforms to ANSI-IEEE 754-1985 standard
  Full set of trigonometric and transcendental functions
  Concurrent execution with host processor (MC68030)
  Concurrent execution of multiple floating-point operations

Digital signal processor: Motorola DSP56001, running at 25 MHz
  Up to 10.25 million 24-bit instructions/second
  24-bit data path to on-chip and external memory
  On-chip X-data, Y-data, and program memory
  Dedicated 8 K x 24-bit high-speed static RAM
  Two 48-bit accumulators, with 8-bit extensions for 56-bit results
  Synchronous and asynchronous serial communications (via DSP port)
  Concurrent execution with host processor (MC68030)
  Extensive internal pipelining

I/O channels: NeXT Integrated Channel Processor (ICP)
  supports 12 direct memory access (DMA) channels
  bandwidth of up to 32 megabytes/second
  128-byte dual buffers

Disk controller: NeXT Optical Storage Processor (OSP)
  controls Canon optical disk drive
  performs real-time Reed-Solomon error correction

Clock/calendar chip:
  32.768 KHz crystal
  3.0 volt removable lithium battery

Memory

  64 kilobytes (KB) EEPROM, containing system configuration information
  128 kilobytes (KB) ROM, containing bootstrap code and NeXT ROM monitor
  32 kilobytes (KB) high-speed static RAM (SRAM), 24 KB used by the DSP56001; 4KB used by the OSP

256 kilobytes (KB) dual-ported video RAM

8, 12, or 16 megabytes (MB) 120ns dynamic RAM (DRAM), using removable 1 MB SIMMs (surface-mounted in-line memory modules); should support 4 MB SIMMs, allowing up to 64 MB of DRAM.

Communications and Interfaces

Video monitor interface (female DB-19 connector)

Provides +12v, -12v power, video signal, sound

Receives keyboard and mouse input

Thin wire Ethernet (BNC connector)

IEEE 802.3 compatible

Two RS-422 serial ports (8-pin min-DIN connectors)

Implemented using SCC chip Z8530

Serial Port B provides +5v for external devices

Small Computer Standard Interface (SCSI) connectors;

Implemented using 53C90 SCSI chip

Internal: 50-pin shrouded vertical header

External: female DB-25 connector

Burst transfer rate: 4.8 megabytes (MB)/second

Printer port (female DB-9 connector)

5 megabits/second transfer rate

Digital signal processor (DSP) port (female DB-15 connector)

Provides both synchronous and asynchronous serial communications

Communicated directly with the DSP56001

Maximum transfer rate of 2 megabits/second.

THE NeXT COMPUTER

Expansion: 4 enhanced NuBus slots (one used for motherboard)

Type C Eurocard connector (96 pins)

10.840" x 10.637" x 0.062" form factor; components can extend 0.85" above and 0.15" below expansion card

Basic cycle rate of 12.5 megaHertz (MHz)

Burst transfer rate of 25 MHz and peak rate of 100 MHz

25 watts of power available per slot

Power: 300-watt, auto-adjusting power supply

Voltage: 90 to 270 volts AC
Frequency: 47 Hz to 63 Hz single phase
Automatically adjusts to line voltage and frequency
Provides power to slots, mass storage, and MegaPixel
Display
Environment:
Ambient temperature: 32° to 104° F (0° to 40° C)
Relative humidity: 10% to 90% non-condensing
Altitude: 0 to 15,000 feet (0 to 4,500 meters)
Size and weight:
Height x width x depth: 12" x 12" x 12" (30 x 30 x 30 cm)
Weight: 25 to 40 lbs (10 to 19 kg), depending on mass storage used
Can hold two full-height 5.25" mass storage devices
Certifications:
UL listed and CSA certified
Complies with FCC Part 15 Class A requirements

MASS STORAGE DEVICES

Magneto-Optical Disk Drive (Canon)
Storage: 256 megabytes (MB) per formatted disk
Average seek time: 92 millisecond (ms), 5 ms within 5 megabyte (MB) range
Raw transfer rate: 1.14 megabyte/second, burst, 0.26 - 0.83 MB/second, sustained
Rotation: 3000 revolutions/minute (RPM)
Disk surface: single-sided, plastic-coated, with rare-earth layer and aluminum backing
Unlimited read/write/erase capability
Removable primary storage and/or backup device
One or two optical disk drives per cube
SCSI Hard Disks (Maxtor)
Storage: 330 MB and 660 MB, formatted
Average seek time: 14.5 ms and 16.5 ms, respectively
Raw transfer rate: 4.8 MB/second, burst
Rotation: 3600 RPM

Platters: 5 and 8, respectively
Rotary voice coil actuator and integrated SCSI controller
45 KB dual-ported FIFO buffer

THE NeXT MEGAPIXEL DISPLAY

Monitor
17" monochrome flat screen
Resolution: 1120 (h) x 832 (v) x 2 bits
Gray levels: black, dark gray, light gray, white
Pixel density: 94 dots per inch (dpi)
Vertical refresh rate: 68.3 Hz
Video bandwidth: 100 MHz

Connectors
Video cable interface (female DB-19) supplies power (+12v, -12v), video signal, digital audio, keyboard and mouse signals
Keyboard jack (5-pin min-DIN)
Dual gold-plated RCA phone line-out jacks
Mini-connector ("Walkman"-style) stereo headphone jack
Monophonic microphone jack

Sound
Internal speaker (mixing stereo signal)
16-bit, 44.1 KHz stereo digital-to-analog (D-to-A) converter chip for sound output (through speaker, line-outs, headphone jack)
8-bit, 8 KHz CODEC (phone quality) analog-to-digital converter chip for sound input (through microphone jack)

Keyboard
85-key, low-profile keyboard
Standard keyboard layout
Modifier keys include Shift, Control, Alternate, and Command
System control keys for power on/off, brightness up/down, and volume up/down
Arrow keys in inverted T-configuration
Numeric keypad with digits, operators, and Enter key

Mouse
> Two buttons distinguishable under software control
> Opto-mechanical ball-and-shaft mechanism

Size and Weight (of monitor)
> Height x depth x width: 17.3" x 16.0" x 14.0" (44 x 40 x 35 cm)
> Weight: 50 lbs (23 kg)

THE NeXT 400 DPI LASER PRINTER

Printer
> Printer connector (female DB-9), with 5 megabit/second transfer rate
> Voltage: 110 or 220 volts AC (switch selectable)
> Frequency: 50 to 60 Hz (autoselecting)
> Output resolution: 300 or 400 dots per inch (dpi), software selectable
> Toner cartridge: EP-S cartridge (approx. 4,000 pages)
> Adjustable toner level (1 [dark] through 9 [light])
> Removable output tray

Paper cartridge:
> Holds up to 200 sheets of letter-sized paper
> Adjustable for a variety of widths (up to 8.5")
> Can accommodate legal size with plastic cover removed
> Plastic cover has adjustable paper guides for manual feed

Size and weight:
> Height x depth x width : 7" x 17"x 14" (18 x 43 x 35 cm)
> With cartridge and tray: 7" x 17" x 32" (18 x 43 x 81 cm)
> Weight: 35 lbs (77 kg)

COMMENTARY

Connectivity is the key to survival and growth, and NeXT has done much to ensure that its cube can be connected to a variety of devices. The NeXT motherboard gives you a wide mix of connectors, avoiding the common pitfall of providing minimal connectivity and then expecting the user to buy additional cards to make things work. The separate printer and Ethernet connectors ensure that the two serial ports aren't tied up doing those jobs; likewise, the separate DSP serial port allows for direct, high-speed access to the digital signal processor without tying up any other ports. And the serial and SCSI ports are identical to those found on the Apple Macintosh, making it easier to share peripherals such as modems and printers with existing systems.

Most of the cables you need for such hookups can be bought "off the shelf." However, the information in this chapters frees you and those you work with to design your own cable and interfaces. Of course, it is wise to use caution when connecting hardware devices to one another, but you should find few problems connecting this system to other equipment.

The NeXT Software Architecture

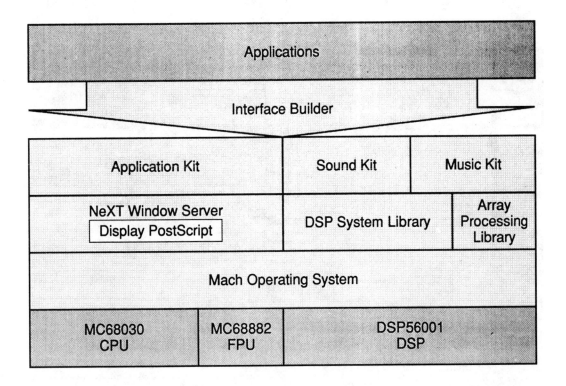

Applications

Interface Builder

Application Kit	Sound Kit	Music Kit

| NeXT Window Server | DSP System Library | Array Processing Library |
| Display PostScript | | |

Mach Operating System			
MC68030 CPU	MC68882 FPU	DSP56001 DSP	

Part II
The Software

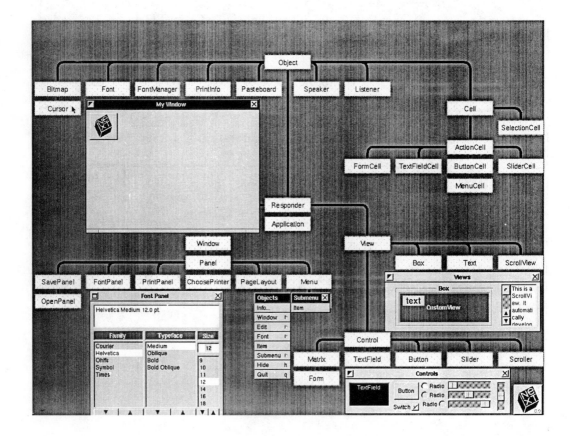

The fastest computer is worthless if you can't use it. Worse yet, excellent hardware can be crippled by mediocre software. The NeXT software, much like the NeXT hardware, is revolutionary, not so much in the advances of its individual elements but in all the components that have been brought together—neatly fitted together—in one system. Coordination and consistency is evident from the lowest to the highest levels. And, yes, like the hardware, the software does have its share of surprises and breakthroughs.

The NeXT system software consists of three major components: a set of bundled applications, the NeXT user interface, and the Mach operating system. The applications, including programs such as WriteNow, Mathematica, and the NeXT SQL Database Server, help you to get work done. The user interface, comprising NextStep and Display PostScript, determines how you interact with the system. The operating system manages resources, organizes files, and coordinates programs running simultaneously. Information flows back and forth between the various components, transformed between various formats. The aim, again: to let you accomplish your goals faster, easier, and better.

6
Applications

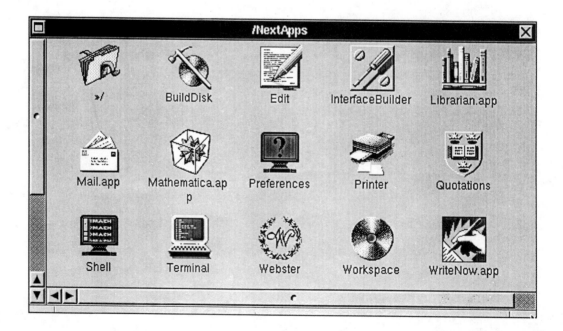

No matter how impressive the hardware is, the true measure of any computer is how much it helps you accomplish. And you can only accomplish work if you have software—computer programs—that run on the computer you're using.

The NeXT system faces the same problem that most new systems face: a lack of software. When the Apple II, the IBM PC, the Macintosh, the Amiga, and the Atari ST all came out, there was very little software available for them. Early purchasers had to wait for third-party software companies to develop the applications they wanted, or write their own.

NeXT decided to avoid that problem, or at least minimize it, by bundling a number of applications with each NeXT computer. **Bundling** means "to include as part of the system," and NeXT included quite a few applications at no extra charge. Some of these programs were developed by NeXT for use on their computer. Others were developed by outside companies; these were usually products already available for other computers, which were then converted (or, in the industry parlance, "ported over") to the NeXT system.

The applications scheduled to be bundled with Release 1.0 of the NeXT system software include WriteNow, a word processor; Edit, a text editor; Digital Webster, an on-line version of *Webster's Ninth New Collegiate Dictionary*; Quotation, an on-line version of the *Oxford Dictionary of Quotations*; Digital Librarian, a general on-line referencing program; the NeXT SQL Database Server, a database "engine"; Mathematica, an interactive symbolic mathematics package; and Allegro Common Lisp, a programming environment. In addition, a number of NeXT utilities are included with the system, such as Mail, Preferences, BuildDisk, Printer, Clock, Terminal, and Shell.

Of the programs given above, all but the NeXT SQL Database Server are present in Release 0.9, though some applications, such as Mathematica and Allegro Common Lisp, are not yet in final form. Finished versions of all applications will be bundled with Release 1.0. This chapter presents a brief overview of all these applications; some, such as WriteNow and Interface Builder, will be discussed in more detail in later chapters.

WORD PROCESSORS

For decades, computers had an image of being "number crunchers," good mostly for complex, high-speed mathematical work. That image has shifted over the past few years, and with good reason: now, the number-one use of computers is **word processing**, that is, creating, editing, and printing text in a variety of formats. A broader term, **desktop publishing**, encompasses word processing along with related tasks such as illustration, page layout, and font design.

The NeXT system comes bundled with two different word processors—WriteNow and Edit—designed for two different types of documents. WriteNow is for document preparation; you would use it to prepare letters, reports, and articles. Edit, on the other hand, is more of a simple text editor; you would use it to write programs or create data files that need to be free of any extraneous formatting information. Let's look at how they differ and when to use each.

WRITENOW

As mentioned above, WriteNow is a complete word processor, designed for preparing documents such as letters, manuals, articles, reports, papers—in short, anything that requires some degree of formatting and layout. In this respect, it's much like the word processors found on the Apple Macintosh and other systems. In fact, WriteNow was originally developed for the Macintosh and is still sold for that computer; this version was rewritten to run on the NeXT system.

WYSIWYG, (pronounced "whizzywig"), which stands for "What You See Is What You Get," is a term used to describe word processor and page layout programs that attempt to show you on the computer screen just what your document will look like when it's printed. WriteNow is a WYSIWYG word processor and, in fact, is better at displaying a document than many similar programs found on other systems. This is because NeXT computer uses the same method—a graphical system called Display PostScript—to display text and images both on the screen and on the printed page. The result: a very close cor-

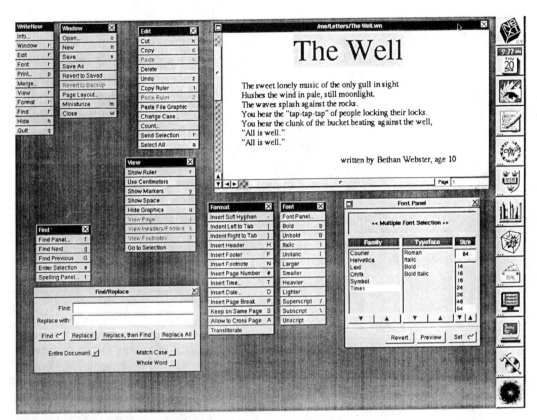

Figure 6.1. The WriteNow application

respondence between what you see on the MegaPixel Display and what comes out of the laser printer, such as seen in Figure 6.1. Most differences are minor, and are due largely to the change in resolution: the screen shows only 92 dots per inch, while the printer supports either 300 or 400 dots per inch.

When you launch WriteNow, you see only a menu in the upper-left corner of the screen, the usual spot for application menus to appear. When you start a new document, you get a "blank sheet of paper" to type on; that is, a window appears with no text in it, and anything you type appears in that window. When you reach the bottom of that page, a new page appears below, with a small break in between. A vertical scroll bar along the left edge lets you move up and down through the document.

You can save the document on your optical or hard disk at any time and then either quit WriteNow, continue working on that document, or open up a new one. For that matter, WriteNow lets you have any number of documents open at the same time. This allows you to transfer text easily from one document to another, or to refer to one while changing another.

WriteNow offers a number of features, including support of multiple fonts and font sizes in the text; insertion of headers, footers, and footnotes; automatic insertion of page numbers, current time, and current date; multiple "rulers" for varying the margins, line spacing, justification, and tab settings within a document; multiple columns; superscripting and subscripting; support of various paper sizes; pasting and resizing of graphics; and, of course, cutting, copying, and pasting text, either within a document or between documents.

EDIT

As useful as WriteNow is, you wouldn't want to use it to write programs or create normal text files; it inserts special formatting codes within the file. These allow it to remember how the document should look next time you open it. Unfortunately, those same codes can confuse programs that just want to read the text and numbers in your file. You don't want or need a word processor; you just want a good old-fashioned text editor.

Edit is a text editor program. Unlike WriteNow, it produces text files than can be easily and clearly read by most other applications on the NeXT system. The user interface is similar to WriteNow, as shown in Figure 6.2, but the set of operations differs. For example, Edit doesn't have headers, footers, and rulers, but it does let you find a specific line number, look up a C function in the UNIX manuals, or indent a selected block of text.

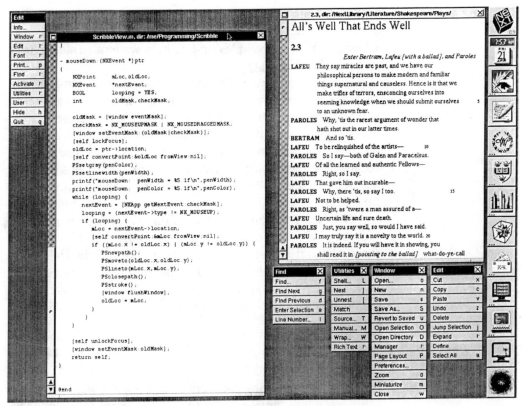

Figure 6.2. The Edit application

A number of the on-line documents are in Edit format, such as all the NeXT and UNIX manuals, as well as the complete works of Shakespeare. This means, of course, that you can read these documents directly (rather than having to work through the Digital Librarian) just by opening them up.

ON-LINE REFERENCES

The concept of electronic books and on-line documentation are not new. UNIX systems traditionally have "manual pages" which you can display with the `man <topic>` command. The CD-ROM market provides various reference works stored on read-only compact discs. And application developers on various computers (such as the Macintosh and the IBM PC) have created larger and more complex on-line help systems to aid the user in using their products.

Each of these systems has limitations, though. On-line help systems are usually available only when the corresponding application is running. CD-ROM products require the user to purchase a separate CD-ROM drive. And while the UNIX man and grep commands provide some powerful search-and-retrieve capabilities, they also have their limitations, not the least of which is the necessity of using the UNIX command line interface.

The NeXT system comes with three applications that provide on-line referencing with an easy-to-use interface. Two of these—Digital Webster and Quotation—are specific to a given reference work, while the third—Digital Librarian—is a general on-line referencing system, capable of searching a variety of documents. Let's look at each of them.

DIGITAL WEBSTER

Five years ago, spelling checkers were a hot software item, and there was some controversy as to whether or not they should be used—some people feared that we would all forget how to spell. Now, they are a standard built-in feature of most major word processors. Many also include a thesaurus to find words similar and opposite in meaning to a particular word.

What these packages don't offer you, however, is any information about the word itself: pronunciation, etymology, and definitions. For those, you have to go to a printed dictionary—or to a NeXT computer.

Digital Webster is an application that lets you access an on-line version of *Webster's Ninth New Collegiate Dictionary*. Each entry for a given word is just as you would find it in the printed version of *Webster's Ninth*, right down to drawings and diagrams, when present; see Figure 6.3 for an example.

Digital Webster can be launched directly by the user or by another application. For example, both WriteNow and Edit let you select a word and then invoke the Define command, which

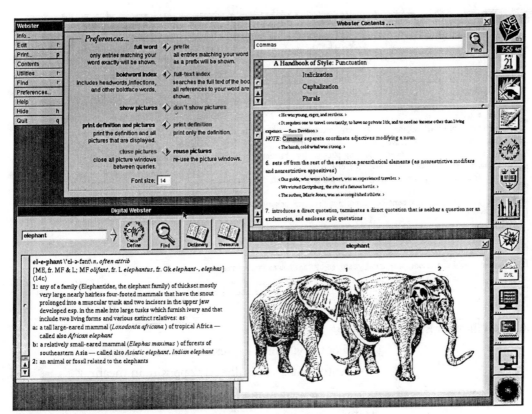

Figure 6.3. The Digital Webster application

brings up Digital Webster (if it's not already running) and passes it that word to look up. Once Digital Webster is up and running, you can quickly cross-reference by double-clicking on any word that appears in the definition area.

Digital Webster includes a built-in thesaurus, and you can choose to use just the thesaurus, just the dictionary, or both at the same time. You open or close each by clicking on the appropriate labeled icon at the top of the window. The thesaurus lists five types of words:

- Synonyms: words very similar in meaning
- Related: words related in meaning
- Idioms: idiomatic words or phrases conveying the same or related meanings

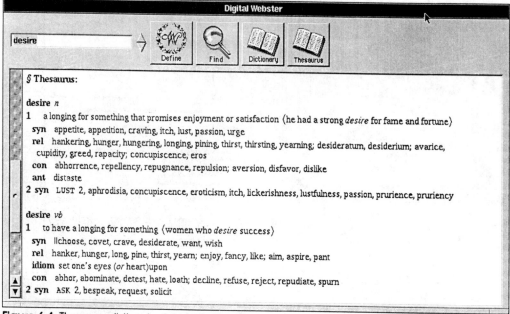

Figure 6.4. Thesaurus listing for "desire"

- Contrary: words expressing contrary ideas
- Antonyms: words directly opposite in meaning

Figure 6.4 shows the thesaurus listing for the word "desire."

Even though the Webster database files occupy some 40 megabytes of disk space, the time it takes to look up a word and display its definition is usually 2 to 5 seconds on a hard-disk-based system.

QUOTATION

Another specialized reference program is Quotation, which lets you search the *Oxford Dictionary of Quotations* (1988 Digital Edition, based on the 1979 Third Edition). Those of you who like to pass the time browsing through quotations will enjoy this program: not only is it far easier to search than a bound volume, but it can bring all the quotations containing a given word together, providing some interesting juxtapositions. Figure 6.5 shows a typical display.

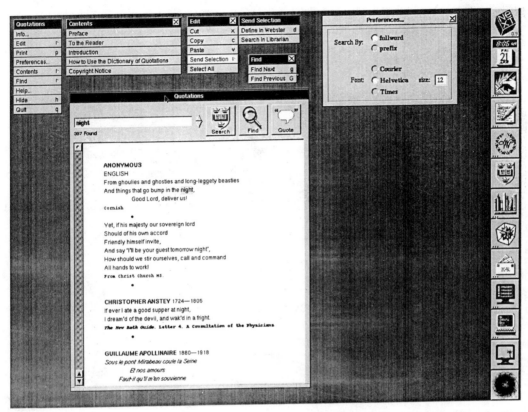

Figure 6.5. The Quotation application

You have a number of options when searching, including whether to look for all quotations with a given word ("night") or all quotations by authors with a given last name ("Davis"); whether to match the word exactly ("night") or to match it with any word beginning with that word ("nights," "nightshade," "nightfall," etc.); and whether to look for all quotations containing a set of words ("night dark").

Quotation has on-line help files to guide you in using it. It also contains the preface and introductions from the bound Third Edition, which are as much a delight to read as the quotations themselves.

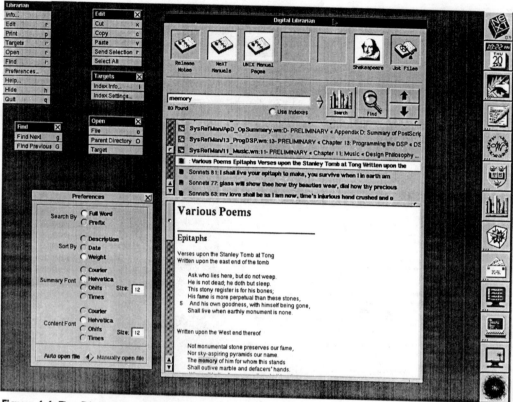

Figure 6.6. The Digital Librarian application

DIGITAL LIBRARIAN

While Digital Webster and Quotation access specific references, the Digital Librarian is a more general application, one that combines elements of the approaches mentioned above. It gives you access to all the NeXT and UNIX documentation, letting you not only find the manual page for a given command but also allowing you to find all references to a given command or topic. It lets you search on-line reference works, either directly or by invoking a utility specific to that reference material. And it provides you with a general help facility for the various applications on the system, and has the potential to do the same for other programs or materials you might acquire. Figure 6.6 shows the Digital Librarian window.

Each icon along the top represents a document or set of documents to be searched. You can select one or more of them to be used in your search. Note that there are blank icon slots. You can drag the icon of a text file (or a directory containing one or more text files) from a directory window into one of these slots; Digital Librarian automatically indexes the files which can then be searched.

Once you've entered a word to be searched for, the Librarian then looks through all the selected documents for that word. If the word is found in one or more documents, those documents are listed in the browser area below the Search and Find buttons. A small icon at the left of each entry indicates the file type (Edit, WriteNow, etc.), and the first line of text in the file is given. Clicking on each entry displays the contents of that entry in the text area below the browser area; you can then scroll through the file. To open the file itself using the appropriate application, select the File command from the Open menu.

NeXT has included a number of on-line references for use with Digital Librarian. These include the complete NeXT manuals and technical documentation; the complete set of UNIX manuals; and the complete works of William Shakespeare, as compiled by the Oxford University Press (1986 Edition), including all plays, poems, and sonnets. Generally, these documents are kept in very small chunks—for example, each scene in one of Shakespeare's plays is a separate text file—making it easy to read or print them.

MATHEMATICA

As was mentioned before, computers have long had the stereotype of being primarily mathematical machines. Ironically, personal computers have only had limited usefulness for any higher forms of math, such as algebra, calculus, differential equations, and so on. This is because these fields require a lot of symbolic math—math based on manipulation of names and expressions—and while computers may add fast, they don't do well with symbolic manipulation on their own.

Mathematica, developed by Wolfram Research, is an answer to that problem. It's a symbolic mathematical environ-

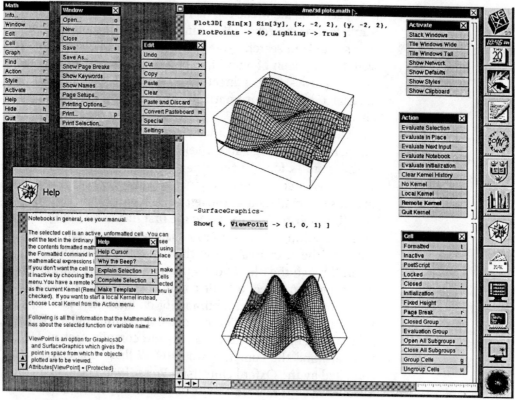

Figure 6.7. The Mathematica application

ment that performs any number of tasks. Mathematica can act like a sophisticated calculator, offering unlimited precision; it can be also used as a programming language, solving problems and printing results. It will do two- and three-dimensional plotting of functions, expressions, and data. It can perform symbolic mathematics, find derivatives, carry out integration, solve series of equations, and do power series expansion. Figure 6.7 shows some of Mathematica's ability to render three-dimensional plots of mathematical expressions.

A working (though not completed) version of Mathematica is included with Release 0.9. The final version in Release 1.0 will include a "math object" that will allow Objective C programs to use Mathematica to perform complex calculations.

NeXT SQL DATABASE SERVER

For serious information storage and retrieval, NeXT has provided the NeXT SQL ("Standard Query Language") Database Server, developed by Sybase.

Database is a general term for a collection of information and covers a broad spectrum: an address book can be thought of as a database, as can the Library of Congress. A database usually consists of some number of records—for example, each entry in your address book. And a **record** usually consists of a set of fields—for example, in your address book, each entry has slots for name, address, and phone number.

In this case, we're talking about a computer database, that is, information stored on your computer, whether it be documents, financial information, personnel and student records, or scientific data. A **database server** is a program that lets you—or your applications—access and update a computer database.

The NeXT SQL Database Server, then, is a utility that allows various users and applications to share and update the same database, all at the same time. It recognizes commands in Transact-SQL, which is a standard set of commands for asking a database program to retrieve or modify information. Programs can send SQL commands to the server and get back the desired information. And NeXT users whose machines are on the same Ethernet network can (with appropriate authorization) access databases on each other's NeXT computers by means of the database server.

The NeXT SQL Database Server wasn't included with Release 0.9; however, it should be bundled with Release 1.0.

ALLEGRO COMMON LISP

The standard NeXT program development system, consisting of Interface Builder, the Application Kit, Display PostScript, and Objective C, will be discussed in the next few chapters. However, another development system will be bundled with the NeXT computer: Allegro CL, a Common Lisp environment from Franz Inc.

Lisp is actually one of the oldest high-level computer languages. It is used heavily in computer science education and research, especially for artificial intelligence (AI) applications. Allegro CL will fully support the object-oriented environment on the NeXT system, including use of the objects in the Application Kit.

Release 0.9 includes a standard UNIX version of Allegro Common Lisp that you run from within the Terminal application (discussed later in this chapter). The final version of Allegro CL, which should be bundled in Release 1.0, will use the NeXT user interface and have full access to the objects defined in the Application Kit.

NeXT UTILITIES

There are a number of lesser programs bundled with the NeXT system, all designed to make life easier in one way or another. These include: Preferences, Mail, BuildDisk, Printer, Clock, Terminal, and Shell. All are included in Release 0.9, though they may undergo minor changes in each system release. Here's a brief rundown of each.

PREFERENCES

Each user likes to customize the system to fit his or her own needs, wants, and habits. The Preferences application, mentioned in Chapters 3 and 4, does just that, letting you adjust mouse and keyboard settings, screen brightness, and speaker volume. All these settings will be remembered and applied each time you log in; each user can have his or her own settings.

As shown in Figure 6.8, you can use the Preferences application to set the computer's clock to the current time and date. This panel lets you set a flag so that the Preference icon will display the current time and date, as seen in some of the figures earlier in this chapter (look under the NeXT icon in the icon dock). You can also change your password and select which device (optical disk, hard disk, or EtherNet) to boot from when you turn on your NeXT system.

Figure 6.8. The system clock/calendar settings in the Preferences application

MAIL

If your NeXT system is connected to a network, you can use the Mail application to exchange messages with other users on the network. Mail is compatible with the standard UNIX mail utility, but gives you a NeXT-style user interface to make things easy. Figure 6.9 shows some of the various windows and options available to you.

If you are exchanging messages with a user on another NeXT system, you can send and receive voice mail. To send voice mail, you just need a microphone that you can plug into the back of the MegaPixel Display. Obviously, you don't need a microphone to receive voice mail; NeXT will play it for you when you read the message, using the MegaPixel Display's built-in speaker. Mail also lets you attach a file (document, program, data file, etc.) to a mail message. This means that you could send a report created using WriteNow to another NeXT user on the network, with a mail message attached as a memo.

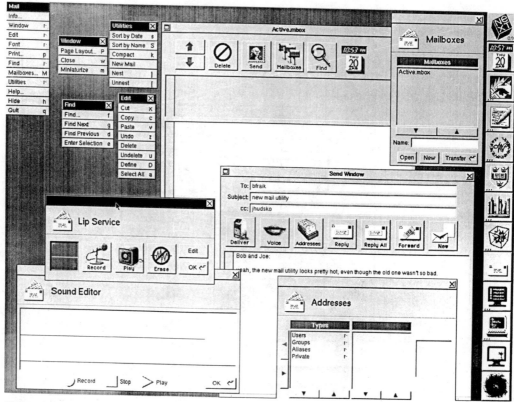

Figure 6.9. The Mail utility

BUILDDISK

BuildDisk is a rarely used application that performs a **system build** on your disk; that is, it formats your disk (either optical or hard), creates all the appropriate directories, and then copies all the appropriate files. You use this in only two cases. First, if you get a NeXT system with a hard disk, you boot off of the optical disk, then run BuildDisk to format the hard disk and copy all the system files onto it. This usually takes about an hour. Second, if you want to create a bootable optical disk, you boot off of your hard disk or the network, and then run BuildDisk to format the optical disk and copy the system files. Running off a hard disk, this takes about three hours; it takes longer if you're running off the network or a second optical drive. Figure 6.10 shows the BuildDisk application window.

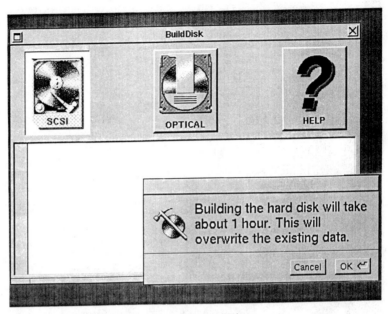

Building the hard disk will take about 1 hour. This will overwrite the existing data.

Cancel OK ↵

Figure 6.10. The BuildDisk application window

PRINTER

The Printer application was discussed in Chapter 4. It lets you manage the print queue. You can view any document in the print queue; you can also remove it from the queue so that it doesn't get printed. You can change the resolution of the laser printer to either 300 or 400 dots per inch. And you can even use the application to test the laser printer.

TERMINAL AND SHELL

Running underneath all these applications is Mach, a UNIX-compatible operating system that supports a regular command-line interface. NeXT provides two different utilities for accessing Mach directly: Terminal and Shell, both seen in Figure 6.11.

The "classic" terminal connection to a UNIX system is a VT-100 terminal (or compatible equivalent), with an 80-character x 24-line display and direct screen addressing. The Terminal application gives you just that: a nonresizable window that uses 12-point Courier font to put up an 80-character x 24-line

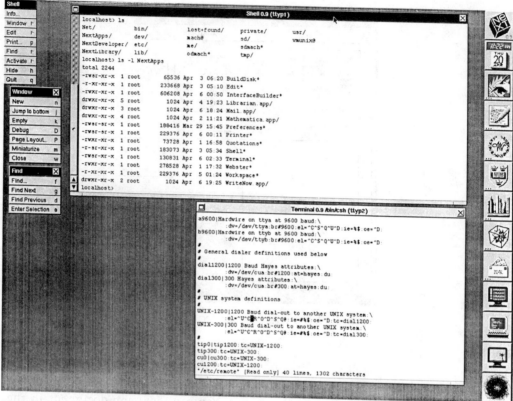

Figure 6.11. The Terminal and Shell utilities

display. Through this window, you get a standard UNIX prompt and access to most (if not all) of the standard UNIX features, commands, and utilities that you'd expect. And the programs that use direct cursor control (such as vi, a commonly used UNIX text editor) work just fine.

Shell, like Terminal, gives you access to the UNIX user interface. Unlike Terminal, though, Shell emphasizes the NeXT user interface. The Shell window is resizable, so that you can make it as tall and as wide as you like. Commands and results—what you typed and how it responded—are saved as they scroll off the top of the window, and you can use the scroll bar to go back and see what was done. For that matter, the Shell menu offers forward and backward searching, as well as copying, pasting, and printing of the Shell window's contents.

COMMENTARY

NeXT has been very aggressive in the amount and quality of software bundled with their system. There is a certain danger in this: third-party developers don't want to compete with free software, and so the bundled programs tend to dominate their respective areas. This is what happened on the Macintosh with MacPaint and MacWrite; third-party paint and word processing programs were slow in coming to market, and they didn't thrive until Apple stopped bundling.

NeXT, of course is in a different position than Apple was in with the Macintosh. The NeXT market is narrower in scope, the installed base will grow much more slowly, and some third-party developers will be scared off by the lack of a floppy disk drive on the NeXT system. So a more aggressive bundling policy makes sense and benefits you, the user, in the short run. The long-term effects are still uncertain.

Having said all that, let's look at what software *isn't* bundled with the NeXT system. The most noticeable lack is a true paint program of some kind. Some demonstration programs bundled with Release 0.9 give you limited image design and output, but there's nothing as simple as MacPaint. The other two common software packages not included are a page layout program and a spreadsheet. In all three cases, there are well-established third-party firms who have announced or implied product development for the NeXT system. The only major obstacle is the software distribution issue; that may slow down release of some products.

The bottom line: NeXT provides most of what you need, and third-party developers should do the rest.

7
The NeXT User Interface

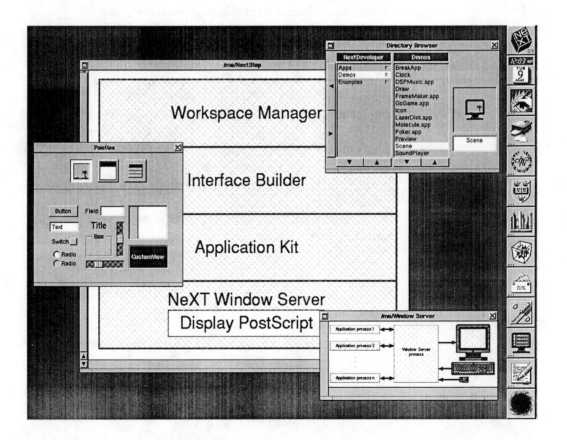

Applications are essential; for most users, they are the entire reason for sitting down at a computer. But both users and applications need to interact with the rest of the computer. Users want to manipulate files and create programs of their own; applications need to interact with the users, with other programs, and with the resources of the computer itself. To aid both programs and people, NeXT created the NeXT user interface, composed of NextStep (developed at NeXT) and Display PostScript (developed by Adobe and NeXT).

NextStep is made up of four software elements, shown on the opposite page. One is **Workspace Manager**, the user interface that displays files and directories, manages the icon dock, and launches applications. Working together with that is **Interface Builder**, a "program construction kit" that aids you in creating your own programs, allowing you to design and lay out much of a program's user interface using just the mouse and the keyboard. Both these programs, as well as most other applications running on the NeXT computer, make use of the **Application Kit**, a software library that defines how objects such as windows, menus, and buttons work. Meanwhile, the **Window Server** manages the display on the screen, handling drawing requests from the various programs running, and determines which programs will be notified about events such as mouse clicks and key presses. Window Server, in turn, calls **Display PostScript** to perform any actual drawing required, either for the display or for the printer.

These elements combine to define and implement the NeXT user interface; before seeing just how they do that, let's look at the concepts behind the NeXT user interface.

THE NeXT USER INTERFACE

The wars being fought by rival computer companies have shifted battlegrounds over the last few years. In the early to mid 1980s, the focus was compatibility: with IBM, naturally; there was no one else to worry about being compatible with. To a lesser extent, there also a focus on hardware performance. That's why the introduction of the Macintosh in 1984 was greeted with scorn by so many people: it was not IBM-compatible and was woefully underpowered. But then the introduction of the Macintosh shifted the focus from hardware to software, and specifically to the **user interface**, that is, the manner in which the user interacts with the computer.

While many of the ideas embodied in the Macintosh user interface were pioneered elsewhere, they didn't gain widespread exposure until the Macintosh was released. Since then, other firms have followed suit with products such as GEM, Intuition, Windows, and Presentation Manager. The realization: it doesn't matter how fast the computer is or what software runs on it if people have a hard time using it.

GOALS

Because of this, the NeXT user interface, as supported by NextStep, was designed with the following goals in mind:

- It should adapt to your level of expertise.

- It should act consistently even in different applications.

- It should give you control of what happens.

- It should feel natural to you.

- It should respond primarily to the mouse.

Each of these represents a significant design decision. Let's take a brief look at each.

Adaptable

When the Macintosh was announced in 1984, its user interface—graphical; using windows, menus, and icons; mouse-oriented—became an immediate source of controversy. It was hailed by people who had long been intimidated by the terse, cryptic nature of **command-line interfaces** (CLIs), such as those found under CP/M, MS-DOS, and UNIX. It was scorned by people who had mastered such systems and found the Macintosh interface agonizingly slow and limiting. The arguments, pro and con, pointed out a fundamental problem in user interface design: how do you make a user interface easy enough for novices to learn and powerful enough for experts to use?

The NeXT user interface attempts to bridge that gap in a few different ways. It starts by providing the type of interface which industry experience has shown is easiest for inexperienced users to learn. This interface uses windows, pop-up menus, and icons, all of which are controlled largely with a two-button mouse.

Power users haven't been forgotten, though. Keyboard equivalents are offered for many commands that would otherwise be selected using the mouse. More important, two different applications, Terminal and Shell, provide direct access to the Mach operating system via csh (for C shell), a standard and widely accepted UNIX command-line interface. Since Terminal and Shell run under Workspace Manager, you get the best of both worlds: a command-line interface in a windowing environment, allowing you to use both at the same time.

Consistent

One of the struggles users have had in the MS-DOS/PC-compatible market is the variety of user interfaces for applications. Each program has its own interface, and proficiency in one program helps little in learning another. Ironically, when efforts have been made to reduce this variation—for example, by one spreadsheet program emulating the user interface of another—the result has been legal action over infringement of "look and feel" copyrights.

The NeXT user interface avoids this by creating a consistent user interface for all programs and applications. This interface is embodied in the behavior of objects such as windows, menus, icons, and applications. Since these and related objects are defined in the Application Kit, a program using those objects will automatically exhibit a certain degree of consistent behavior. Interface Builder reinforces this consistency by setting up certain default objects when you start to create a new program with it. And the NeXT technical documentation contains a detailed list of guidelines as to how programs should behave.

The result: once you know how the user interface works, you can learn each new program or application with a minimum of effort.

User-Controlled

Many applications and user interfaces found on other systems work in a **modal** fashion. This means that at any time you are limited to a given set of actions, that is, you're in a given mode: insertion mode, data entry mode, update mode. And even if the application is **non-modal**, the operating system may be modal. For example, you might only be able to work on one application at a time; switching to another application, or wanting to use directory commands, requires you to save your work and exit the current program.

Because the NeXT user interface is designed to be largely non-modal, you have as much freedom as possible to decide what to do next. In short, you're in control of your environment. You can have multiple applications running simultaneously, and switching applications requires only a mouse click. Within a given application, you usually have access to all pertinent commands. There are instances of modal behavior, such as an attention panel asking you to verify some action that could have irreversible consequences. Even in those cases, though, the application doesn't have control of the system; you can still switch to another application, or use Workspace Manager to examine or modify your files and directories.

Natural

Command-line interfaces, for all their power, suffer from some inherent limitations: they are one-dimensional, myopic, and cryptic. "One-dimensional" because they focus your attention on a single line of text, no matter how large the screen. "Myopic" because they force you to deal with a single event or command at any given moment. "Cryptic" because they cause all information going into (or coming out of) the system to do so as text, which doesn't convey information as quickly or, often, as understandably as graphics do.

The NeXT user interface, like most graphical interfaces, avoids these limitations. It takes advantage of our visual orientation—the fact that it's easier to show or do than to describe. It takes advantage of the full screen, and allows a number of things to go on at once. At the same time, it conveys the illusion of dealing with physical objects in a real two-dimensional space: you pick up, drag, resize, and otherwise manipulate the "objects" on the screen. Instead of having to memorize long lists of commands and options to be typed in, you just perform the action directly. All this corresponds to how you work in the real world, so that the actions required of you seem as natural and intuitive as possible.

Mouse-Oriented

A command-line interface is, by necessity, text-oriented. You type in commands, press Return, and the computer responds appropriately. There's nothing inherently wrong with this, and, in fact, there are tasks and operations for which a command-line interface is demonstrably superior. The point is that a keyboard is best (and a mouse would be largely useless) for a command-line interface because of the one-dimensional text orientation of a CLI.

By the same token, a graphical interface works best with some type of positioning device that lets you move freely in two dimensions, select, pick up, and release objects. A number of such devices exist—light pens, trackballs, graphical tables—but the most popular and most common is a mouse, which is the device shipped with the NeXT system. This doesn't mean that the keyboard isn't important, just that the mouse is a necessary and useful tool for the user interface.

USER ACTIONS

The two devices you use to interact with the user interface are the mouse and the keyboard. Let's talk briefly about how you use each one.

The mouse is associated with the cursor. The cursor is usually an arrow, but may change to another shape, or even disappear, under certain circumstances. The mouse has two buttons, one left and one right. All actions described here involve using either button, though you can assign one button a special function, as described in Chapter 9.

There are three basic mouse operations, though a number of secondary operations can be described (and are, in Chapter 9). The first is **clicking**: moving the cursor over some object, then quickly depressing and releasing the mouse button. This is analogous to touching, selecting, or choosing some object. Clicking twice rapidly is known as **double-clicking** and has some special uses.

The second operation is **pressing**: moving the cursor over some object, depressing the mouse button, and holding it down until the desired result is obtained. This is analogous to holding down a control, such as a tuning button or an accelerator pedal.

The third basic operation is **dragging**: moving the cursor over some object, depressing the mouse button, moving the cursor to another location, and releasing the mouse button. This is analogous to picking up an object and moving it, or dragging an object (such as a pencil) over a surface.

Keyboard actions mostly fall into two categories. The first is text (or numeric) input; you type, and the resulting letters, digits, symbols, etc., get sent to the application, usually to be displayed somewhere. The second is command selection; you hold the Command key down and type some character. The result is interpreted as a command to the application, usually corresponding to a menu item.

SCREEN ELEMENTS

These operations interact with the elements displayed on the screen. There are four independent elements or objects that you are presented with by the NeXT user interface: icons, menus, panels, and windows, all shown in Figure 7.1. Other elements, such as buttons, switches, sliders, and scrollers, appear within these objects.

An **icon** is a small graphical image used most often to represent a file—application, document, or data file—or a directory. There are two typical actions with icons. First, you drag an icon from one window to another, symbolizing moving the file; you can also drag application icons out to the icon dock (more on

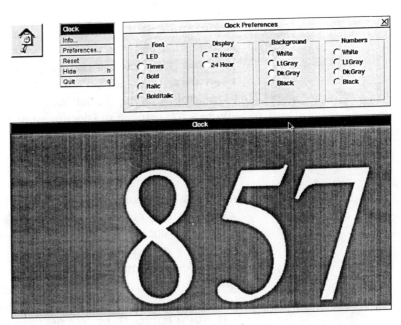

Figure 7.1. Elements of the NeXT user interface

this later). Second, you can double-click on an icon, launching the application associated with that icon.

A **menu** is a list of commands associated with a particular application or program. You select a command by clicking on it; the command is highlighted while it is being carried out, then reverts to its normal shade. Some commands bring up **submenus**, which act just like menus. Other commands may cause panels to appear. Menus and submenus have **title bars** at the top; you can use them to drag the menus around the screen.

A **panel** is a rectangular area displaying information and some number of **controls**, such as **buttons**, **switches**, and **sliders**. The controls are operated by clicking on them with the mouse. Panels have title bars; you can drag them around, too. A panel may have a **close button** in the title bar; if you click on it, the panel disappears.

A **window** is a central work area for an application, also rectangular. This is where you are most likely to see and manipulate data—text, images, numbers—in a document. Like a panel, a window usually has a title bar and can be dragged or, if a close button is present, closed. A window may also have a **resize bar** along its bottom; you can then resize the window by grabbing this bar with the cursor and dragging it. It may also have a **miniaturize button**, used to turn the window in an icon. This icon is called a **miniwindow**; it can be expanded back into a full window by double-clicking on it. A window may also have scrollers along the left and/or bottom edges; these allow you to scroll through the document being displayed.

WORKSPACE MANAGER: MANAGING FILES

When you use a computer, you need to have some way of interacting with it, of giving it commands to carry out, such as "delete this document," "move that file to this area," "run this program," and so on. To accomplish these things, you press keys; on some computers, you also move mice and click buttons. But those actions, in and of themselves, don't really do anything. Instead, the computer needs to be running a program that will interpret these actions, then take appropriate action. On a workstation running UNIX, this program is called the shell (usually sh or csh); on an IBM PC running MS-DOS, it could be COMMAND.COM, GEM, Windows, or Presentation Manager; on a Macintosh, it's the Finder; and on a NeXT computer, it's Workspace Manager.

It's easy to confuse Workspace Manager with the NeXT user interface. This is because the term "user interface" is used in a variety of ways, one of which is to describe the programs mentioned above. Workspace Manager is just another application running on the NeXT system; the NeXT user interface, as described in the previous section, refers to the manner in which all applications, including Workspace Manager, present themselves to you.

When you start using—or **log into**—the NeXT system, it launches Workspace Manager. Workspace Manager remains up and running as long as you are using the system. In fact, you end a work session by quitting Workspace Manager, or logging off.

EXAMINING DIRECTORIES

Workspace Manager provides three major services for you. First, it lets you examine the system of directories and files on your mass storage devices (hard disk, optical disk, etc.). It does this by providing a series of **directory windows**, windows that show you the contents of a given directory in a variety of formats.

One such window, in the **Directory Browser** format shown in Figure 7.2, is automatically opened when you log in; you can open additional directory windows as desired and can select the format for each. Using a few of the commands in the WM (Workspace Manager) menu, you can get even more information specific to a given file or directory.

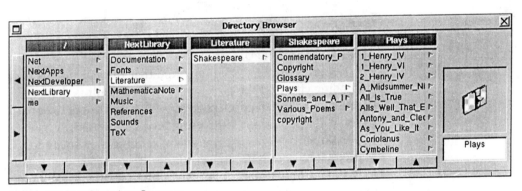

Figure 7.2. The Directory Browser

MANAGING FILES AND DIRECTORIES

Workspace Manager also lets you manage files and directories. Using these directory windows, you can copy, move, and delete both files and directories, just by dragging an icon from one window to another. You can create new directories and rename existing directories and files. You can examine and change the various protection levels for individual files or directories, determining who can read, write, execute, or search them.

LAUNCHING PROGRAMS

Finally, Workspace Manager lets you **launch** (load and run) applications and programs. You can do this by using a directory window to find a particular application and then double-clicking on its name or icon. Workspace Manager also maintains the icon dock along the right edge of the display. This is a place where you can drag and leave the icons associated with applications, so that you can launch or select them without having to browse through directory windows.

For more details on using Workspace Manager, see Chapter 9.

INTERFACE BUILDER: CREATING PROGRAMS

The advent of graphical user interfaces has been a boon to users, who find them much easier to learn and use, for all the reasons given earlier. Unfortunately, they are a bane for developers and programmers, who now find that they spend most of their coding effort on the user interface. The result is that products are often delayed or released with bugs because of the complexity of developing and supporting the user interface.

NextStep addresses that problem, offering a two-part solution. The first part is Interface Builder, a utility that lets you create the user interface for your program from a large palette of predefined objects, such as windows, menus, buttons, sliders, text fields, and icons. As you can see in Figure 7.3, Interface Builder lets you use the "physical world" metaphor of the NeXT user interface to drag, resize, arrange, and otherwise manipulate these objects until your program's interface looks the way you want it to.

Interface Builder provides three major functions in developing a program. First, it lets you lay out the user interface using the screen and the mouse. Second, it lets you define connections between the various objects in the user interface. Third, it creates Objective C source code files that can then be expanded to provide the functionality required. Let's see how these functions help you in creating applications.

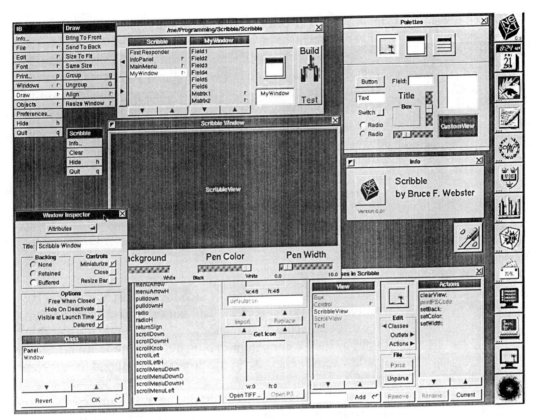

Figure 7.3. Interface Builder

LAYING OUT THE INTERFACE

If you're a programmer, you know that one of the most tedious tasks can be getting the visual interface for your program laid out just right, especially in a graphical environment. Whether you're using a separate resource file or putting commands right into your code, you find yourself going through a cycle of adjusting, compiling, and running the program to get everything just right.

Interface Builder lets you do this interactively. To add a new window or panel, you just drag one off the palette. You can then resize it until it's just right. Likewise, you can drag buttons, sliders, and other controls, placing them right where you want them and resizing them as desired. The menu can be expanded and rearranged as you wish, with items and submenus added or deleted. You can position labels, text fields, and other text-oriented objects.

Besides arranging objects, you can also customize them. A special panel, called the Inspector, allows you to modify various attributes for specific objects. For example, you can use the Inspector to edit a window's title, determine which controls are present in the title bar (resize, miniaturize, and close buttons), and set options such as whether or not it's visible when your program is first launched. You can use the Inspector to determine how a button works, how (and if) it's labeled, what key will trigger it, what sound will play when you press it, and so on.

MAKING CONNECTIONS

Interface design and layout is nice, but is just the start. Once you have the various objects laid out, you have to decide how they are connected to one another. For example, it's one thing to put a Clear command into a menu; it's another to get, say, a window somewhere else in the program to respond to that command.

Interface Builder lets you do this as well. Some connections are established automatically for you; when you start a new project, the Hide and Quit commands in the default menu are already hooked up to the underlying application, while the Info command will trigger the appearance of the predefined information panel. You can set up other connections yourself.

CREATING SOURCE CODE

Interface Builder does more than just permit you to lay out your interface and connect elements in that interface. It actually generates all the files necessary for an application: a file containing the layout and connection information, Objective C source code files, and a makefile that the Objective C compiler uses to compile and link all the right files in the right order. This automatic file generation means that you can create a working program from what Interface Builder creates. The program won't do much—the only functionality will be that inherent in the objects used (such as resizing a window) or defined by the connections made (such as the effects of the Hide and Quit commands in the menu). But it does provide a framework for you to build on.

THE APPLICATION KIT: PROVIDING OBJECTS

In the last section we referred to the various elements in a program's user interface as "objects" and talked about connections between objects, or objects sending messages to one another. These terms weren't used casually. NextStep provides an object-oriented environment for application development, and the Application Kit is the foundation of that environment. But before you learn just what the Application Kit does, let's talk a bit about the term "object-oriented."

OBJECT-ORIENTED DESIGN

Traditional application design— for command-driven programs —focused on algorithms and command prompts. An algorithm is just the set of steps required to solve a particular problem, like a recipe or an industrial process. The application would prompt you for a command, wait until you type something, take the appropriate steps—carry out the necessary algorithms—and then prompt you again. This approach was easy to implement, but not always satisfying for the user, and the program spent most of its time waiting for the user to press Return.

Over the last five years, the focus has shifted to event-driven program design, in parallel with the shift to graphical user interfaces. An event-driven application is constantly scanning for events—pressing a key, clicking a button, moving the mouse—which it then handles appropriately. While this scanning is going on, the program can be carrying out other tasks. Combined with a graphical user interface, this approach is more satisfying for the user. However, it puts a tremendous burden on the programmer, who has to handle all possible events (closing windows, menu selections, and so on). Indeed, much of the programming effort is spent figuring out what the event is, where it happened, what it affects, and how to handle it. The resulting code is often complicated and tortuous.

Because of this burden, there has been a recent shift toward object-oriented program design. An object-oriented application can be thought of as a collection of objects that send messages back and forth, getting information about each other and telling each other what to do. These objects may be visible items —windows, buttons, menus, drawing areas—or nonvisible data structures, such as the internal representation of a chess board. In an event-driven environment, these objects get passed the events that apply to them, which they either handle or pass on to other objects. This approach provides a logical approach for breaking large, event-driven programs down into smaller, self-contained object definitions that can be updated or modified independent of one another.

CLASSES AND INHERITANCE

When you define an object, you actually create an object class. For example, you might create the object class Window. This class describes what information a Window object holds—size, location, title—and what messages you can send to it—close, resize, change title. One of those messages has the instructions on how to create an **instance** of a Window, that is, an actual Window object. This is the message sent to the Window class to create windows as they are required in your program. Once you've create an actual instance, you can send it the other messages, telling it what to do.

One key concept in object-oriented design is that of **inheritance.** Suppose you want to create a special kind of window, called MyWindow, that behaves just a bit differently than the Window class you've already defined. Rather than duplicate all your Window code, you just declare MyWindow to be a subclass of Window. As such, MyWindow inherits all of Window's data and message definitions. All you have to do then is add whatever new data and message definitions you want MyWindow to have, as well as redefining any inherited messages that you want to behave differently.

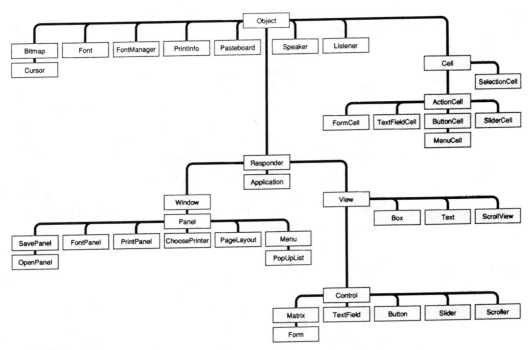

Figure 7.4. The Application Kit inheritance hierarchy

A LIBRARY OF OBJECTS

While object-oriented programming has some definite benefits, it doesn't solve the problem of defining all those objects in the first place. That's where the Application Kit comes in. It's a library of over thirty major objects, including all the objects required to implement the NeXT user interface. Figure 7.4 shows the objects defined in the Application Kit.

The "family tree" diagram in Figure 7.4 indicates which objects descended from (are subclasses of) other objects. The fundamental object class is Object; all other objects are descended from this class. Most visible objects are descended from the Window and View classes, while the Cell class defines most objects that hold information.

These objects are fully defined and implemented, including all event-handling behavior. That means, for example, that objects of the class Window (or one of its subclasses) already know how to handle being dragged, resized, miniaturized, or closed. Likewise, buttons know when they've been pressed, sliders know how to update themselves and keep track of their current values, and so on.

This predefined behavior serves two major purposes. First, it greatly reduces the time and effort required to implement the user interface, especially when used in combination with Interface Builder. If you want to change how one of these objects behaves, you can always subclass it and add only those changes that you desire; otherwise, you don't have to worry.

Second, it standardizes the NeXT user interface. All applications use the objects in the Application Kit, and so they behave the same—except, of course, where the object has been subclassed and the behavior modified.

OBJECTIVE C

Even with tools such as Interface Builder and the Application Kit, you still have to do a fair amount of programming to bring up a significant application. To this end, NeXT has bundled the Objective C compiler from Stepstone Technology with every NeXT system. While Objective C is not part of NextStep per se, it is an important and necessary tool for anyone wishing to write programs for the NeXT computer. Interface Builder produces Objective C source code, and the object definitions in the Application Kit are set up to be used with Objective C programs.

Objective C is based on the Gnu C compiler developed by Richard Stallman. Release 0.9 has merged the Objective C syntax with the Gnu C compiler to speed up compilation and to produce faster, more efficient code. Of course, you still have full access to the usual C library routines and can freely mix normal C functions and variables with the Objective C routines. More details on Objective C, as well as some sample routines, are given in Chapter 12, Creating Applications.

WINDOW SERVER: MANAGING EVENTS

The NeXT user interface lets you have multiple applications running at the same time, each application having multiple windows open. All these windows can have drawing and other changes going on at the same time, and you are free during all this to click on different windows, panels, icons, and menus, triggering various actions. The obvious question: how does this all get handled correctly?

The answer is Window Server, the bottom layer of NextStep. Window Server performs a number of functions. It receives all events from the mouse, keyboard, and computer, determines which application they belong to, and sends them on. It maintains the separate windows on the screen, moving and updating them as necessary. And it accepts all drawing commands, using Display PostScript to perform the actual image creation.

EVENT HANDLING

NextStep is an **event-driven** environment. This means that the user interface and all the applications respond to events. Most of these events you create: pressing keys, clicking buttons, moving the mouse. A few, such as a "power off" warning, come from the system itself. Information about these events comes in to Window Server, which then decides what to do with them.

In most cases, Window Server passes these on to the appropriate application. For example, if you click on a button in a panel, Window Server notes the location of the mouse when the click occurred, determines which program owned that area of the screen, and sends an event record to the Application object in that program. The **event record** is a data structure that contains information about the event: what type it was, where it happened, and any other pertinent information. The Application object then determines which of the program's other objects should receive the event record—in this case, the Panel object. In turn, the Panel object checks if there is some other object within its bounds that should get the event record. In this case, there is—the Button object—so the Button object gets sent a "mouse down" message, which it processes accordingly.

In real life, the process just described is optimized for speed, and the Button object gets the "mouse down" event record without a lot of intermediate processing. This is done by building a data structure describing all the objects within a program that can respond to such an event and their relative positions. When the application receives the event record, it can directly check to see which object should get the event and passes it on to that object.

Likewise, there are a few events directly handled by the Window Server. For example, when a "mouse down" occurs in the title bar of a window or panel, Window Server (with help from Display PostScript) directly intercepts that event and handles moving the window or panel around the screen. When the mouse button is released, Window Server sends a "window moved" event to the appropriate application.

WINDOW MANAGEMENT

Window Server sees everything on the screen as a set of windows. A **window**, as defined here, is simply a rectangular area on the screen into which images are drawn. The four independent objects mentioned earlier—icons, menus, panels, and windows—are all considered windows by Window Server. The actual appearance and behavior of each of those objects is controlled by the Application Kit; Window Server simply draws what it's told to.

In keeping the screen properly organized, Window Server uses a **screen list**. Every window (icon, etc.) visible on the screen is in that list. The list itself is sorted from back to front. Using that list, Window Server can calculate how much of each window is visible at any given time. That way, it can correctly update the display as windows are created, moved, or closed.

Window Server uses the screen list to determine which application should receive a given event. For example, when you click the mouse somewhere on the screen, Window Server compares the location against the screen list to see if it's in any of the windows. If it is, then it sends the event to the application owning that window.

DRAWING UPDATES

Communication between Window Server and the applications goes both ways. While Window Server sends events to the applications, the applications send drawing commands to Window Server, which then uses Display PostScript to create (or render) the actual bitmap images within the appropriate window. These images are then compared against the screen list, and the visible portion of that window is updated.

This raises a question about what happens in the non-visible portion of the window being updated. Is the drawing information for that portion lost, or is it saved somehow? The answer depends on what kind of storage (memory) you set up to back up that window. Window Server supports three kinds of **backing store**; let's talk about each.

The default type of backing store is **buffered**. In this case, memory equivalent to the window's full size (uncovered) image is set aside in main memory. Whenever you draw to that window, Display PostScript actually renders the image in the off-screen area. When you then tell Window Server to "flush window," the part of that image corresponding to the visible portion of the window is **blasted** to the screen, that is, copied at a high rate of speed to the appropriate location in video RAM. Should more of the window be uncovered later, then the corresponding part of the off-screen image can be blasted over.

This method has two advantages. First, it avoids the flicker or "tearing" that sometimes happens when you draw directly to the screen. Instead, it lets you do all your drawing ahead of time, and then moves the complete image over all at once. Second, it avoids the hassle encountered on other systems, such as the Macintosh; on these systems, the application has to be able to redraw any portion of the screen at any time. Developers there often end up implementing this approach themselves—that is, they always draw to an off-screen buffer, and then "redraw" by copying from that buffer to the screen—but the Window Server makes that all transparent.

The next type of backing store is **retained**. This is just like buffered, except that the visible portion of the image is drawn directly on the screen, and the non-visible portion is drawn to the backing store. This has the advantage of being slightly faster than the buffered approach while still maintaining the off-screen information, but you still run the risk of tearing or flickering while the image is being drawn.

The last type of backing store is **none**. In this case, all drawing is done directly to the screen and only in the visible portion of the window; the rest of the image is thrown away. This method is faster, and it avoids using any memory for an off-screen buffer. However, you run the risk of flicker while drawing, and should more of the window be uncovered, the application will have to redraw the entire image again.

REMOTE OPERATION

One consequence of the design of NextStep and the use of the Mach operating system is that the Window Server running on your NeXT computer can actually serve applications running on other NeXT systems. To do this your NeXT system must be hooked up to an Ethernet network. You also must have the proper authority (and UNIX skills) to do a remote log-in onto another NeXT system on the network. Once you're logged in, launch a NeXT application over there. The result: that application's menus and windows appear on your display, but the application itself is running on the other NeXT system. Response will be a bit sluggish, since all event records and drawing requests are being sent over the network, but it will work.

At this point, it's time to look briefly at what actually does all the drawing on a NeXT system, both on the screen and through the printer: Display PostScript.

DISPLAY POSTSCRIPT: DRAWING IMAGES

Much has been said in this chapter about the trend toward graphical user interfaces. These interfaces make it easier to vary how text looks and to integrate text and graphics in the same document. As the resolution and quality of displays has increased, there has been a corresponding trend in printed output; laser printers have supplanted dot-matrix printers, much as high-resolution graphic displays are taking over from the traditional 80-by-25 character-based display. The goal in all this has been WYSIWYG output—What You See Is What You Get. In other words, the document as seen on the screen should match the document as it comes out of the printer.

Unfortunately, these two devices for rendering text and images—high-resolution displays and laser printers—have followed divergent paths. Various manufacturers have come up with different software package for drawing to the screen: QuickDraw on the Macintosh; X-Windows on UNIX systems; GEM on the IBM PC and the Atari ST; Windows and Presentation Manager on the IBM PC; Intuition on the Amiga; and so on. On the other hand, a completely different set of packages has been developed for laser printers, dominated largely by PostScript, from Adobe Systems, and the HP standard, from Hewlett-Packard. The result is that programs that draw to the screen and produce printed output have to support two different drawing methods: one for the screen and one for the printer.

To minimize this problem, NeXT took the pioneering step of using the same imaging routines—Display PostScript—for both the screen and the printer. Developed jointly by Adobe Systems and NeXT, Display PostScript incorporates all the drawing capabilities of PostScript and adds a number of extensions, including a special graphics operation called "compositing." The result is an imaging system that can handle both interactive graphics and hard copy output, producing a very high correlation between what you see on the MegaPixel Display and what comes out of the NeXT Laser Printer.

THE POSTSCRIPT LANGUAGE

PostScript is an imaging language developed by Adobe Systems, Inc., designed originally for use in printer and similar output devices. It is a true programming language, very reminiscent of FORTH because of being stack-oriented. It is an **interpreted** language: commands are sent down as text strings, which are then interpreted and the instructions carried out. Display PostScript, however, recognizes two forms of **binary encoded commands**, which can be executed more quickly; NextStep and NeXT applications use these formats almost exclusively.

Room does not permit an extensive discussion of PostScript, but here are a few of the concepts that you're likely to run into while using the NeXT system.

Graphical Objects

PostScript commands work on three types of graphical objects: text, geometric figures, and bitmaps. **Text** consists of characters: letters, digits, punctuation, and special symbols (such as "©"). Each character can have a specified **font**, that is, a typeface, such as Helvetica, Times Roman, or Courier. It can also have a point size, indicating how large the type is. And it can have a style, such as **bold**, *italic*, or ***bold italic***.

Geometric objects are constructed by PostScript commands. For example, a solid light-gray circle could be created by a few PostScript commands:

```
newpath
  150 150 100 0 360 arc
closepath
0.333 setgray
stroke
```

Bitmaps are actual scanned, sampled, or generated images. A bitmap is a list of values for every dot within the image; each value ranges from 0.0 (black) to 1.0 (white), indicating the dot's shade. Most of the icons used in the NeXT user interface are examples of bitmaps.

Operations and Paths

Once you have a graphical object defined, you can perform a number of operations on it. You can **translate** it: move it to another location. You can **scale** it: make it bigger or smaller. You can **rotate** it: turn it clockwise or counterclockwise. And you can **clip** it: draw only that portion falling within another image.

PostScript operates on the idea of paths. A **path** is a sequence of drawing instructions that can involve any or all of the graphical object types mentioned above. To draw in PostScript, you first create the path, and then either **stroke** it (draw it with lines) or fill it (paint it in). You can define a **clipping path**; drawing will then take place only within the region defined by the path.

THE DISPLAY POSTSCRIPT IMPLEMENTATION

Display PostScript is a superset of the PostScript programming language. In addition to all the standard PostScript commands, it contains a number of extensions requisite for an interactive, multitasking environment. These can be accessed in your Objective C programs by two means: the Client Library and pswrap functions.

The Client Library

All the Display PostScript operators, including the PostScript operators, are available as C function calls; this collection of functions is called the Client Library. These functions send binary object commands down to the Window Server, which passes them on to Display PostScript.

Most of these functions have names in the form `PSfunc-name()`, where *funcname* is the name of the corresponding PostScript function. For example, the PostScript code to draw a gray circle (shown above) would translate into the following calls:

```
PSnewpath();
PSarc(150.0, 150.0, 100.0, 0.0, 360.0);
PSclosepath();
```

```
PSsetgray(0.333);
PSstroke();
```

In a similar fashion, those calls specific to Display PostScript have names in the form `DPSfuncname()`, where *funcname* is the name of the corresponding Display PostScript function.

All these functions are documented in the NeXT *Technical Reference Manual*.

pswraps

There is yet another way in which you can send commands down to Display PostScript: pswraps. A pswrap is a sequence of Display PostScript commands that you can "wrap up" into a single C function call and then use repeatedly. For example, suppose you wanted to modify the commands above so that you could draw disks of a given color. You might define the following pswrap:

```
defineps drawdisk(float x,y,radius,gray)
   newpath
   x y radius 0 360 arc
   closepath
   gray setgray
   stroke
endps
```

You could then call your routine within a C program like this:

```
drawdisk(150.0,150.0,100.0);
```

The pswrap `drawdisk()` would then send binary encoded PostScript commands down to Display PostScript. Details on how to create and use pswraps are given in the NeXT *Technical Reference Manual*.

Compositing

While Display PostScript is available on a number of systems, there are some extensions specific to the NeXT system. Perhaps the most significant of those extensions is **compositing**. This is a mechanism for combining two bitmap images rapidly. A typical use is animating an image (such as a ball) over a static background (a brick wall). By compositing the ball image with the brick wall image repeatedly, with the ball's position moving a little each time, you achieve an animation effect.

Each pixel in the "higher" image (such as the ball) has an alpha value, which signifies how transparent the pixel is. The alpha value ranges from 0.0 (transparent) to 1.0 (opaque). **Transparent** means that none of the pixel's original shade comes through; **opaque** means that all of its color comes through. When you combine the higher and lower images on a pixel by pixel basis, the result is based on the alpha value of the higher image's pixel. If the alpha value is 0.0, then the lower image's pixel shows through completely; if the alpha value is 1.0, then only the upper image's pixel shown; if it's somewhere in between, then the two pixels combine according to the alpha value and their respective shades.

Further options involve a set of logical operators determining just how the images are combined. The result is a tremendous variety of combinations that allow you to mix complex, shaded objects of varied transparency.

For a simple demonstration of compositing, use Workspace Manager to open up the directory window for /NeXT/Apps, then change that window's viewing style to Icon (using the View submenu in the WM menu). Now, find the WriteNow icon, grab it with the mouse, and drag it over some of the other icons. You'll find that you can see through the dark gray areas around the borders of the icon.

ADDITIONAL INFORMATION ON POSTSCRIPT

For more information on PostScript, you should get the official PostScript reference manuals, all published by Addison-Wesley and usually identified by the color of their covers (given in parentheses):

- *PostScript Language Program Design* (green)
- *PostScript Language Reference Manual* (red)
- *PostScript Language Tutorial and Cookbook* (blue)

These are known as the Green Book, the Red Book, and the Blue Book, respectively. They're not only the official manuals, they are also very well written and worth having if you plan to do any programming or image design on the NeXT system. If you can only get one, get the tutorial (the Blue Book).

COMMENTARY

Just as the motherboard is the real heart of the NeXT hardware, NextStep is the heart of the software. Workspace Manager, which is still being modified and improved, manages to capture and surpass many of the strengths of the Macintosh user interface while avoiding imitation. Interface Builder, itself built on ideas and concepts pioneered elsewhere, sets a new standard for interactive program design. The Application Kit, with its object-oriented approach to system routines, relieves much of the burden inherent in programming an event-driven system with a graphical user interface. Window Server, with Display PostScript wrapped inside, manages the events and graphics for multiple applications running simultaneously.

Together, these four components provide a consistent, powerful environment for applications and programming. As happened with the Macintosh system software, what NeXT has done here will be closely studied and widely imitated for some time to come.

8
The Mach Operating System

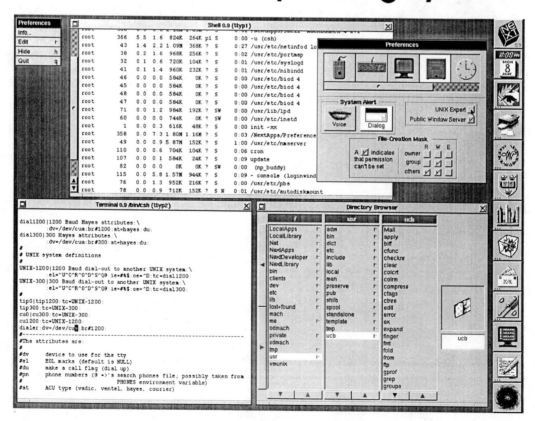

The most active program on a computer is the one that users are often least aware of: the **operating system**, sometimes called the **OS**. This is the first program to run when you power up the system; it remains running as you load and execute applications; and it's the last program running as you turn the system off. In fact, it is so pervasive that most users don't think of it so much as a program as just what the computer does when it's on.

The operating system provides a number of functions, including the following:

- It loads programs from the disk into memory and starts them executing.

- It maintains the directory and file structure on mass storage devices.

- It provides a standard set of routines that programs can use to locate, read from, and write to disk files.

- It manages access by programs to system resources, such as memory, input/output ports, and mass storage devices.

- It schedules task priority in a multitasking system, deciding how much CPU time each program gets.

- It performs swapping and handles page faults in a virtual memory system, deciding how much real memory each program gets.

- It provides a mechanism for programs to exchange information.

Not all operating systems provide all these facilities, especially those found on microcomputers and some minicomputers. However, the Mach operating system, which is designed to be UNIX-compatible while avoiding many of UNIX's problems, does. Let's look at why NeXT chose to use Mach, what special features Mach offers, and what the implications of Mach's UNIX compatibility are for you.

WHY MACH?

When the designers at NeXT, Inc., started thinking about an operating system for their computer, they were faced with a simple choice: they could either write their own, or they could use or adapt an existing operating system. Since they wanted to include all the features given earlier, they realized that writing their own OS wasn't feasible; it would just take too long and tie up too many programmers within the company.

Once they decided to go with an existing OS, their choices were fairly limited. Most operating systems of the complexity desired are specific to a given computer, processor, or hardware architecture, so the choices were quickly narrowed down to one family: the various implementations of the UNIX operating system.

WHY UNIX?

The UNIX operating system was originally developed at Bell Labs in the late 1960s and early 1970s in an effort to bring an interactive operating system onto Digital Equipment Corporation (DEC) PDP/11 minicomputers. The original idea was simple: a small kernel would provide the low-level input/output and task-scheduling functions, while a large set of **utilities**—each a separate program—would do most of the actual work. The user interface would just be another program, called the **shell**; it would let the user run the various utilities and examine files being stored on the disk.

Because of AT&T's willingness to distribute UNIX (including the original source code) cheaply to universities, UNIX became very popular in the academic and research environment. More important, the authors of UNIX rewrote most of it in C, a high-level computer language they had developed. This meant that UNIX could be made to run on other computers, so long as those systems had a C compiler available and someone was willing and able to convert those portions of UNIX that were machine-specific. The result was that UNIX was brought up on a wide range of computers—again, mostly in academic and research environments.

In the intervening years, UNIX has migrated to the work-station and personal computer markets. At the same time, the source-code availability has resulted in a large number of enhancements and variations. Indeed, one of the major issues facing vendors and users of systems running UNIX is: which version of UNIX should I use? Large corporations, such as IBM, AT&T, DEC, Apple, Sun, and others, have lined up behind dif-ferent versions, each group seeking to establish their implemen-tation as "standard." And the question NeXT faced now became: which UNIX?

THE VIRTUES OF MACH

UNIX was originally designed to run on a small, simple com-puter system; one of the earlier implementations used only 16 KB of memory for the kernel while running. However, UNIX has grown enormously over the last 20 years, adding major fea-tures and adapting to more sophisticated and complex environ-ments, including features such as virtual memory and multiple processors. The UNIX kernel, originally intended to be small and simple, became large and convoluted. Adding new features, or modifying old ones, became a serious challenge.

A group of researchers at Carnegie-Mellon University decided to go back and start all over again. Their goal was to write a small, tight kernel that performed some fundamental tasks very well. All other operations would be handled with code that, like the original UNIX utilities, would reside outside the kernel. This project went through several phases; the final result was the Mach operating system.

Because of these features, NeXT selected the Mach operat-ing system to use on its computer and hired one of the principal developers, Dr. Avadis Tevanian, to polish up Mach for com-mercial release. Because of the wide acceptance of UNIX in the higher education market, NeXT also decided to focus on a UNIX-compatible implementation of Mach, while adding those features and attributes that make Mach competitive with other UNIX implementations.

THE MACH KERNEL

The Mach kernel is designed to handle three basic tasks:

- **virtual memory management**—allocating system memory resources to each program

- **processor scheduling**—allocating system computing resources to each program

- **intertask communication**—allowing separate programs to share information or send messages to one another

It does these things with an abstract, object-oriented approach, allowing Mach to be readily ported from one system to another. Also, by limiting the functions of the kernel to the essentials, the Mach design allows easier modification of the other functions of the operating system.

MACH OBJECTS

Mach is based around a set of objects, somewhat abstract, which describe executing programs. These objects are tasks, threads, messages, and ports.

A **task** is the basic unit of execution; you can think of a program or an application as being a single task. A task encompasses not only the program code itself (see the next paragraph), but all system resources allocated to that program: memory, processors, mass storage devices, ports.

A **thread** is an independent set of CPU instructions, always embedded within a task. The thread is the actual program code contained within a task. Most tasks contain a single thread, but it is possible for a given task to have more than one; for example, a simulation program might have several threads running simultaneously, each one representing some element of the simulation. A thread always belongs to and is contained within a single task.

A **message** is a collection of information to be sent from one task or thread to another. The message can contain data, instructions, or whatever is appropriate. For example, the WriteNow application can send a message to the Webster application, passing it a word and asking it to show the definition of that word.

A **port** is the place where a task receives messages. For one task to send a message to another, it has to have permission to access that task's port. Use of ports allows one task to send a message to another one without having to know much of anything about the receiving task—which could be running on a different system.

VIRTUAL MEMORY MANAGEMENT

Mach is a **virtual memory** operating system. This means that a task can have more memory assigned to it than is actually available in the computer system. This has three major advantages. First, it lets you run a program that requires more memory than you have installed in your system. Second, it lets you have several programs running simultaneously, even when there isn't enough memory for all of them to be resident simultaneously. Third, it makes it relatively simple to run programs that have large, sparse memory spaces.

A task's memory space is divided up into **pages**, equal-sized chunks of memory. Some of these pages are resident in physical memory at any time; the rest are stored on the mass storage device (hard or optical disk) in a **swapping file**. When a thread within a task requires a page that's not currently in memory, a **page fault** occurs; the kernel suspends execution of the thread while it loads in the necessary page, swapping out other pages if necessary, then lets the thread continue execution.

Mach offers a number of virtual memory features to enhance performance over standard UNIX systems. One such feature involves sending messages from one task to another. Mach can handle this by simply changing the virtual memory mapping of the two tasks, so that the page(s) containing the message are removed from the sending task's memory map and added to the receiving task's memory map. This avoids the time and overhead normally required by UNIX to copy the message into the kernel's memory space, and from there into the receiving task's memory space.

A related feature allows you to have memory-mapped files. In other words, a task can add an entire file to its virtual memory map, and then access any portion of that file as if it were residing in memory. The appropriate sections of the file are swapped in and out of memory as required.

PROCESSOR SCHEDULING

Mach is a **multitasking** operating system, that is, it allows more than one task to be loaded into memory and executing at any given time. It does this by determining how much CPU time each thread in each task gets. By giving little chunks of CPU time to each thread on a rotating basis, it creates the illusion of several programs running simultaneously. The amount of CPU time that each thread gets, and how often it gets CPU time, depends on that thread's priority—how important the system thinks it is—and whether or not that thread is blocked, that is, waiting for something else to happen (data to be read in from disk, a key to be pressed, a sound to finish playing) before it can continue.

Mach is also designed to support **multiprocessing**, that is, to work on a system containing several CPUs. This means that overall system performance can be improved by adding CPU chips to a given system.

INTERTASK COMMUNICATIONS

The Mach kernel handles messages being transmitted from one thread to another, from one task to another, and from a task to the kernel (or vice versa). It sets up and controls the ports for each task or thread, keeping track of messages sent and received.

Ports are separate objects from threads and tasks, which access ports based on the privileges granted. For example, a task (or thread) can have **send access** to a port, meaning that it can send a message to that port; likewise, it can have **receive access**, allowing it to read any messages sent to that port. While several tasks can have send access to a port at the same time, only one task can have receive access at any given moment.

Essentially, all intertask communications are handled using messages and ports. By using this approach, Mach can ensure synchronization between the sending and receiving tasks, blocking access by the receiving task until the entire message has been sent. This approach also allows Mach to transparently implement communications between tasks on different systems.

UNIX COMPATIBILITY

The Mach kernel in and of itself has no inherent UNIX compatibility. However, because of its size and focus, it easily allows a UNIX-compatible system to be set up on top of it. This is just what has been done for the NeXT computer. The resulting version of Mach is said to be **source-compatible** with the BSD (Berkeley Standard Distribution) 4.3 release of the UNIX operating system; in other words, programs that can run on 68000-based computers using BSD 4.3 UNIX will also run on the NeXT system with recompilation.

Entire books have been written about the UNIX operating system, and you may well want to do some extra reading in that area. In the meantime, here are some basic concepts about using UNIX, which you'll find handy.

USERS AND GROUPS

A typical microcomputer operating system assumes a single user; when you turn on the computer and boot up the system, it comes up, ready to do work. It doesn't distinguish between different people using it; each user is granted full access to all files and can copy, modify, and delete files at will.

UNIX, however, is designed as a **multi-user** operating system. It assumes that different people will be using it, possibly at the same time. It also assumes that you, as a user, may want some degree of protection for the files you create and use, so that another user doesn't accidentally delete your files. Likewise, it assumes that the person managing the computer system (called the **system administrator**) may want to restrict who can use the computer to an approved list, and may want to prevent accidental or deliberate alteration of system files by those users.

Each user of a UNIX system, then, typically needs permission to use that system. This permission comes in the form of a **user login ID**—such as jdow—and a **password**—such as amiga2K. When you boot up the system, it prompts you for the login ID and the password; if you give both correctly, you are allowed to use the system. This process is known as **logging in**. Likewise, when you are done using the system, you **log out**, that is, you tell the system that you're finished. It then shuts off access to all files, waiting for the next user to log in.

Once you've logged in, you may face certain restrictions concerning file access and manipulation. Typically, you have full control over files that you've created, including those you've copied from other user's files. As a general rule, you can read and execute other users' files, as well as the system files, but you can't delete or change them. In some cases, you may not even be able to read or execute them.

On UNIX systems, several users often need to be able to work together, accessing and changing each other's files while still protecting those files from unauthorized access. Such users can be made members of a **group**, automatically inheriting the same privileges and restrictions. UNIX typically predefines several groups (such as staff) and allows the system administrator to create new ones.

The system administrator needs to be able to set up, change, and delete accounts; access and change system files; and perform other critical system tasks. Because of this, the system administrator typically has a **superuser** account, that is, one that supersedes all protections and limitations. On the NeXT system, this superuser account has the user login ID of `root`. The differences between a user and a superuser, and how to log in as a superuser are discussed in more detail Appendix B.

FILES

Information in your NeXT system is organized into files. A **file** is a collection of associated information stored on a mass storage device, such as a hard disk or optical disk. There are numerous types of files, but they can usually be grouped into three broad classes: **text files**, containing information in readable text format; **data files**, containing information in non-readable binary format; and **object files**, containing CPU instructions in binary (machine code) format. There are various exceptions and special cases—for example, WriteNow files contain both readable text and binary-encoded formatting data—but you'll find that most files you work with fall into one of the these three categories.

A file has a **file name**, that is, some string of letters, digits, and punctuation that identifies it. Many file names also have an **extension** at the end, consisting of a period (".") followed by one or more letters or digits. The extension is used to identify what kind of file it is. For example, the name of the file that this chapter was stored in is "mach.wn"; the extension ".wn" means that it's a WriteNow document.

Note that Mach (like UNIX) is **case-sensitive**, that is, it considers upper- and lowercase letters to be different when used in file names. For example, the file name "Mach.wn" is different than the file name "mach.wn". This is important to remember, because if you type in "Mach.wn" when the file you want is "mach.wn", the system won't be able to find it.

File Ownership and Protection

Each file has an **owner**, usually defined as the person who created it. More precisely, the owner is the user login ID used by the person who created it. For example, if you log in using the ID jdow, that ID will be given as the owner of that file.

Each file has its protection status stored with it, that is, a set of bits determining who can read it, write it, or execute it (if it's an object file). This protection status is stored for three different sets of people: the file's owner, members of the owner's group, and everyone else. You can change the protection status for files which you own, or which belong to your group. A superuser can access any file, regardless of protection, and can change its protection status.

DIRECTORIES

Files are organized into directories, that is, a collection of files, usually related in some way: same owner, same type, and so on. You can think of a directory as being like a file folder: you can place an assortment of documents into the folder, and can remove them as well. If you move the file folder itself, then all the documents inside are moved with it.

A directory is really just a special type of file, and so shares most of the same traits. For example, a directory has an owner; it has protection status bits, though the "execution" status refers to the ability to search the directory; and it can be copied, moved, or deleted.

Besides holding files, a directory can also hold other directories, much as you can store one or more file folders within a given folder. A directory stored within another directory is sometimes called a **subdirectory**. Because of this organization, which allows directories to contain directories, which can hold other directories and so on, the NeXT computer is said to have a **hierarchical file system**.

The "topmost" directory—that is, the directory enclosed by no other directory—is called the **root directory**; its actual name is "/". This directory contains a number of files and subdirectories; the subdirectories, in turn, contain files and/or subdirectories, and so on. The **full path name** for a file consists of the file name itself preceded by the names of all the enclosing directories, with those names separated by slashes ("/"). For example, the file "mach.wn" is stored in the directory Software, which is stored in the directory NeXTBook, which is stored in the directory Library, which is stored in the directory bwebster, which is stored in the directory Homes, which is stored in the directory MyDisk, which is stored in the root directory ("/"). Thus, the full path name for "mach.wn" is: "/MyDisk/Homes/bwebster/Library/NeXTBook/Software/mach.wn".

DEVICES

Hardware devices, such as the printer, the disk drives, and the serial ports, are treated like files. Most of these devices "files" are found in the directory "dev", which is contained in the root directory. For example, the printer can be refered to by the path name "/dev/printer". By using these path names, programs can read from and write to various hardware devices.

THE SHELL

The standard UNIX user interface is a type of program called a **shell**. This is a **command line interface** (or **CLI**) that works by prompting you for a command, processing that command, printing any results, and then prompting you for the next command. The shell performs some commands directly, but most "commands" are actually separate programs that the shell loads and executes.

The NeXT system comes with a **graphical user interface** (**GUI**), that works by allowing you to manipulate images on the screen with the mouse, so you don't need the shell in most cases. However, the Shell and Terminal applications allow you to use the standard UNIX shell when desired for direct access to UNIX commands and utilities. Chapter 11 talks about the shell in more detail and gives instructions on how to use some of the more common commands.

UTILITIES

UNIX typically comes with a large set of utilities, including text editors and formatters, compilers, communication and mail programs, and on-line documentation. Most of these standard utilities are included with the NeXT computer; major exceptions are the FORTRAN, Lisp, and Pascal compilers (and associated libraries) usually bundled with UNIX.

COMMENTARY

Success often involves learning from others' mistakes and problems. The single greatest problem confronting the various families of personal computers is that of an insufficiently powerful and complete operating system. Each product line has had its OS go through several generations, and in a few cases an entirely new OS has attempted to replace the old one. This process has left a trail of broken software and confused users, while developers have had to scramble to ensure that their products remain compatible with the latest offerings.

NeXT appears to have learned from the rest of the industry. By using Mach, NeXT has started out with functionality, toward which the personal computer industry (and, for that matter, the workstation industry) is still striving. At the same time, NeXT has gained the benefits of UNIX while avoiding many of its weaknesses. As always, there is a danger of being "left out" if the workstation industry settles on some other *de facto* standards for UNIX, and criticism of NeXT's choice of Mach has focused on that possibility. But many people said the same thing about the Macintosh not being MS-DOS-compatible, and in the long run that's proven to be an asset, not a liability. By putting features and performance over adherence to a mythical industry standard, NeXT has probably done itself a big favor.

Part III
Using the System

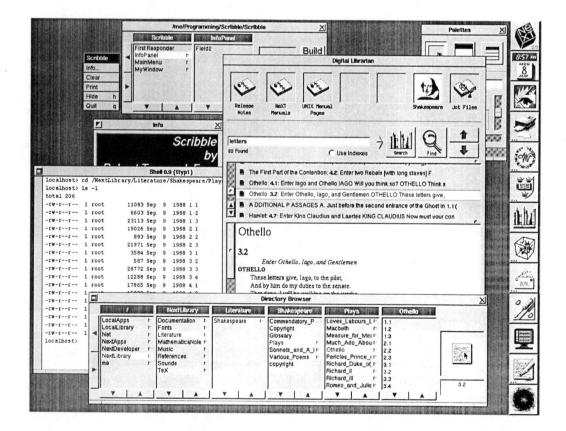

The purpose of this section is to introduce you to using the NeXT system. You may have a system assigned for your own use. You may have one that you're sharing with a few other people. You may know where there are NeXT systems that you can access. Or you may simply want to know what it's like to use a NeXT computer, as opposed to using a Macintosh, an IBM PC, a Sun workstation, or even a minicomputer or mainframe. Whatever your reasons, by the time you finish this section, you'll have a good idea of what it's like to actually sit down and use a NeXT computer.

Chapter 9, Working with NeXT, teaches you how to use Workspace Manager, the NeXT user interface. Chapter 10, Using Applications, gives you step-by-step instructions on accomplishing basic tasks using some of the applications bundled with the NeXT computer. Chapter 11, Exploring the Shell, talks about the UNIX shell, a command-line interface available through the Shell and Terminal applications, and shows you how to use the UNIX shell to perform some important system management tasks. Finally, Chapter 12, Creating Programs, helps you to write an application of your own—a simple "scribble" program—using Interface Builder and Objective C.

9
Working with NeXT

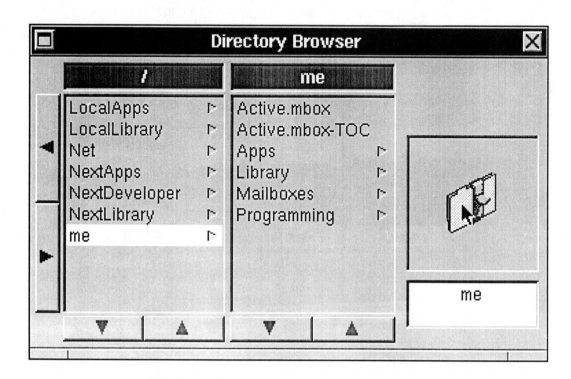

In this chapter, you're going to learn just what it's like to use the NeXT system, from powering up to powering down. You'll find out how to log in to the system, interact with what you find there, and then log back out again. You'll discover how to drag icons, select menus, scroll windows, and push buttons. And you'll come out of this chapter feeling confident about your ability to sit down and get work done on a NeXT computer.

Much of this material is covered in detail in *The NeXT User's Reference Manual*, which you should read; the intent here is to explain enough to make you feel comfortable with the NeXT system, particularly the **user interface**, that is, the set of concepts and techniques by which you interact with the NeXT computer.

UNPACKING AND SETTING UP

The basic NeXT system comes in two boxes, one containing the NeXT computer itself (along with user manuals and optical disks), the other holding the MegaPixel Display (with keyboard and mouse). If you've purchased a NeXT 400 dpi Laser Printer, it will be in a third, smaller box.

The first box you should open is the one containing the NeXT computer. Open the top of the box carefully; you want to keep all the boxes in good condition, should you need to move your system to another site or return it to your dealer for maintenance or repair. Once the box is open, you'll see a smaller box inside labeled "Accessories." Remove this box and open it. Inside it is a manual called *Getting Started on the NeXT Computer*. This manual has full and careful details about unpacking your system and setting it up. **Follow these instructions carefully.** There's nothing really complicated about them, but they do tell you exactly how to proceed.

Once you have your system unpacked and set up, you're ready to turn it on and do some work.

POWERING UP

It's easy to turn on the NeXT system: just press the Power key. This key is located along the top row of the keyboard, between the Sound and Brightness keys, directly above the arrow keys. It has on it a circle with a vertical bar through the middle.

When you press this key, it closes a circuit that goes from the keyboard, through the display, and down the video cable to the cube. This circuit then causes an internal power switch to close, sending power to the motherboard, any mass storage devices, and back to the display.

When the motherboard powers up, it executes a testing program located in read-only memory (ROM). This goes through and verifies that the normal memory (the RAM) on the motherboard is working properly, as well as performing a few other diagnostics. All this takes 20 seconds or so, depending upon how much memory you have.

Once the testing routine is done, the motherboard then executes the bootstrap code that's in ROM. This is a small program that goes out to a predetermined device—the optical disk, the hard disk, or the Ethernet network—loads a larger program into RAM, and then starts executing that program. That program then loads the operating system (Mach) into memory, reading the files from that same device, and then switches execution to Mach. This entire process was originally called "bootstrapping," as in "lifting yourself up by your bootstraps"; nowadays, it's usually just called **booting**.

The booting process can take from 1 to 3 minutes, depending upon which device you're booting from: optical drive, hard disk, or from another system connected to yours over Ethernet. The window that appears on the screen shows you your boot source: different icons are used for each device. And the icons are animated—for example, the disk platters rotate in the optical and hard disk icons—to entertain you while all this is happening and to reassure you that work is actually being done.

If the NeXT system expects to boot from an optical disk, and you haven't yet inserted one, you'll get a message in the Loading Files window asking you to do so. If you examine the optical disk closely, you'll find that it has the word "top" etched into the plastic on one side, with a triangular arrow pointing toward the nearest end. Insert that end of the disk into the optical disk drive slot, with the word "top" facing up. When the disk is about three-quarters inserted, you'll encounter some resistance. Push harder; when the disk is almost all the way in, the NeXT disk drive will pull it inside the cube and begin to read from it.

LOGGING IN

After Mach is loaded, then the other system files—Display PostScript, Window Server, and Workspace Manager—are read in off the boot device. Once these files are all in memory, the system is ready for you to **log in**, that is, to identify yourself and establish that you are an authorized user of this particular system. Let's discuss for a minute why this might be necessary.

Mach is a true multitasking, multiuser operating system. It is, for example, possible to have someone sitting at a terminal connected to the system through one of the serial ports, using it as they would any minicomputer or mainframe computer, while you're working on the MegaPixel Display. Even without that connection, different people might use the same NeXT system at different times. In either case, the issue of *security* comes up: how do you identify which files and directories belong to you, and how do you prevent them from being modified or even accessed by others?

Mach, being UNIX-compatible, supports the concept of **user login accounts**. The idea is simple, and probably familiar to anyone who has worked with larger computers: in order to use the computer, you must log in, that is, provide a user identifier (telling who you are) and a password (proving that it's really you). The **user login ID** is a single word, consisting of letters and (if you want) digits, that is your personal identifier while you're on the NeXT system. It's usually related to your name; examples include `jdow`, `bobsmith`, `ericm`. The **password** is also a single word, composed of letters, digits, and punctuation marks; you can think of it as a secret code that lets you (and no one else) log in using your user ID. Examples might include `ZZZeiry`, `dog!fat`, or `alpha421`. Each user ID has a specific password associated with it; when you log in, you're asked to enter both. If the user ID and password check out, then you're allowed on the system; otherwise, you can't use it at all. Once you're on, there are usually limits as to the **privileges** that you have: which system commands you can use, whether you can read, write, and/or execute a given file, and so on.

Your system is shipped with only a single user account set up; the user ID is me, and there is no password defined. Because of that, you are automatically logged in when the system is done booting. However, you can create a password using the Preferences application; you'll learn how to use this program in Chapter 10, Using Applications.

If you have done this, or if you already have a separate account set up on the NeXT system, you'll get the Login window shown in Figure 9.1, with the vertical bar cursor blinking in the top field. You type your user ID, such as me (without the quotation marks, of course), then press Return. The vertical bar now goes to the lower field, you type your password (which is not echoed to the screen), then press Return again. If you made a mistake, the window will "jitter" for a second or two, and then you'll be prompted for your user ID and password again. *Important note:* the Mach operating system is case-sensitive, that is, it distinguishes between upper- and lowercase letters. If you're logging into the me account and you type Me, ME, or, for whatever reason, mE, Mach won't recognize it. The same goes for your password.

Figure 9.1. NeXT Login window

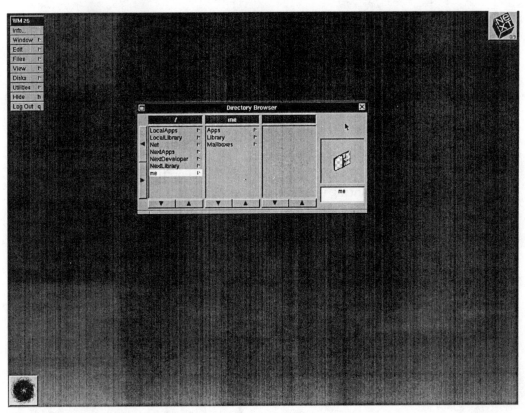

Figure 9.2. The Workspace Manager display

Once you have correctly entered your user ID and password, the login box disappears, the screen goes blank for a few seconds, and then you are up and running under Workspace Manager. You'll see a display similar to that in Figure 9.2. The Workspace Manager menu is in the upper-left corner of the screen; the Directory Browser window, which lets you see and use the files (programs, documents, and so on) on your disk is in the middle; and the application dock, which holds symbols representing commonly used applications, is on the right edge. You'll learn how these work below, but first you need to learn how to use the mouse.

USING THE MOUSE

The mouse is your main device for interacting with Workspace Manager. You are presented with a wide variety of objects on the screen—icons, menus, windows, buttons, text fields, scroll bars—which you select or otherwise manipulate. You do this by moving the mouse around, while pressing and releasing the large square buttons found on the mouse itself. Here's how this works.

As you look at the screen, you'll see a small black arrow, pointing up and to the left. This is the **cursor**. As you move the mouse around, you'll find that the cursor moves correspondingly. Notice that the distance the cursor moves is proportional to how fast you move the mouse: slow mouse movements produce small cursor displacements, fast mouse movements produce large displacements. You will be able to adjust this relationship using the Preferences utility.

The mouse also has two buttons on it, a left and a right. Normally, both buttons work identically. However, the Preferences application lets you assign a special function—which will be described later—to one of the buttons. For now, though, we'll assume that you're using the buttons in their normal fashion. There are a number of actions you can perform using the buttons and the mouse itself; let's take a look at them.

CLICKING

The first action is **clicking**: pressing and releasing the mouse button once. This is how you select items in a list, press buttons, choose menu commands, pick a window to come forward, and so on. Also, a number of controls are or can be activated by clicking on them or on some portion thereof; for example, clicking in the portion of a slider not occupied by the slide bar itself causes the slider to move to that spot.

PRESSING

The second, closely related action is **pressing**: moving the cursor over some object, pressing the mouse button, and not releasing it until the desired result is obtained. For example, the scroll bar controls found in the lower-left corner of windows work this way: you press on the selected control until the window has scrolled the desired distance.

DRAGGING

The third action is **dragging**: moving the cursor over some object, holding the mouse button down, and then moving the cursor, dragging the object along with it. With this method, you can move icons around within a window, drag application icons to and from the icon dock, and move windows and menus by dragging their menu bars along.

DOUBLE-CLICKING

The fourth action is **double-clicking**: clicking twice in rapid succession. This is used primarily to launch applications or to open files, in both cases by double-clicking on their icons, or on their names in a file list. It can also be used to select a single word within a text field, by double-clicking on any portion of the word. People unaccustomed to using mice often delay too long between the clicks. This has the same result as performing a single click, waiting, and then performing another single click. The Preferences utility lets you adjust the acceptable delay between clicks (see Figure 9.3).

GROUPING

The fifth action is **grouping**: selecting a number of objects within a window. To do this, move the cursor to some point that's near the objects and still within the window—say, above and to the left. Press the mouse button, hold it down, and drag the cursor toward the opposite corner (in this case, down and to the right). A rectangle appears, with one corner anchored at the spot where you first pressed the button, and the other corner "pinned" to the cursor; as you move the cursor, the rectangle grows and shrinks accordingly. When you release the button, all the objects within the rectangle are selected. Note that you can achieve the same effect by holding either Shift key down and clicking once on each of the objects; likewise, you can "deselect" by this same means.

SELECTING

The sixth action is **selecting**: choosing a section of text for cutting, copying, or modifying. This works on any text object (such as a word processing document) or editable text field. You move the cursor to the starting location, hold the mouse button down, and drag the cursor. Text gets selected, letter by letter if you're moving left or right, line by line if you're moving up or down.

THE "MENU BUTTON" FUNCTION

As mentioned above, both the left and right mouse buttons normally behave identically. However, using the Preferences application, shown in Figure 9.3, you can make one or the other the "menu button." This means that when you press it, a copy of the main menu of the current application appears underneath the cursor. As you keep the button pressed, you can drag the cursor down through the menu; each item will be highlighted as you move the cursor over it. If it represents a submenu, that submenu will appear, and you can move the cursor over the items in it. The item that is highlighted when you release the button is selected, and the menu disappears; if you don't want to choose a command, just move the cursor off the menu before releasing the button. This feature allows you to select menu commands quickly, without having to move the cursor up to where the main menu is.

To enable this feature, bring up the Preferences application as described in Chapter 10. If you click on the mouse icon in the Preferences window, you'll get the display shown in Figure 9.3. The "Enable Menu Button" switch controls this feature; clicking on the little box to the right of the word "Button" turns it on and off, with the "on" state indicated by a checkmark within the box. The two icons labeled "Left" and "Right" within the "handedness" box determine which of the two buttons will be the menu button; for example, if the icon labeled "Right" is highlighted (has a white background), then the right button will be the menu button. That way, if you are using the mouse with your right hand, your index finger rests naturally on the left button, which performs the "normal" button function, while the right button pops up the current application's menu. Likewise, if you click on the "Left" icon in the "handedness" box, the right button becomes the regular button, while the left button performs the special menu function.

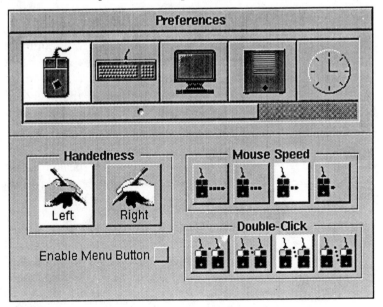

Figure 9.3. The mouse settings in the Preferences application

USING THE KEYBOARD

The keyboard, described in Chapter 3, serves three major functions. The first, obviously, is to allow you to send text and numbers to the computer, or, more accurately, to the applications currently executing on your computer. As you type, the characters—letters, digits, punctuation marks, special symbols—displayed on the keys are sent, one at a time, through the video cable to the motherboard; there they are received by the Window Server (see Chapter 7), which then forwards them on to the key window (explained later), which then handles them appropriately. As shown in Chapter 3, you can use the Alternate key to generate special characters, such as "Æ," "«," and "¢."

The second function allows you to issue commands to applications, using the Command key. Most commands are given to applications using menus, that is, by clicking on the commands listed there. Many of these commands have a letter, digit, or symbol on the right-hand side. This means that you can send the same command by holding down either Command key (there's one on each side of the spacebar) and typing that character. It's important to note that upper- and lowercase letters are considered different in commands; in other words, Command-r is different from Command-R (which is generated by holding down both the Command key and the Shift key, and then pressing "R").

The third function of the keyboard is to control the NeXT system itself. As you've already seen, you power up the entire computer by pressing the Power key; you'll use the same key to turn the system off. The two keys to its left let you raise and lower the volume of the speaker inside the MegaPixel Display; pressing the bottom key while holding the Command key down mutes the speaker completely. The two keys to the right of the Power key let you adjust the brightness of the actual screen.

SPECIAL KEY COMBINATIONS

In addition to its regular functions, the keyboard has some special key combinations that let you perform certain system functions. A few are somewhat mundane. One, Command-Return produces the same keycode as pressing the Enter key in the numeric keypad. Another, Command-period ("."), is treated as a Cancel or Abort command by a number of applications.

Command-space (" ") is recognized by the standard File Selection panel as a command to complete the file name being typed in. For example, if you are opening a file in a given directory, you can type just enough letters of that file's name to uniquely identify it, and then press Command-space. This will finish out the file's name for you. You'll see an example of using this feature in Chapter 10, Using Applications.

Two combinations perform special functions for the MegaPixel Display. As just mentioned above, pressing Command-Mute (where "Mute" is the Volume Down key) turns off the display's internal speaker; pressing Command-Mute again turns the speaker back on. Likewise, pressing Command-Shift puts the keyboard in "alpha lock" mode, so that every lettered key (A–Z) produces an uppercase letter only. A small green light-emitting diode (LED) build into each Shift key will light up, signifying that you're in "alpha lock" mode. Pressing Command-Shift again gets you out of "alpha lock" mode and turns off the LED.

The keyboard also lets you reset the computer if you have a **system crash**, that is, if program or system errors cause your machine to lock up, so that it no longer responds to the mouse or the keyboard. To do this, hold down the right Command key and press the upper-left key in the numeric keypad (the key with the tilde ["~"] on it). A small box appears, asking if you wish to restart the system—that is, go through the boot process again—or to power down. You can even press "n" to cancel the request and go back to where you were.

The next level of reset occurs when you hold down *both* Command keys, and then press the tilde key. This causes a

non-maskable interrupt (or **NMI**); simply put, it's an interruption that the operating system can't ignore. This will bring up a window in the middle of the screen, letting you run the NMI mini-monitor, a program designed to let system gurus check to see what's wrong. You can go back to where you were by entering the command `continue`, or you can make some simple requests to examine the system status.

If you type the command `monitor` while within the NMI mini-monitor, you will execute the NeXT ROM Monitor. This program, which resides in the motherboard's ROM, lets you examine and modify memory locations and various system parameters. You also can use it to force your system to boot from a different device; thus, if something trashed your hard disk, you could use the command `bod` to force it to boot from an optical disk, or `ben` to make it boot from Ethernet. Likewise, if you wanted to force it to boot from the hard disk when it might be expecting to boot from the optical disk or Ethernet, you can type in the command `bsd` (boot SCSI disk).

If things are so far gone that even this won't work, you can do a **hard reset** by holding down the left Alternate and Command keys, and then pressing the "*" key in the numeric keypad (the upper-right-most key). The NeXT system will then act as if you had just powered up, going through the test and loading sequences described above.

SCREEN ELEMENTS

Now that you know how to use the mouse and the keyboard, you need to learn what to use them on. Workspace Manager (WM) presents a number of graphical elements or objects on the screen for you to see and manipulate. The basic ones are icons, menus, lists, panels, and windows. These are all similar: rectangular display objects that present information and handle events (such as mouse actions). But each has a specific function, and, for the most part, a distinct appearance. Let's discuss the function and role of each.

ICONS

An **icon** is a small object that usually represents a file, either a document or an application (computer program), though a few have special functions. Figure 9.4 shows a window containing some of the icons that you are likely to see on the NeXT display. They appear most often in one of three places: in the Directory Browser; in a directory window; or in the icon dock. In addition, the icons of applications that are currently executing, or of windows that have been miniaturized, can be placed anywhere on the screen.

As mentioned above, icons are used most often to launch applications, either directly or indirectly. When you double-click on an icon representing an application, the icon is highlighted—turns white—and remains so until that program has been loaded into memory and has started running. If the program's icon isn't in the icon dock, then it appears elsewhere on the screen (usually along the bottom edge) and remains visible until the program has finished executing. If you select the Hide command in that program's main menu, then all the windows, panels, and menus associated with that program disappear, leaving just the icon; when you double-click on the icon, everything appears again.

If you double-click on an icon representing a file specific to a given application (such as a WriteNow document or an Interface Builder project), that application is launched just as if you had double-clicked on its icon and behaves the same in all

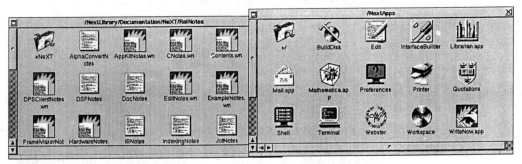

Figure 9.4. Typical NeXT icons

respects, with one addition: that file is automatically opened, as if you launched the application directly and then requested that the file be opened. Note that document file icons appear only in directory windows, never on the screen or in the icon dock.

The Application Dock

The **application dock** is the column of icons along the right edge of the display. This dock always has at least one icon in it: the NeXT logo. This icon cannot be moved from its position at the top of the dock; however, you can drag it straight down with the mouse, sliding the entire dock (except for the NeXT icon) off the bottom of the screen.

The only other icons that can be in the dock are application icons and the Black Hole. The application icons, as mentioned, represent programs that you can execute; you can drag them to the dock from a directory window or browser. The Black Hole is used to delete files; its use is explained a little later.

When you place an application's icon in the dock, three small dots appear in its lower-left corner. These tell you that the application isn't running. When you launch the application, either by double-clicking on its icon or by double-clicking on a related document icon, the dots disappear. That way, you can tell by glancing at the dock which of the applications are running and which aren't.

The configuration of the dock is saved when you log out and restored when you log back in, so that you can put icons of frequently used applications in the dock and have them there each time you use the system. You can examine this configuration using the Utilities/Dock Info... command in the WM menu. Figure 9.5 shows the application dock along with the Dock Info panel. Note that by clicking in the boxes along the left side, you can select which applications will be launched automatically when you log in.

Icons in Windows

Icons displayed in a directory window can represent either files or subdirectories (see Figure 9.6). The subdirectories are uniformly represented as folders, with the enclosing directory (the next level up) shown as an open folder, always in the upper-left

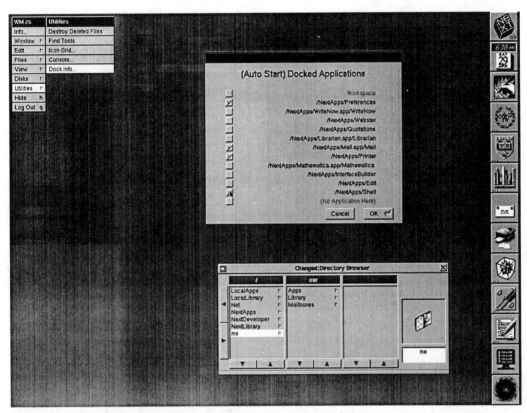

Figure 9.5. The application dock and the Dock Info panel

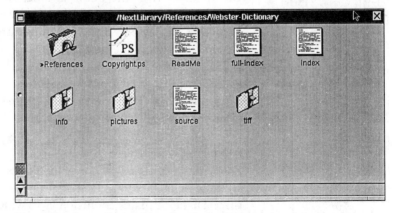

Figure 9.6. Icon display in a directory window

corner. To move down into a subdirectory, double-click on the appropriate closed folder; to move back up, double-click on the open folder. To move files (and entire subdirectories) from one directory to another, open up a window for each directory and drag the appropriate icons from one window to the other.

Icons sitting on the screen have a light gray background that's 64 pixels wide by 64 pixels high. The actual pictures can be no larger than 48 pixels wide by 48 pixels high. Icons displayed in a directory window or browser consist only of the picture; they do not have a background unless they are moved into the icon dock or appear on the screen because of being launched. Document and folder icons can never be placed on the screen or in the icon dock; if you attempt to do so, they will just "snap back" to where they were. Icons of applications that are not currently running can be placed in the icon dock, but not anywhere else on the screen. As mentioned, the icons of applications currently running can be anywhere on the screen.

MENUS

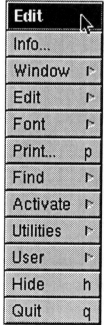

Figure 9.7. A typical menu

Each currently running application has its own menu, a means by which you tell the application what to do. A **menu** is a rectangular image, usually taller than it is wide, consisting of a title bar at the top and one or more menu items, arranged as a single column, as shown in Figure 9.7. The **title bar** has the name of the application (if the name is long, an abbreviation is sometimes used). While menus will typically appear in the upper-left corner of the display, you can move them anywhere on the screen by dragging the title bar.

The **menu items** represent the actual commands to the application. You can think of them as a column of buttons; to carry out the action, you move the cursor over the appropriate item and click the mouse button once. The item will be highlighted—its background will turn white—until the command is complete.

Workspace Manager normally allows only one set of menus, all those belonging to a given application, to be visible at any one time. That eliminates confusion as to which menus are currently active and what application you're currently working with.

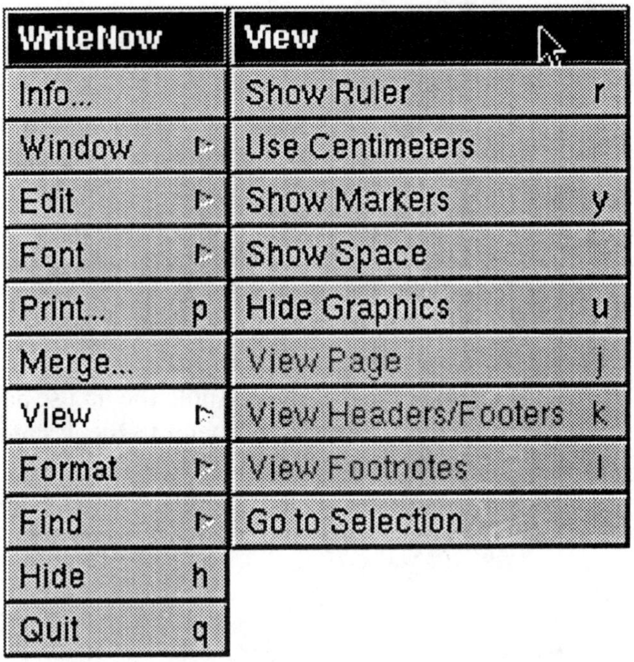

WriteNow	View	
Info...	Show Ruler	r
Window ▷	Use Centimeters	
Edit ▷	Show Markers	y
Font ▷	Show Space	
Print... p	Hide Graphics	u
Merge...	View Page	j
View ▷	View Headers/Footers	k
Format ▷	View Footnotes	l
Find ▷	Go to Selection	
Hide h		
Quit q		

Figure 9.8. WriteNow menu, with View submenu opened

In some cases, the text in a menu item will be gray, instead of black. This indicates that the item is currently **disabled**, that is, if you click on it, nothing happens. Why? Because for some reason that command isn't applicable. For example, in the View submenu in WriteNow, the View Footnotes command is disabled as long as there are no footnotes in the document, as shown in Figure 9.8. Once you add a footnote, WriteNow enables the command, and you can then use it.

SUBMENUS

To avoid long menus and to better organize the commands, Workspace Manager allows you to have **submenus**. When you click on an item that has an indented arrowhead near the right edge, a submenu appears to the right of it, and the item remains highlighted (see Figure 9.8). The submenu remains there until you click again on the highlighted item, or you select another item in the same menu. If you want, you can "tear off" the submenu by dragging it by its title bar (which has the name of the item that created it) and moving it to where you'd like it. At that point, the highlighted item reverts to normal, and you can select other items in that menu without making the submenu go away. The submenu now has a **close button** at the right end of the title bar; if you click on it, the submenu disappears.

If you don't want the submenu to hang around—you just want to choose some command in it, and then have the submenu disappear—then you can use a different method. Move the cursor over the item that creates the submenu, and press the mouse button, holding it down. When the submenu appears, continue to hold the mouse button down and move the cursor into the submenu to the desired item. You'll notice that each item becomes highlighted as you move the cursor over it. When you have the one you want, release the mouse button. That command will be executed, and the submenu will disappear.

LISTS

While a menu offers a freestanding assortment of options or commands, a **list** offers a selection within the context of a panel or window. The NeXT user interface provides for two types of lists: pop-up lists and pull-down lists, both of which are shown in Figure 9.9.

A **pop-up list** serves much the same function as a set of radio buttons (which are described later in the "Controls" section). It lets you choose from a set of mutually exclusive options. In its normal state, the pop-up list consists of a button containing the currently selected option and a small "handle" icon, indicating that this is a pop-up list. When you move the cursor over the button and press the mouse button, the entire list appears, with the current selection highlighted. While keeping the mouse button pressed, you can now move the cursor up and down, highlighting each of the choices. When you have

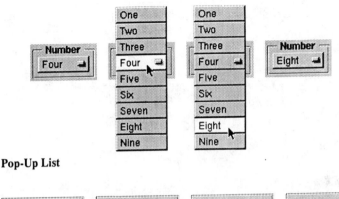

Pop-Up List

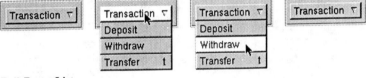

Pull-Down List

Figure 9.9. Pop-up and pull-down lists

highlighted the one you want, release the mouse button. The list collapses into a single button displaying your new selection.

A **pull-down list** behaves more like a menu. It contains a set of actions or requests that can be selected repeatedly. In its normal state, the pull-down list looks much like a pop-up list: a button with a label and a special icon, this one looking like an arrow pointing down. When you move the cursor over it and press the mouse button, the entire list appears below the button; you can then drag the cursor down and make your selection. However, the title never changes, and the choices denote actions rather than settings.

PANELS

Some menu items cause **panels** to appear. A panel is a window, usually relatively small, that contains a set of **controls** and

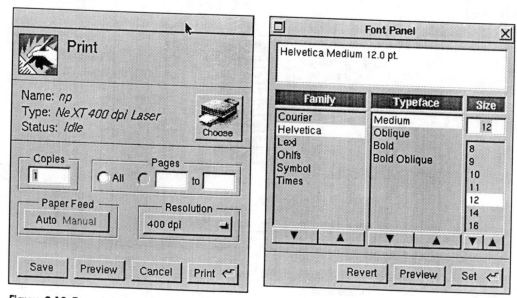

Figure 9.10. Two standard panels: the Print panel and the Font panel

fields. Figure 9.10 shows two typical panels. Controls include such things as buttons, sliders, radio buttons, and check boxes. Fields are areas (often enclosed) that contain text and numeric information. The purpose of a panel is to allow you to have additional input into a program, often by changing some settings and then clicking on a button labeled "OK." Panels usually have title bars, which you can use to drag the panels around the screen; many also have close buttons to make them disappear.

Modal Panels

There are two basic types of panels: modal and non-modal. A **modal panel** is so called because it puts you into a "mode," a state that you can't get out of until you do something. For example, most applications that have a Print command in the menu bring up a panel like the one on the left in Figure 9.10. The menu item remains highlighted, and you can't do anything else with the application until you select one of the action buttons along the bottom of the panel. At that point, the panel disappears, and the menu item reverts to normal.

An **attention panel** is a special kind of modal panel, so called because it usually signals some important decision that you have to make, such as whether or not to save the current file to disk before exiting the application that created it. In other words, your action might have undesirable consequences, and the panel is basically saying "Are you sure?" or "Don't you want to do this first?" An attention panel is distinguished by the lack of a title in its title bar and by the fact that you can't cover it with any other object. Note that for both types of modal panels, you can always switch to another application; you just can't do anything else in the application putting up the panel until you've made the panel go away.

Non-modal Panels

A **non-modal panel** is one that hangs around without interfering with the operation of the application. The panel on the right in Figure 9.10 is an example of a non-modal panel. It's used by an application to set the font type, size, and style of a text document. When you select the Font Panel item in the application's Font menu, the panel appears, and the item reverts to normal. You can then continue your work as before. When you want to change any of those aspects, you just select the desired settings, then click on the set button. When you want the panel to disappear, you just click on its close button.

WINDOWS

A window—in this discussion, at least—is a large area in which you do most of the work involved with a given application. The windows are either brought up automatically when you launch the application—such as the windows for Shell or Digital Librarian—or are created as you open specific documents, such as text files opened using Edit or WriteNow.

How do windows differ from panels? In some cases, the distinction is arbitrary, since the application's main window may have a number of controls on it, and, in fact, panels are just a species of the window family. Philosophically, though, a window occupies one of the two roles mentioned above: it either corre-

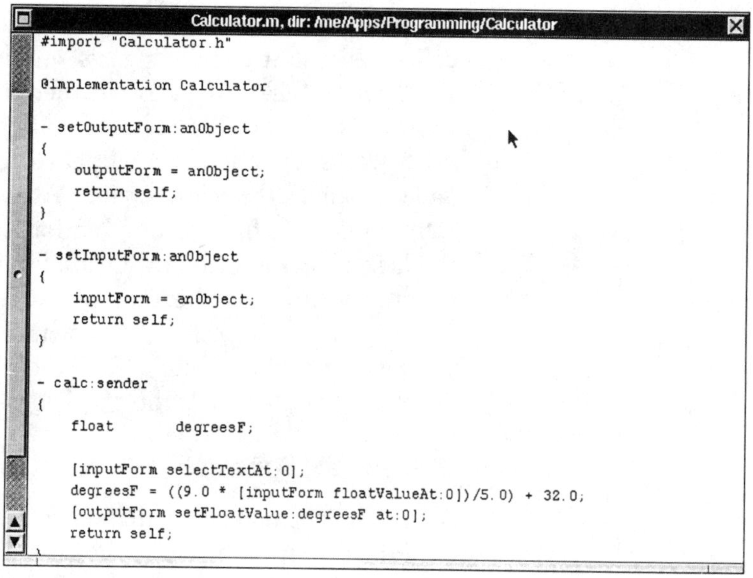

```
Calculator.m, dir: /me/Apps/Programming/Calculator            ☒
#import "Calculator.h"

@implementation Calculator

- setOutputForm:anObject
{
    outputForm = anObject;
    return self;
}

- setInputForm:anObject
{
    inputForm = anObject;
    return self;
}

- calc:sender
{
    float       degreesF;

    [inputForm selectTextAt:0];
    degreesF = ((9.0 * [inputForm floatValueAt:0])/5.0) + 32.0;
    [outputForm setFloatValue:degreesF at:0];
    return self;
```

Figure 9.11. Sample window

sponds to an opened document or it is the main work area of the application. A basic rule of thumb: if you can't get any work done with it closed, it's probably a window. Also, while both windows and non-modal panels may have close buttons, a window often has two additional controls that a panel almost never has: a miniaturize button (in the title bar) and a resize bar (at the bottom of the window), both of which can be seen in Figure 9.11.

Miniaturizing Windows

Clicking on the **miniaturize button** of a given window causes that window to disappear and a small icon (called a **miniwindow**) representing it to appear on the screen, usually down near the bottom. You can then make the window reappear by double-clicking on the miniwindow. This technique lets you easily manage several windows that are open simultaneously. Even while miniaturized, the window is still considered active; any drawing done or changes made will be seen when the window is re-enlarged. You can move these miniwindows around the screen, much like the icons of currently running applications; however, they will not "snap" into the icon dock, and you cannot put them into a directory window.

Resizing Windows

The **resize bar** allows you to change the size of a window. This bar, if present, is found at the bottom of the window; it is set off from the rest of the window by a horizontal "grooved" line and it has two small sections at either end. You can make the window taller or shorter by grabbing the bar with the mouse and dragging it up or down. A dotted outline will follow the cursor; when you release the mouse button, the window will redraw itself within its new size. The sections at either end of the resize bar can be dragged horizontally, allowing you to make the window longer or shorter on either side. They can also be dragged in a diagonal fashion, so that you can adjust both height and width simultaneously.

ORDERING SCREEN ELEMENTS

Since Workspace Manager allows you to have many windows open and active at the same time, certain questions arise. How are windows (and panels and menus and icons) ordered; that is, which ones go in front? How do you bring a window in front of the others? When you type on the keyboard, which window gets what you type?

Workspace Manager has some definite answers to each of these questions. On the issue of ordering, for example, there are some well-defined rules:

1. Pop-up and pull-down lists appear in front of all other screen elements; if they didn't, then you might not be able to see all your choices. These lists only appear as long as you keep the mouse button depressed, so you can't work with anything else until they disappear anyway.

2. Attention (modal) panels always appear next, that is, behind pop-up and pull-down lists, but in front of everything else. It is possible to have several such panels on the screen at once, though it requires a bit of work (bring one up in Application A, switch to Application B, bring one up there, and so on). In such a case, these panels are reordered the way you would reorder windows: by clicking on them.

3. The main menu of the active application comes next. As mentioned above, there is only one set of menus on the screen at any given time, representing the application that the user is currently working with. The main menu of that application stays in front of everything else (except items 1 and 2).

4. After that come any submenus that are currently on the screen. Submenus can cover each other, as well as everything below, but they remain behind all the items in 1, 2, and 3.

5. Next come icons in the icon dock. Lists, attention panels, and menus will cover them up, but everything else slides behind.

6. Last comes everything else on the screen: non-modal panels, windows, miniwindows, and undocked icons.

The next question is, how do the objects in category 6 get ordered; that is, what determines which one is in front, which one is behind that one, and so on? The answer? For the most part, *you* do. How? By moving the cursor over that object and clicking on it. If, for example, you click on one window that is partially behind another, that window will "come to the front" and be fully visible, while the other window will "go behind" it and be partially (or even fully) hidden.

There are usually some additional effects when reordering windows. For example, if the two windows mentioned in the example above belong to different applications, then bringing one to the front will cause the menus and open panels of its application to appear, while causing the menus (and, often, the panels) of the other application to vanish. This helps reduce the "visual clutter" on the screen.

THE KEY WINDOW AND THE MAIN WINDOW

Another effect of clicking on a window is that it makes it the key window. The **key window** is the one that gets all keyboard events; in other words, when you type something, that's the window you're typing to. This doesn't mean that the window will necessarily do anything with those keystrokes, just that it's getting them. Note that a panel can be the key window. The key window is distinguished by having a black title bar.

Suppose you're doing word processing with several documents open, and you want to change the font used in a title in one of them. You click on that document's window (making it the key window), select the title, then click on the Font panel. The Font panel's title bar goes black, indicating that it's now the key window—so how does it know which document it's going to change? If you were to look at the title bar of the document that was previously the key window, you'd find that the bar was dark gray (instead of light gray like the others). That's because this window is still the **main window**—that is, the one being worked on. In other words, clicking on a window makes it both the key window and the main window; clicking on a panel only makes it the key window and does not change the main window.

CONTROLS

There are a number of different **controls** found in panels and windows. Some you've already learned about, such as the close and miniaturize buttons that appear in title bars, or the resize bars found at the bottoms of windows. But these are specialized instances of a general type of control—a button—and various types and uses of controls can be found in a variety of applications. Figure 9.12 shows the most common types of controls; let's look at each of them.

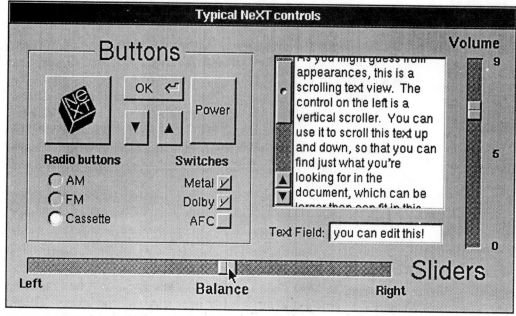

Figure 9.12. Controls found in panels and windows

BUTTONS

A **button** is the most general type of control. It can have a variety of shapes and forms, can be labeled or unlabeled, and can even change in appearance as it is used. The general use of a button is to carry out some action. You move the cursor over the button and click once; the appropriate action then takes place. A menu, for example, is simply a window with a single column of buttons in it.

Buttons are often used in panels to apply a number of settings. For example, in a Font panel you select the font type, the font size, and any style settings (such as bold and italic), then click a button to apply all those to a document or some selected text.

Some buttons work **continuously**. In other words, you move the cursor over them, press the mouse button, and keep it pressed. As you do, some action keeps happening. The scrolling buttons in the Directory Browser are of this type.

SWITCHES

A **switch** is a button used to toggle some state or condition, that is, to turn it on or off. When you click on the switch itself, a check mark appears; when you click on it again, the check disappears. The label for the switch indicates the state or condition that's in effect when the check mark is visible.

RADIO BUTTONS

Sometimes you want to select one of a set of mutually exclusive options or conditions. The control for this is a set of **radio buttons**, so called because they act like the control buttons on car radios: each one selects a particular channel, to the exclusion of the others. There is always one button selected in a set of radio buttons, indicated by the ball-shaped object inside of it; the others are all empty circles. To select a different one, just move the cursor over it and click; it will now have the "ball" in it, and the others will all be empty.

SLIDERS

Sometimes you need a continual range of settings, much like using a tuning knob on a radio, rather than a set of discrete ones. The control that best emulates this is a **slider**. As you can see, a slider is an empty track with a slider button inside. The button can be dragged from one end of the track to the other using the cursor and the mouse. As you drag the slider button, it sends its current location to the application, which then updates whatever it needs to. You can also make the slider button jump directly to a given spot in the track by clicking on that spot.

SCROLLERS

A **scroller** is a specialized combination of slider and buttons, used to scroll through a text or graphic document too large to be seen all at once. The scroll button works just like the slider button—you drag it back and forth, and you can click on the track to make it jump to a given spot. Unlike the slider button, the scroll button changes its size to reflect how much of the total document you're actually seeing. The larger the document, the smaller the scroll button gets—up to a point; otherwise, it could become too thin to handle effectively. Likewise, the smaller the document, the larger the scroll button becomes; and if the entire document fits within the window, the button disappears altogether.

A scroller also has two "fine control" buttons at one end. These let you move the scroll button by some incremental amount (a pixel, a line of text, etc.) defined by the application. A single click scrolls the document by that amount; keeping the button pressed lets it scroll continuously. Holding down the Alternate key changes the increment to some larger amount (a page, etc.), again as defined by the application.

As with sliders, there are both vertical and horizontal scrollers. The fine control buttons of a vertical scroller appear at its bottom, while those of a horizontal scroller appear at its left end. When you have both types together, the vertical scroller appears to the left of the document, while the horizontal one appears at the bottom. The result is that all four fine control buttons are in the lower-left corner of the document, making it very convenient to use them for fine adjustments.

TEXT FIELDS

A text field isn't quite like the other controls, but it is a way of interacting with an application. A text field displays a numeric value or text string, representing some setting within the application, or it may be empty. In either case, you are expected either to enter a value—a file name, a starting value, a string to search for—or to accept what's already there. Text fields are found in file selector panels, find/replace panels, and similar places.

When you click on the text field, a vertical bar cursor appears; you can now edit the value or string, adding and deleting characters and/or numbers. You can usually select a particular word or number by double-clicking on it, and you can select the entire entry by dragging the cursor from one end of the field to the other; in both cases, whatever you type next will replace the selected portion. When you're done, you can press Return or just click somewhere else.

BROWSING THROUGH THE FILE SYSTEM

As described in Chapter 8, Mach implements a **hierarchical file system**. This means that your mass storage device—optical disk or hard disk—is divided up into a set of **directories**, which you can think of as file folders. In fact, that's what the icon for a directory looks like: an expandable folder. And like an expandable folder, a directory can hold any number of files and/or subdirectories. A **file** is actual stored information: a program, a document, a data file. A **subdirectory** is a directory that's located inside of another directory. And the **path name** for a file is the list of the directories that enclose it.

THE DIRECTORY BROWSER

When you log in under Workspace Manager, you are greeted by whatever icons you have in the dock, the WM menu, and the Directory Browser. The last is a window that allows you to "browse" or scan through the file system on your NeXT system, so that you can find a particular file. It displays the hierarchical file structure, with each column representing the contents of the directory named at the top. The "root" directory—that is, the one at the topmost level of the hierarchy, the one that encloses all other files and directories—is just referred to with a slash ("/"), and is shown in the leftmost column of the browser. The names with an indented arrowhead to the right of them are directories; the others are files. To select a directory, just click once on its name. That name is then highlighted, its name appears at the top of the next column, and that column now displays its contents.

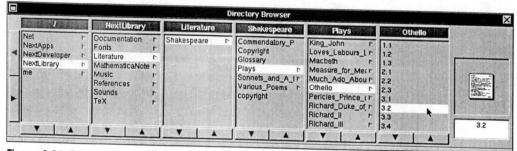

Figure 9.13. The Directory Browser, showing the file
"/NextLibrary/Literature/Shakespeare/Plays/Othello/3.2"

In Figure 9.13, the Directory Browser has been resized so that you can see the complete path to the Edit file containing Act 3, Scene 2, of Shakespeare's play, "Othello." Note that some directories have only directories in them, some have a mix of directories and files, and the last one (Othello) has only files. Also notice that under each column there are buttons with arrows pointing up and down. These are used to scroll through the list in a given column if all the names can't fit. Likewise, there are arrows along the far left edge; these let you scroll through the directory columns if the Browser is too narrow to show the full path.

Finally, there is a box at the far-right end of the Browser. This holds the icon of the currently selected file or directory. If this is an application icon, you can drag it over to the application dock, or double-click it to start it executing. If it's a document icon and there's an associated application, then you can double-click it to open it, launching the application automatically. And if it's a directory icon (folder), then you can double-click it to open up a directory window.

Directory organization

When you first start using the Next system, the Directory Browser window shows you a number of directories. There are three basic sets: the Next directories, the Local directories, and the user directories.

The Next directories contain all the NeXT system files. The directory NextApps contains the bundled applications, such as WriteNow, Mathematica, and Shell, along with their associated files. The directory NextDeveloper contains both demonstration programs (in the Demos subdirectory) and sample source code (in the Examples subdirectory). NextLibrary contains all the on-line documentation (Shakespeare, Webster's Dictionary/Thesaurus, NeXT and UNIX manuals), as well as standard system resources, such as fonts and sounds. IMPORTANT NOTE: do not store files that you wish to save in these directories, at least not without keeping copies elsewhere. Future releases of the NeXT system software will overwrite the contents of these directories.

The Local directories parallel the Next directories. There are two, LocalApps and LocalLibrary, which contain much the same things as NextApps and NextLibrary. The difference is that these applications and files are intended to be accessed just by users on your machine or (in some cases) on your local network.

The user directories are all those named the same as the various user login IDs for your system. For example, the directory me already exists on each system; as you add new users, they will each get their own directory. Each user directory typically has at least three subdirectories: Apps, for holding private applications; Library, for holding private documents, fonts, and sound files; and Mailboxes, for holding private mail.

The parallel sets of Apps and Library directories are searched when you require a particular application, document, sound, font, or whatever. The private directory is searched first, then the Local directory, and then the NeXT directory. Note that if the system is looking for an application, it will check the application dock before any of these directories.

One other directory which you'll see is Net. This directory lets you access other systems on the same Ethernet network as your system. Each system shows up as a subdirectory within the Net directory.

User versus Expert Mode

The Mach operating system requires a lot of directories and files that you don't need to know about, such as /etc, /dev, and so on. If you're not familiar with UNIX, these directories and files can be confusing; you could even potentially mess up the system

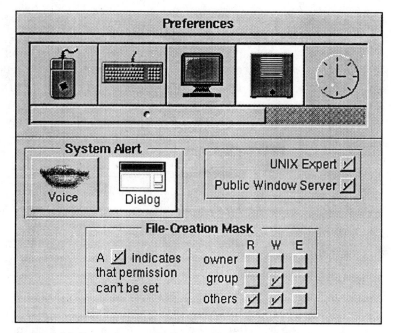

Figure 9.14. The system settings in the Preferences application

files to the point of having to rebuild your disk. Because of that, these directories (and the files they enclose) are normally hidden from you, hence you only see the directories mentioned above when using Workspace Manager, though you can still access these other directories using the UNIX command line interface available through the Shell or Terminal applications.

You can, however, tell Workspace Manager to let you see all the files and directories on the disk through the usual Directory Browsers and windows. To do this, bring up the system panel in the Preferences application, shown in Figure 9.14. Check the box labeled "Unix Expert," log off the system, and then log back in. The Directory Browser will now show all the directories and files in the file system.

DIRECTORY WINDOWS

A **directory window** is a window displaying the contents of a given directory. The Directory Browser you see when you first

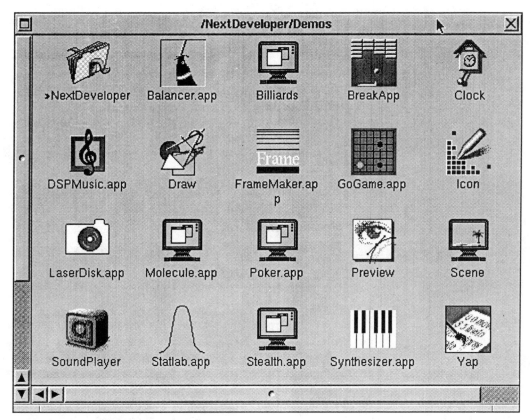

Figure 9.15. Directory window in icon format

log in is just a directory window that's using the browser format; Figure 9.15 shows the same window using the icon format. You can have several directory windows open at the same time, each representing a different directory. Using these windows, you can perform various operations on files and subdirectories, including copying or moving them from one directory to another, deleting them, renaming them, or creating new directories.

There are various formats for displaying the files and subdirectories in a directory window. The three basic formats are: browser (the Directory Browser); iconic (rows and columns of file icons, with names underneath); and list (a list of file names, with additional information provided as requested). You select the format for a given directory window by clicking on it (making it the main/key window), then choosing the desired format from the View submenu of the WM menu. Here are the options provided:

- Fastest: lists the names of the files and directories in a single column, in alphabetical order, with just a miniature icon at the left to indicate the type.

- Icon: displays the full-sized icon for each file and directory, with its name underneath, as shown in Figure 9.15.

- Name: like Fastest, but also shows read/write/execute privileges, file owner, file size (in bytes), and date of last modification; an example is shown in Figure 9.16.

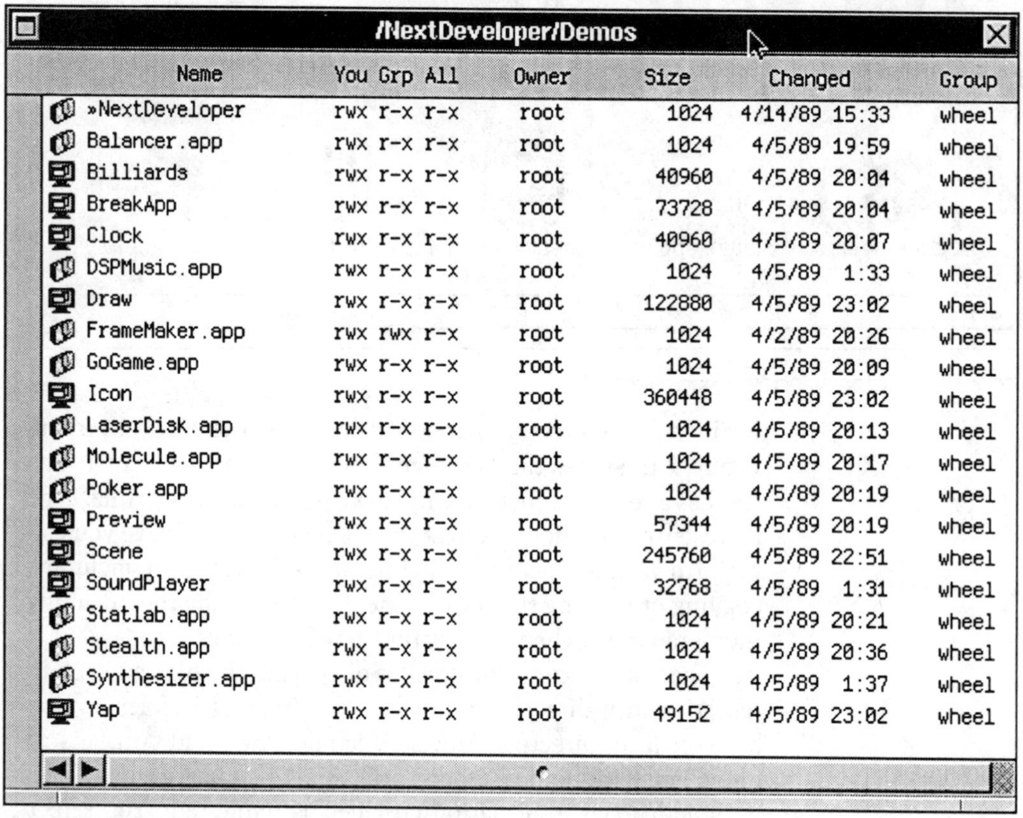

Name	You Grp All	Owner	Size	Changed	Group
»NextDeveloper	rwx r-x r-x	root	1024	4/14/89 15:33	wheel
Balancer.app	rwx r-x r-x	root	1024	4/5/89 19:59	wheel
Billiards	rwx r-x r-x	root	40960	4/5/89 20:04	wheel
BreakApp	rwx r-x r-x	root	73728	4/5/89 20:04	wheel
Clock	rwx r-x r-x	root	40960	4/5/89 20:07	wheel
DSPMusic.app	rwx r-x r-x	root	1024	4/5/89 1:33	wheel
Draw	rwx r-x r-x	root	122880	4/5/89 23:02	wheel
FrameMaker.app	rwx rwx r-x	root	1024	4/2/89 20:26	wheel
GoGame.app	rwx r-x r-x	root	1024	4/5/89 20:09	wheel
Icon	rwx r-x r-x	root	360448	4/5/89 23:02	wheel
LaserDisk.app	rwx r-x r-x	root	1024	4/5/89 20:13	wheel
Molecule.app	rwx r-x r-x	root	1024	4/5/89 20:17	wheel
Poker.app	rwx r-x r-x	root	1024	4/5/89 20:19	wheel
Preview	rwx r-x r-x	root	57344	4/5/89 20:19	wheel
Scene	rwx r-x r-x	root	245760	4/5/89 22:51	wheel
SoundPlayer	rwx r-x r-x	root	32768	4/5/89 1:31	wheel
Statlab.app	rwx r-x r-x	root	1024	4/5/89 20:21	wheel
Stealth.app	rwx r-x r-x	root	1024	4/5/89 20:36	wheel
Synthesizer.app	rwx r-x r-x	root	1024	4/5/89 1:37	wheel
Yap	rwx r-x r-x	root	49152	4/5/89 23:02	wheel

/NextDeveloper/Demos

Figure 9.16. Directory window in name format

- Date: like Name, but sorted by date of last modification (most recently modified files listed first).

- Size: like Name, but sorted by size (largest files listed first).

- Browser: the Directory Browser format described above.

List Formats

For all the list formats—fastest, name, date, size—a directory window behaves consistently. A double-click on an application or a document behaves just as described for the browser format, that is, it launches the application, or it attempts to open the document by launching an associated application. A double-click on a directory, however, doesn't open up a new directory window; instead, it displays the contents of that directory in the same window, replacing the old display. If you really do want to open a new directory window, then click once on the directory and select the Window/Open Directory command from the WM menu (or press Command-Shift-O).

A means for going back up to the enclosing directory is also provided. There is always an entry whose name is that of the enclosing directory preceded by the character "»". It will usually be the first file in a window using the name format. When you double-click on this directory, the current display disappears and is replaced by that of the enclosing directory.

Icon Format

For the icon format, double-clicking on a directory icon opens up a new window for that directory. Likewise, double-clicking on the "open folder" icon of the enclosing directory causes the entire directory window to disappear.

Unlike the list formats, the icon format lets you rearrange the layout of the icons by dragging the icons around within the window. A certain amount of order is maintained, since the icons snap into alignment with an invisible grid. There are also a few WM menu commands, both found in the View submenu, to help you straighten things up. The Clean Up Icons command does some general grouping, pulling all icons toward the upper-left corner of the window. The Sort Icons command orders the icons alphabetically in a series of rows. Note, however, that the ordering is case-sensitive, and that uppercase letters are presumed to come before lowercase letters. This means that the file "ReadMe.wn" will come before the file "myList.txt", since "R" comes before "m" in the ASCII character set. This same rule holds true for directory windows using the name format.

File Filters

Much as Workspace Manager normally screens out those system-specific directories that you don't need to worry about, you can also ask Workspace Manager to only show you certain file types in a given directory window using the Filter... command in the View submenu. Figure 9.17 shows the panel that the Filter... command brings up.

To use this command, click on the directory window or browser which is to be affected, then select the View/Filter... command. Once the panel appears, click on one or more icons. If you are going to select multiple icons, hold the Shift key down as you do so. Each icon selected will be enclosed in a highlighted box. When you're done, click on the OK button. The panel will vanish, and the directory window will be redrawn, with only the selected file types showing. Note that applications and directories are *always* shown; this command only affects document and data file types.

When might this command be handy? Here's an example from creating this book. The screen figures used in this book were saved as both EPS (Encapsulated PostScript) and TIFF (Tag Image File Format) files, with files of each type saved in different directories. As it turned out, however, some files of each type ended up in the wrong directory. It was very simple to track these down using the Filter... command. For example, the directory that was supposed to hold only EPS files was opened, the Filter panel brought up, and only TIFF files selected for display. A few errant TIFF files appeared and were quickly moved over to the correct directory.

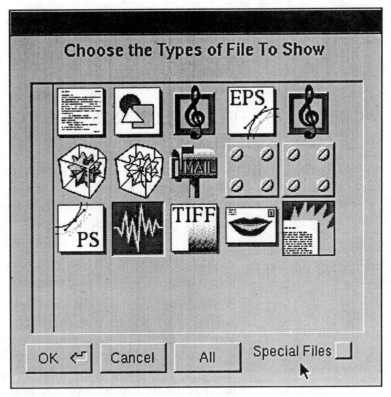

Figure 9.17. The Filter panel for the View/Filter... command

UPDATING THE DIRECTORY WINDOW

Suppose you have a particular directory, called MyDocs, displayed in a directory window. You launch the WriteNow application and use it to create a new document. You save it out as a file named "newstuff.wn" in the MyDocs directory. You then click on the MyDocs directory window. No file named "newstuff.wn" is there! Why not?

To help minimize system overhead, directory windows and browsers are not updated automatically when files or directories are created, moved, or deleted by other applications. Instead, you need to click on the appropriate directory window, which, if it needs to be updated, will have the word "Changed:"

up in the title bar. In that case, select the Window/Update command (or press Command-u). This will force Workspace Manager to redraw the contents of that window, reflecting the current changes.

WORKING WITH FILES, DIRECTORIES, AND VOLUMES

You've spent a fair amount of time learning all the different ways you can look at what's stored on your system. Now it's time to learn how to do something with all that information. You'll start at the bottom level—files—then work up through directories and on to volumes.

WORKING WITH FILES

A **file** is the basic unit of stored information that you manipulate at the Workspace Manager level. The files you work with generally fall into one of three categories: **applications** (programs you run), **documents** (text and/or graphics and/or data that you create and modify using an application), or **resources** (such as sound, font information, or graphics used by an application or by the system itself). Note that the last two are sometimes interchangeable; one application might be used to create a document (such as a sound) that becomes a resource for another application. Also, the operating system maintains a large number of files that contain information about how the system operates, but those are beyond the scope of this chapter.

File Information

A given file has a lot of information associated with it, as you can see in Figure 9.18. You can bring up this panel by clicking on a file name or icon in a directory window or browser and then selecting the Files/More info... command in the WM menu.

Each file has a **file name**, that is, a string of characters, numbers, and punctuation symbols that somehow identify it. As you might imagine, it's good practice to pick file names that

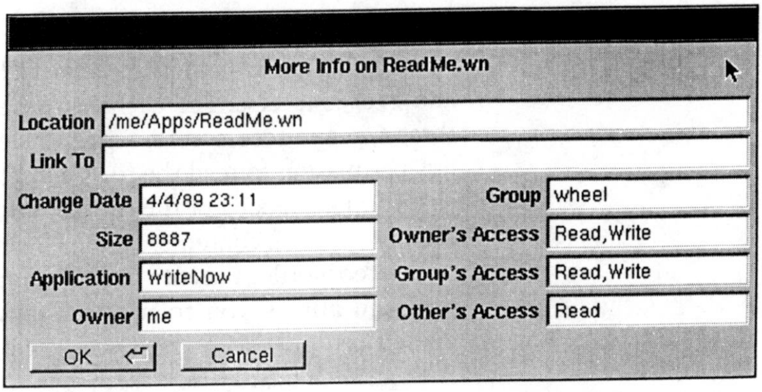

More Info on ReadMe.wn	
Location /me/Apps/ReadMe.wn	
Link To	

Change Date 4/4/89 23:11		**Group** wheel
Size 8887		**Owner's Access** Read,Write
Application WriteNow		**Group's Access** Read,Write
Owner me		**Other's Access** Read

OK ↵   Cancel

Figure 9.18. The File Information panel for the Files/More Info... command

make sense and bear some relationship to the file's purpose and contents. Thus, a name such as "January_Sales" generally conveys more information than one named "irc89x01", though the latter might be appropriate in a situation where each letter or digit in the name had well-known (or, at least, well-documented) significance.

Many file names end with an **extension**, which consists of a period (".") followed by one or more characters. These extensions are used to identify the file's type or purpose, such as what kind of data it holds or with what application it is associated. For example, the file "ReadMe.wn" is presumed to be a WriteNow document, while the file "Figure9.18.eps" should contain an image encoded as Encapsulated PostScript. NeXT reserves all possible extensions up to four (4) characters (lowercase letters and/or digits) in length and adds the appropriate extension automatically to the file name. This is because the NeXT system uses a file's extension to determine what icon is used to represent that file and which application is launched should you double-click on the file or its icon. Any non-executable file using an undefined extension or with no extension at all is assumed to be associated with the Edit application and will be given the edit document icon.

A file has an **owner**, which usually (though not always) is the user login ID of the person who created the file in the first place. That owner is associated with a **group**, a collection of users who share certain privileges.

The file has certain **privileges** defined for the various people who can access it, namely its owner, those in its owner's group, and everyone else. For each of those categories, the file has three types of access: read, write, and execute. **Read access** confers permission to read the file's contents, which includes being able to make a copy of the file elsewhere. **Write access** lets you modify the file's contents, which also means that you can move or delete the file. **Execute access** defines the file as an application and allows you to run it; though, of course, if the file doesn't contain executable code, setting this access won't make it magically able to run.

Finally, the file has a **file size**, which is the size of the file's contents measured in bytes, and a **change date**, which is the last time the file was modified and those changes saved to disk. You change neither of these directly; instead, they change as you edit or modify the file using some application and save those changes out to disk.

Renaming Files

You can rename a file using any directory window or browser. The principle is pretty much the same, regardless of what format is used. You click on the file's entry or icon to select that file; you then point at one end of the file's name, press the mouse button down, and drag the cursor to the other end. The file's name is now selected, and you can type in the new name. You can make minor changes by replacing or deleting selected portions of the file's name, or by clicking at a given spot in the name and inserting text. Once you've made the changes, pressing Return or clicking the mouse elsewhere is sufficient to implement them.

Note that if you change a file's extension, it can change the file's presumed type and associated application. For example, if you rename "ReadMe.wn" to "ReadMe.doc" or even just "ReadMe", you'll get an attention panel that points out that you're changing the file type, asks you if you're really sure you want to do this, and gives you a chance to cancel the name change.

Changing File Ownership

Workspace Manager, at least as of Release 0.9, doesn't provide a direct way to change a file's ownership, which is probably just as well. Done inadvertently or unwisely, it could cause any number of problems.

However, it is possible to change file ownership using the chown (Change Owner) command with one of the UNIX shell applications, Shell or Terminal. For more details on how to do this, see Chapter 11, Exploring the Shell.

Changing Privilege Status

Workspace Manager does give you a simple mechansim for changing the access privileges for a given file. To do so, simply click on that file or its icon in a directory window or browser, then select the Files/Protect... command in the WM menu. You'll get the attention panel shown in Figure 9.19.

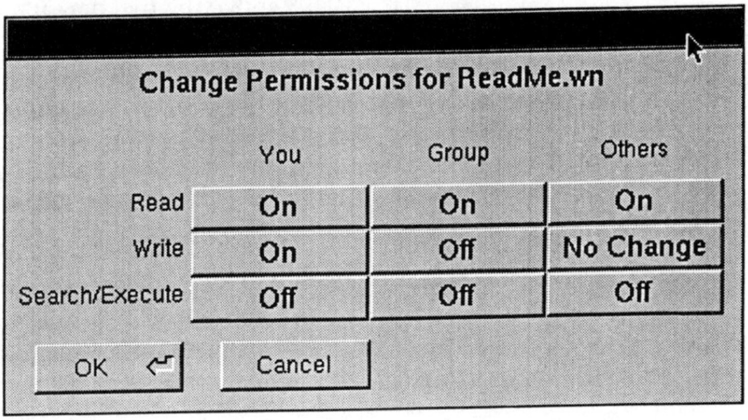

Change Permissions for ReadMe.wn			
	You	Group	Others
Read	On	On	On
Write	On	Off	No Change
Search/Execute	Off	Off	Off
OK ⏎	Cancel		

Figure 9.19. The File Access panel for the Files/Protect... command

To use this panel, just click on the appropriate button to change it to the desired status. Each click on a given button rotates it through three values: ON, meaning you do want to allow that access for that particular person or group; OFF, meaning you do not want to permit that kind of access; and NO CHANGE, meaning that you want that particular access privilege to be what it was before you tried to make changes.

Moving Files

To move a file, you need two directory windows or browsers open, one for the source, one for the destination. If you're using browsers, set them up so that the icon representing the file or directory to be moved is showing in the icon box in one, and the icon for the directory it's being moved into is showing in the icon box of the other. If you're using directory windows, set up one so that the name and icon of the file or directory being copied is visible, then set up the other to show either the folder icon of the destination directory, or the contents of the destination directory. You can also mix and match, that is, do it with one browser window and one directory window.

To actually move the file, drag its icon from the browser or directory window where it's located to the destination browser or directory window. If the destination directory is just shown as a folder icon (in a browser or the window of an enclosing directory), then drag the icon being moved on top of the folder icon. The folder will then change so that it appears "open"; at that point, release the mouse button. If the destination directory was opened as a window, then just drag the icon so that it's over that open window and then release. In either case, the file or directory is now moved to the destination directory, which means that it no longer exists in the directory where it was originally located.

Copying Files

To **copy** a file—that is, to make a copy elsewhere while retaining the original—you must first **duplicate** it. Do this by clicking once on the file or directory (so that it's highlighted), and then selecting the Edit/Duplicate command in the WM menu (or by pressing Command-d). This will create a copy of that file (or directory) named "Copy_Of_oldname," where oldname is the name of the original. You can then move the copy (or the original, if you wish) to the destination directory, using the method described in the previous paragraph. Once there, you can edit the file's name if you wish, deleting the "Copy_Of_" portion.

Workspace Manager also allows you to **link** files, that is, to create another entry for a file in a different directory without actually making a new copy. To do this, hold the Control key down and drag the file's icon to the new destination. The new entry appears, while the old one remains in place. If you now click on the new file entry and bring up the More Info... panel, you'll see the full path name of the original file in the "Link To" field.

Deleting Files

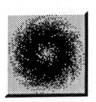

Figure 9.20. The Black Hole icon

The safest way to delete a file is to drag its icon into the Black Hole icon, shown in Figure 9.20. When you get the file's icon over the Black Hole icon, the latter starts swirling. When you release the mouse button, it stops swirling, and the file's icon disappears.

At this point, the file in question hasn't been deleted. Instead, it's been moved to a special directory, which you can examine by double-clicking on the Black Hole icon. This will cause a directory window containing all your deleted files to appear. You can then drag files back out of this window if you desire.

If you wish to permanently destroy all the files in the Black Hole, select the Destroy Deleted Files command in the Utilities submenu of the WM menu. The files in the Black Hole will irretrievably vanish. You can get the same results in fewer steps by clicking on the file to be destroyed, and then selecting the Destroy command in the Files submenu (or by pressing Command-r). You'll get an attention panel asking if you really want to delete the selected file; clicking on the OK button causes that file to vanish forever.

WORKING WITH DIRECTORIES

A **directory** represents a collection of files, usually somehow related, which can be examined, moved, and deleted as a group. Given the hundreds and hundreds of files present on a typical NeXT system, it would be nearly impossible to effectively work with them if you couldn't group them into directories. Furthermore, since directories can contain other directories, you can group related directories and form a hierarchical file structure that's much easier to navigate.

Directories are treated just like files in many respects and, in fact, are implemented as a special file type by the underlying file system. Like files, directories have names, owners, access privileges, and other attributes. Because of that, many of the directions below for working with directories will refer you back to the previous section on working with files.

Creating Directories

As you create new files with your applications, you'll probably also want to create new directories to hold them. The process is simple: select the directory in which you want the new directory to appear (that is, as a subdirectory). To do this, either click once on that directory's name (in a browser column) or open a window for that directory. Then select the Files/New Directory command from the WM menu. This will create a new directory named "NewDirectory." You can then change the name to suit your needs, move files and other directories inside of it, and so on.

Renaming Directories

You rename directories the same way you rename files: click on the directory entry or icon, select the directory's name with the cursor, and edit it as you wish.

Changing Directory Ownership

As with files, there is currently no mechanism in Workspace Manager to change a directory's owner. However, you can use the chown command using Shell or Terminal to change directory ownership, just as you would to change file ownership.

Changing Directory Privileges

Directories have access privileges, too. You can control read access and write access, just as you can with files. However, it's obvious that you could never "execute" a directory, so no such privileges are defined. Instead, you can determine the **search access** that others have, that is, whether or not they can even see what's in the directory. You do this just as you would with files, using the Files/Protect... command in the WM menu.

Moving, Copying, and Linking Directories

As you might guess, you can move, copy, and link directories just as you would files, and you do so using exactly the same methods of dragging and (when necessary) duplicating. However, note that duplicating a directory prior to moving it elsewhere can eat up a tremendous amount of disk space if the directory contains a lot of files and subdirectories. This can be a problem if you're copying a large directory from a device that is relatively full. In such a case, your best bet may be to go into Shell or Terminal and use the cp (Copy) command, which is described in Chapter 11.

Deleting Directories

Again, you can delete a directory the same way you delete a file, either by dragging its icon into the Black Hole, or by clicking on the directory entry or icon and selecting the Files/Destroy command. If you choose the former, you can retrieve the directory or any of its contents out of the Black Hole until such time as you select the Utilities/Destroy Deleted Files command.

   As with duplicating directories, there are some dangers in deleting them, and for much the same reasons. Since a directory can contain so many other files and directories, it's easy to accidentally throw out something you wanted to keep. Before deleting a directory, you should first browse through it to be sure that there are no files in it or in its subdirectories that you wish to save.

WORKING WITH VOLUMES

A **volume** is a collection of directories, such as you find on your NeXT system master. Each optical disk you format represents a single volume; to reference the files on that disk, you must mount it, that is, graft its volume into your directory tree. When you're done, you can then unmount that volume; it and all its directories and files then vanish. Since most such operations you perform will be with optical disks, that's what this section focuses on. However, be aware that volumes can also be accessed over networks (such as Ethernet), and that it is possible to have multiple volumes on a single mass storage device.

Initializing Disks

Your NeXT system comes with an optical disk already initialized and containing all the system files and directories required to run your computer. However, you should not use that disk any more than is necessary. Instead, you should either initialize another optical disk (if you have a one- or two-drive optical-only system) or initialize your hard disk (if you have an internal hard disk).

To do this, boot off of your NeXT system master optical disk. Once you are booted up, find the application BuildDisk in the directory NextApps and run it. In its display, shown in Figure 9.21, you'll be able to choose whether to build a complete system on your hard (SCSI) disk or on a second optical disk. Pick the appropriate choice and follow the instructions. NOTE: this process takes a long time, on the order of one to three hours. If you're building a hard disk, or an optical disk on a two-drive system, then you can start it and go do something else. If you're building an optical disk on a one-drive system, you may be in for some time and effort.

Suppose you don't want to make a complete system copy. Instead, you just want to initialize an optical disk to store files on, or to use for backup purposes. In this case, select the Initialize command in the Disks submenu of the WM menu. You'll be prompted to insert an optical disk, which will then be formatted, erasing forever any data that might have been on it. You can now use that disk as you wish, building whatever directory structure you desire.

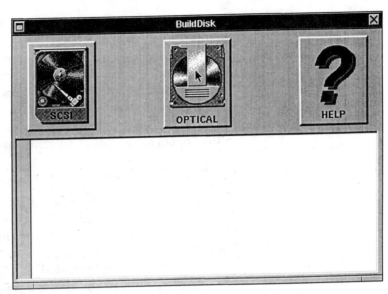

Figure 9.21. The BuildDisk application

Mounting Disks

If you are running off of one disk and wish to access files on another, or to transfer files between the two, you must first **mount** the second disk. If you have a system with two optical drives, or if you are running off of an internal hard disk, then all you need to do is to insert the second (optical) disk into the open disk drive. The system will automatically mount that second disk as a subdirectory in your home directory ("/me" or whatever). You can then access it as if it were just another subdirectory, transferring files and directories. If you look at that disk in a directory window or browser, you'll see that its icon is that of an optical disk, as seen in Figure 9.22.

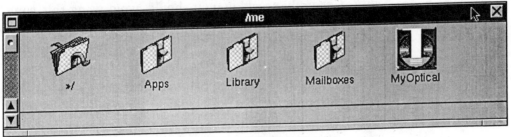

Figure 9.22. A directory window showing a mounted disk icon

If you're running on a one-drive system and wish to access another optical disk, just select the Disks/Mount command in the WM menu. This will eject the optical disk you're currently working with and ask you to insert another one. That second disk gets mounted onto your directory system. You can now access files on either disk, and even transfer files between them, but at a cost: you'll find yourself having to swap disks manually as the system reads from or writes to one disk or the other.

Changing Disk Names

A disk gets a specific name when it is initialized or built. If you use the BuildDisk application, then the disk gets the same name as that disk which did the building. If you use the Disks/Initialize command, then you are prompted for the disk's name when the initializing is done.

Regardless of how the disk got its name, you can change that name without having to reformat the disk. To do so, mount the disk, click on its icon or entry, and select the Disks/Change Disk Name command. You will be prompted for the disk's new name; just type it in and press Return.

Ejecting Disks

There are times when you may want to eject the optical disk you're using without having to shut down the system or unmount the disk. You can do this using the Disks/Eject command in the WM menu. This will eject the disk, which you can then remove for whatever purpose you require. If you have only one drive, the system then goes into a waiting mode in which it ignores any requests or actions that require it to read from or write to the disk. This continues until you re-insert the optical disk. Generally speaking, you should avoid using this command, but be aware that it's there if you need it.

Unmounting Disks

When you are finished with a second volume, you can unmount it by clicking on its entry in the Directory Browser and selecting the Disks/Unmount command in the WM menu. This removes the volume's entry from your directory structure and ejects the optical disk.

LOGGING OUT

When you are finished using the NeXT system, you should **log out**, that is, end your work session. This tells the system that you are done; it then takes whatever steps are necessary to make sure all your applications are terminated and any open files are saved out to disk.

To log out, just select the Log Out command from the WM menu (or press Command-q with the WM menu visible). You'll get the attention panel shown in Figure 9.23, warning you that any documents or other files that you are still using must be saved to disk or your changes will be lost. If you didn't mean to log out, or if there's a file still open that you want to close just to be safe, then choose Cancel; this will stop the entire process. Otherwise, click on the " log out" button in the panel.

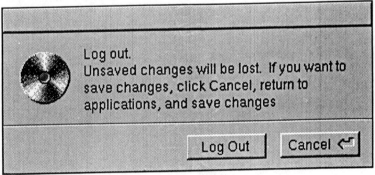

Figure 9.23. Attention panel for logging out

Workspace Manager will then send messages to any active applications, asking them to quit in an orderly fashion. Another attention panel comes up, with a button that allows you to speed the process along by telling the system not to wait for any running applications to shut down. When the log out procedure is done, the screen clears, and the login window reappears. The NeXT system is now ready to be powered down or to have someone else log in.

POWERING DOWN

To turn your NeXT computer off, you simply press the power button after logging out. A panel will appear, asking if you are sure that you want to power down. If you booted from an optical disk, you will also be given the option of having the disk ejected before the system turns itself off.

Should you press the power button while still logged on, you'll get the same choice of options. In almost all cases, you should cancel the power-down and, if you really do want to turn the system off, log out first. If you have a drastic need to interrupt the applications currently executing—for example, if a rogue program is methodically deleting your files, and you can't figure out how to stop it—then you should use the Command-Command-` sequence to bring up the NMI mini-monitor, then type `monitor` to get into the ROM monitor, and from there type either `bod` (boot from optical disk) or `bsd` (boot from SCSI disk).

COMMENTARY

The Macintosh computer, introduced over five years ago, led to the general acceptance of graphical user interfaces. While Apple didn't originate all the concepts, many of which came from the Xerox Palo Alto Research Center (PARC) labs, they did popularize them in a way no one else had done. The Mac's success also led to the tacit acknowledgment by rival computer firms (like IBM) that such interfaces are easier to learn and use than the more traditional command-line interfaces. In fact, many of those firms adopted similar—though usually inferior—inter-faces, leading to several controversial "look-and-feel" lawsuits.

By contrast, the NeXT user interface manages to capture the power of a graphical user interface while imitating little of Apple's style. In fact, it shows significant innovation in a num-ber of areas, and some of its concepts are starting to drift over to other systems. The critical difference for you as a user, though, is that NeXT has taken an operating system—UNIX—which has long been known for being "user-unfriendly" and put a very powerful, yet easy-to-learn, user interface on top of it. The resulting combination gives you the advantages of UNIX while eliminating many of the traditional criticisms.

10
Using Applications

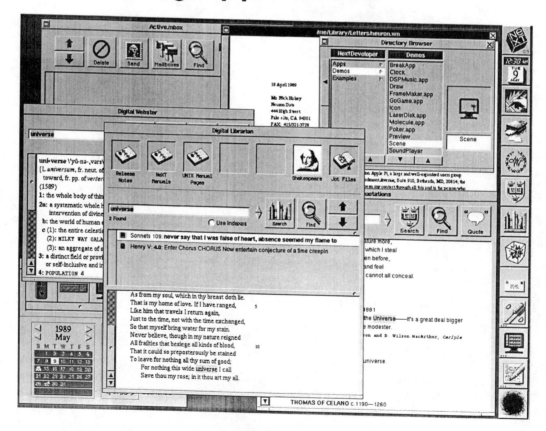

Now that you know how to use Workspace Manager, you're prepared to get some work done. The NeXT system makes that easy; it comes with a wide variety of applications, programs designed to help you solve problems. This chapter will show you, step by step, how to perform some of the basic tasks, such as personalizing your system configuration, creating and printing documents, looking up information in the on-line reference libraries, and sending and receiving mail.

SETTING UP THE APPLICATION DOCK

To make your life easier, you're first going to drag the icons of a number of applications over to the application dock. In case you've forgotten, the application dock is the area along the right edge of the screen where you can "dock" application icons. The NeXT icon is fixed at the top, leaving you room for twelve more icons.

If you want, you can drag the Black Hole icon—normally found in the lower-left corner of the screen—over and put it in the dock. Note that as you move it close to the dock, a highlighted copy of it appears in the dock itself. This shows what position it will snap into as soon as you release the mouse button. If you drag the Black Hole up and down the dock, you'll see

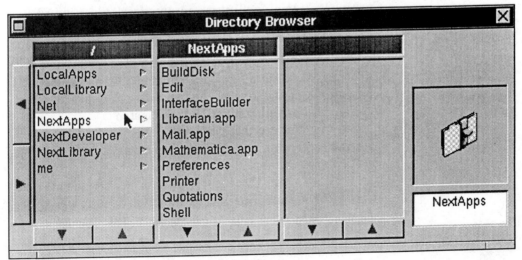

Figure 10.1. The contents of the directory /NextApps

it highlight each of the available positions. Move it down to the very bottom of the dock and lift your finger off the mouse button. It's now in place; time to add some applications.

To find those applications, go to the Directory Browser window and click on the NextApps entry in the first column (the root directory, labeled "/"). At this point, you'll see something like Figure 10.1, showing a list of the bundled applications.

SELECTING APPLICATIONS FOR THE DOCK

Now you're ready to load up the application dock. To move an application's icon over to the dock, click once on that application's name (for example, "Preferences") in the "NextApps" column in the Directory Browser. The corresponding icon will appear in the icon box in the Browser. Drag that icon over to the dock, then release it; it will snap into place and remain in the dock. Note that it hasn't been removed from the "Next-Apps" column, as it would have been were you moving it to another directory.

Perform this action for the following applications: Preferences, WriteNow, Printer, Webster, Quotation, Librarian, Mathematica, and Mail. If you're going to work through Chapter 11, Exploring the Shell, then you'll want to drag Shell or Terminal over there. Likewise, if you plan to work through Chapter 12, Creating Programs, you'll also want InterfaceBuilder and Edit.

As you move each icon into the dock, three little dots appear in its lower-left corner. This indicates that the icon's application isn't currently loaded and running. When you launch any of these applications, the dots in that application's icon will disappear, so that you can tell at a glance which of those applications are running and which aren't.

You might notice that not all these applications are visible in the Directory Browser window. There are two buttons below the NextApps column, the left one pointing up, the right one pointing down. Note that the left arrow is black, while the right arrow is dark gray. This means that there are more entries below the last one (Shell), but none above the top one (Build-

Disk). Move the cursor over the left arrow and click the mouse button once. The list scrolls up by one, and now both arrows are black, meaning that you can scroll in either direction. Leaving the cursor over the left (down) arrow, hold the mouse button down. The list scrolls for a second or two, and then stops; you've reached the bottom of the list for the NextApps directory. Use the two arrows to scroll up and down through the list in order to find the applications you want to move over to the dock.

USING THE DOCK INFO PANEL

Once you've got the dock set up the way you want it, go into the WM (Workspace Manager) menu, bring up the Utilities submenu and select the Dock Info... command. This will bring up the Dock Info panel, which you read about in Chapter 9 and which is shown again in Figure 10.2. Note that each entry in the panel matches the corresponding icon in the dock. Also note that the NeXT icon is labeled as being "Workspace"; this means that you can always bring up the WM menu and any currently open directory windows or browsers by double-clicking on this icon.

The check boxes along the left side of the Dock Info panel let you select any applications to be launched automatically when you log in. For now, just click on the Preferences application; as you become more familiar with the NeXT system, you can determine which other applications (if any) you want automatically launched.

Once you've got the dock set up the way you want it, log out of Workspace Manager using the Log Out command in the WM menu, then log back in. You'll notice that Workspace Manager remembers your application dock configuration and brings it up for you when you log in. Also notice that the Preferences icon turns white, the Preferences window appears, and the three dots on the Preferences icon have vanished. Preferences is now up and running, so let's use it to customize your system a bit more.

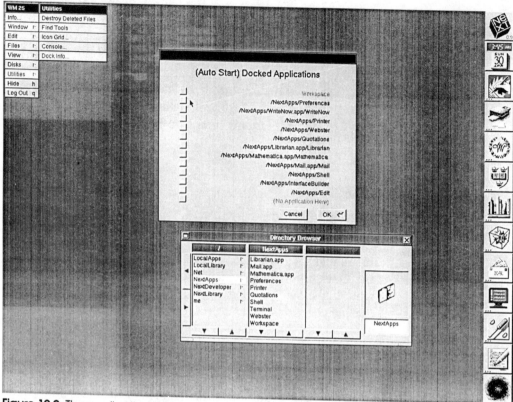

Figure 10.2. The application dock and Dock Info panel

ESTABLISHING PREFERENCES

As you've probably seen elsewhere in the book, the Preferences application lets you customize various system attributes and responses. The Preferences window has a scrollable set of icons across the top; to adjust settings for a particular area (mouse, keyboard, etc.), just click on the appropriate icon, and the window's contents are changed accordingly. Here's a look at the different settings and how to use them.

MOUSE SETTINGS

The mouse settings, shown in Figure 10.3, have four different sections. Let's start with the one in the lower-left corner, the

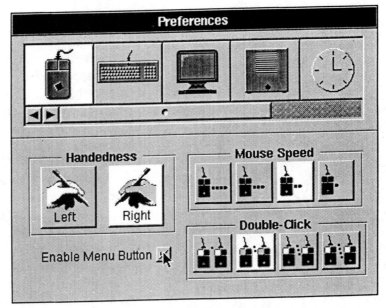

Figure 10.3. The mouse settings in Preferences

"Enable Menu Button" switch. If you turn this option on, then one of the two mouse buttons is given a special function: when you hold it down it, a menu appears under the cursor and remains there until you release the mouse button, allowing you to select any command on that menu if desired. This menu is a copy of whatever main menu is currently on the screen; since main menus are usually located in the upper-left corner, this option saves you from having to drag the mouse up there all the time to select menu items.

In the upper-left corner is the "handedness" box. As discussed in Chapter 9, you must "turn on" the "Enable Menu Button" switch to use this box. It determines which mouse button will pop up a copy of the main menu; that is, if Right is highlighted (has a white interior), then the right mouse button will call up the menu, and likewise for Left. This is based on the idea that if you're using the mouse with your right hand, then your index finger will naturally rest on the left mouse button, which still has the normal button function, so the lesser used right button will have the menu function; and, of course, everything swaps if you're using the mouse with your left hand.

When you move the mouse slowly, the cursor moves a relatively short distance; when you move the mouse quickly, the cursor travels much farther. You can adjust this speed/distance factor using the "mouse speed" buttons. There are four settings, with one to four dots in them. The more dots in a button, the greater the distance traveled for a given speed. The current setting is highlighted. Experiment with the four settings to see which one you like best.

Certain actions require you to perform a double-click with the mouse, that is, clicking the mouse button twice in rapid succession; for example, you typically double-click on an application's icon in order to launch it. The double-click buttons let you determine how short the delay between the clicks must be in order for them to be recognized as a double-click instead of as two separate single clicks. Again, there are four settings, and the number of dots between the mouse images in each button indicate how long a delay will be tolerated. In other words, if you select the button with four dots, the NeXT system will recognize a double-click with a much longer delay between the clicks than if you select the button with one dot.

KEYBOARD SETTINGS

The keyboard settings, shown in Figure 10.4, have just two sections. Both deal with the auto-repeat function of the keyboard: when you hold a key down beyond a certain length of time, it starts automatically repeating, as if you were pressing it again and again. The top section, Key Repeat, controls how quickly the key presses are repeated. There are four buttons, showing the letter "a" separated by two to five dots; the number of dots indicates how quickly the keys are repeated. In other words, the button with five dots will repeat keys more quickly than the other settings. As with most settings, you select your preference by clicking on the appropriate button.

The lower control, Initial Key Repeat, governs how long you have to hold a key down before it starts repeating. Again, there are four buttons; the more dots in the button that's currently selected, the longer you must hold a key down before it starts repeating.

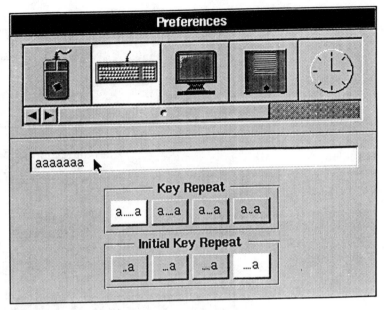

Figure 10.4. The keyboard settings in Preferences

Note that this panel provides a text field at the top to allow you to test your settings. Just move the cursor over the field and click on it; a vertical bar cursor will appear, and you can now type into that field. Try it out by selecting both of the leftmost buttons, then holding down the letter "a"; now select both of the rightmost buttons and do it again. To clear the text field, hold down the Delete key, which will also auto-repeat. You can also clear it by **selecting** all the text in the field, that is, by moving the cursor to one end, holding the mouse button down, and dragging the cursor to the other end. The selected text will now have a gray background instead of a white one; if you now press Delete once, the entire selection will be deleted.

DISPLAY SETTINGS

The display settings, shown in Figure 10.5, let you adjust values for the MegaPixel Display. The first one, Automatic Dimming Delay, controls how long the system will go without any action (keyboard or mouse) on your part before automatically dimming the display's screen. Once the screen is dimmed, it

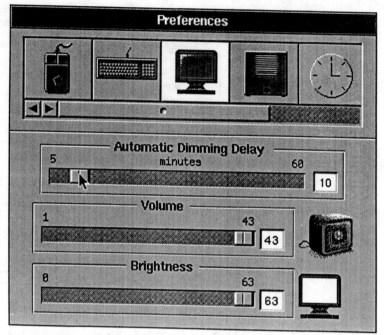

Figure 10.5. The display settings in Preferences

remains that way until you press a key or move the mouse, at which point it's restored to its previous brightness level. You can set this value either by using the slider (dragging the button left or right) or by entering a value in the text field to the right of the slider.

The second control, Volume, lets you adjust the loudness of the display's internal speaker, while the third one, Brightness, lets you adjust the brightness level of the display screen. As before, you can set either of these levels by moving the slider button or by typing a value directly into the text field. Note that both these controls are overridden by the Volume and Brightness keys on the NeXT keyboard.

SYSTEM SETTINGS

The system settings, shown in Figure 10.6, represent a collection of system and user interface settings that you can control.

The first one, System Alert, determines how the system notifies you about a system alert, such as the printer being out of paper. You can select voice messages (which come through the MegaPixel Display's internal speaker), dialog boxes (which appear on the screen), or both.

The File-Creation Mask, shown at the bottom of the window, indicates which file access privileges can or cannot be set by users of a given file. For example, the mask shown in Figure 10.6 indicates that a file's owner can modify all three privileges; members of the owner's group can change read and execute privileges, but not write privileges; and anyone else can only change the execute privilege.

When you start using the NeXT system, you are normally shown only those files and directories that directly concern you, such as the NeXT, Local, and user directories. The UNIX Expert switch lets you tell Workspace Manager to show you the complete UNIX file system in its directory windows and browsers.

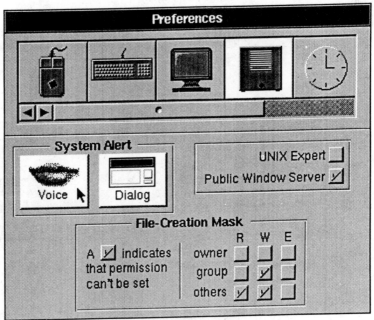

Figure 10.6. The system settings in Preferences

CLOCK/CALENDAR SETTINGS

The clock/calendar settings, shown in Figure 10.7, let you set the time and date for the clock/calendar chip on the NeXT motherboard. The calendar area on the left lets you set the year, month, and day. You can adjust the year and the month by clicking on the arrows to either side of them; as you do so, the monthly calendar changes to reflect the month/year combination. To set the day, just click on the appropriate day in the calendar. You adjust the clock in much the same manner, that is, by clicking on the arrows to either side of the hour, minute, and second values.

All changes are reflected in the time-and-date icon shown above the clock settings. By selecting the "Show Clock When Hidden" switch, you can have the Preferences icon show the time-and-date display whenever you select the Hide function in the Preferences menu. This is a handy way of putting a clock up on the screen, especially if you have the Preferences icon in the application dock.

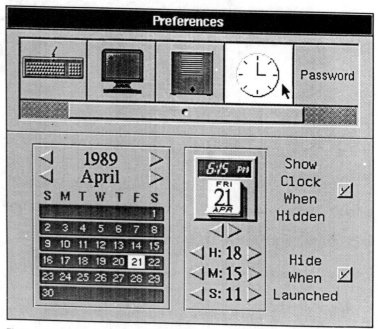

Figure 10.7. The clock/calendar settings in Preferences

The final switch, "Hide When Launched," makes this all even more convenient when used in conjunction with the Dock Info panel. You've already selected Preferences to be launched automatically when you log in. If you click this switch on, then when you log in, Preferences will be launched and then automatically hidden. And if you have the "Show Clock When Hidden" switch on, the Preferences icon will then start showing the current time and date, updated continuously as you work.

CHANGING PASSWORDS

Another function of Preferences is that it allows you to change your password. Remember that when you start with freshly installed system software, there is only one user account, me, and that account has no password. This means that anyone booting up the system will have immediate access, bypassing the login window. Also, the superuser account, root, has no password at first. Instead, you must set the password to help prevent unauthorized access to your files. Likewise, users who do have passwords can use this option to change their passwords from time to time.

Figure 10.8. Changing passwords using Preferences

When you select this option, you are asked to type in your old password as a verification that you are, indeed, that user. You then press Return or click on the OK button to have the system check your old password. If your account currently doesn't have a password, then just click on the OK button. After that, you'll be asked for your new password, which you'll type in, following with Return or a click on the OK button. You'll then be asked for your new password again, just to make sure you didn't misspell it the first time you typed it in. In all three steps, what you type is **not** echoed to the screen, so that people standing behind you can't read your password (new or old) over your shoulder.

CHANGING STARTUP DEVICES

When you get a brand new NeXT system, it is set up to boot from an optical disk, even if you have an internal hard drive. This is because you still need to install all the NeXT system software on the hard disk first, using the BuildDisk application (as described in Chapter 9). But even after that, the NeXT system will still expect to boot from an optical disk. How do you change this? By using the Startup panel in Preferences, shown in Figure 10.9.

Using this panel, you can select one of three startup devices: an optical disk drive, a SCSI (hard) disk drive, or an Ethernet file server. The NeXT system remembers this information even after you power down; the next time you turn on the system, it goes to that device to load in the operating system.

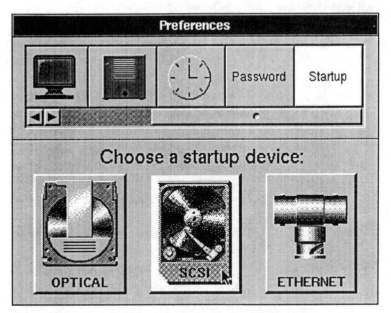

Figure 10.9. Changing startup devices using Preferences

USING AN APPLICATION: WRITENOW

The most common use of computers today is word processing, so it's only fitting that the first real work described here involves creating a document. You'll do that using WriteNow, one of two word processing programs bundled with the NeXT system (the other is Edit). In the process, you'll learn how to perform most standard application functions, such creating, opening and closing files, editing text, setting font types, sizes and styles, manipulating windows and controls, printing documents, and so on.

LAUNCHING AN APPLICATION

There are several ways to **launch** an application, that is, to load it from disk into the computer's memory and start it executing. One way, which you've already seen, is to drag the application's icon into the application dock, select it for automatic launching using the Dock Info panel, then log out and log back in. This is convenient for those applications (such as Preferences) that you want up and running each time you log in, but it's obviously not the method you would use in most circumstances.

It is more simple and practical to drag over to the application dock those applications you most commonly use. These will then be displayed there each time you log in. When you want to use one, double-click on its icon. If it hasn't been launched yet, it will be. While it's being launched, its icon will be highlighted; once it's ready to use, its main menu will appear in the upper-left corner of the screen, and its icon will revert to normal, though (if in the dock) without the three little dots that had marked it as a nonlaunched application. Note that if you double-click on the icon of an already-launched application, you'll simply make its menu and associated windows appear instead of launching a new copy of the application.

Of course, you don't have to drag an application over to the application dock in order to be able to launch it. All you have to do is to find the application in a directory window or browser and double-click on its entry or icon. That application's icon will then appear on the screen outside of the directory window and will remain there until the application is finished executing. Note that you can drag this icon over to the dock and place it there, provided there are open slots available.

There is yet another way to launch an application: using the UNIX shell, within either the Shell or the Terminal application. Details on how to do this are found in Chapter 11, Exploring the Shell.

CREATING A NEW DOCUMENT

Now that you know all the ways to launch an application, use one of them to launch WriteNow. Your screen should look something like Figure 10.10; WriteNow has not only brought up its main menu, but it has also opened a window for a new

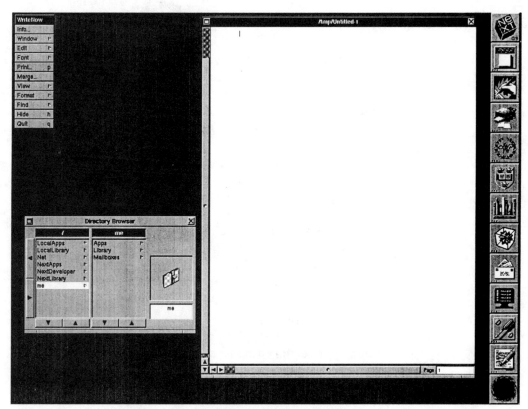

Figure 10.10. The WriteNow application right after launch

document. As you can see, the document window has a title bar with buttons for miniaturizing and closing, vertical and horizontal scrollers, and a resize bar at the bottom.

In the upper-left corner of the document window is a vertical bar that blinks on and off. This is the **text insertion cursor**. Unlike the arrow cursor, this one doesn't change location as you move the mouse. Instead, it shifts to the right as you type, always indicating where the next character will appear. Likewise, as you press Delete, it moves to the left, deleting characters as it goes.

You can now start typing in the window. Type in a paragraph or so of text without pressing Return. You'll notice as you reach the right margin, the text wraps around to the next line by itself. This continues as you type; it allows text to be automatically reformatted if you change the margins, text size, or any other parameters that could affect how the text is laid out. When you're done typing, press Return to signal the end of the paragraph.

SAVING THE DOCUMENT

Before you go any further, you should save your document to disk. Everything you've typed so far is sitting in the computer's memory; if you were to power down the computer, or if the system were to "crash" somehow, your work would be lost. This is not to say that such an event is likely, but it never hurts to be safe (and it can hurt badly not to be).

As you look at the WriteNow menu in the upper-left corner, you'll notice that there isn't any Save command. In fact, there are very few actual commands; most of the menu items bring up submenus. One of those submenus—Window—has the command you want. Click once on the Window item in the WriteNow menu, and you'll get a display like that in Figure 10.11. Most applications have a Window submenu with the same basic set of commands—Open, New, Save, Save As, Miniaturize, and Close—as well as any related commands specific to the application.

To save the document, select the Save command in the Window submenu, either by clicking directly on the menu item

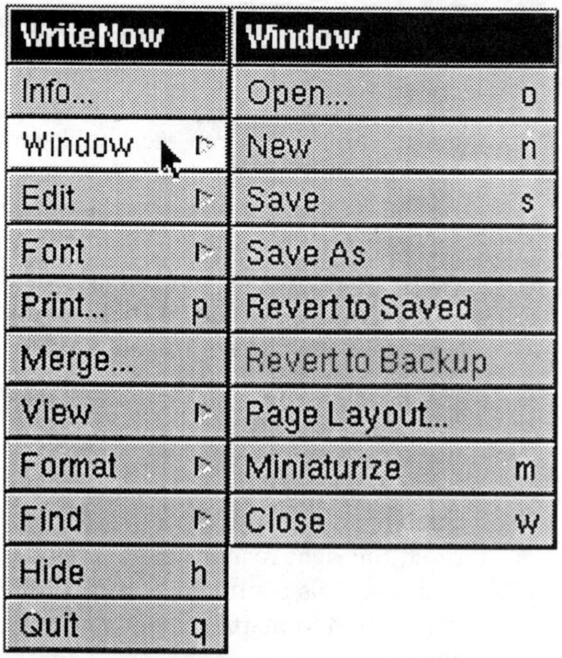

WriteNow		Window	
Info...		Open...	o
Window	▷	New	n
Edit	▷	Save	s
Font	▷	Save As	
Print...	p	Revert to Saved	
Merge...		Revert to Backup	
View	▷	Page Layout...	
Format	▷	Miniaturize	m
Find	▷	Close	w
Hide	h		
Quit	q		

Figure 10.11. The WriteNow menu with the Window submenu

labeled "Save" or by pressing Command-s. Since your document hasn't been saved to disk yet, it doesn't have a file name. To help you name it, WriteNow will bring up a typical File Selection panel, as shown in Figure 10.12.

This panel acts like a compact, two-column Directory Browser. Each column displays the contents of a given directory or subdirectory, with that directory's name at the top of the column. Each entry in a column represents a file or a subdirectory; a subdirectory entry is indicated by an indented arrowhead at

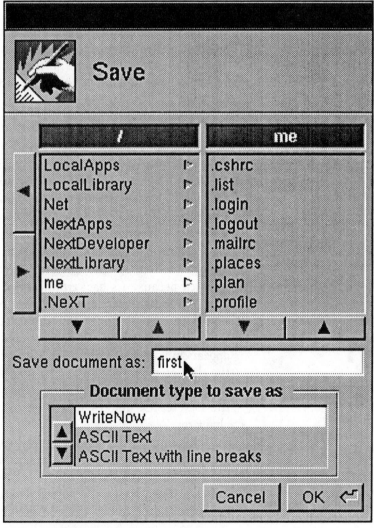

Figure 10.12. Typical File Selection panel

the far right. You can display the contents of a given subdirectory by clicking on its name; its contents will then appear in the right column, with the entire display scrolling left if necessary. The two buttons on the left side allow you to scroll through the directory columns; the buttons underneath each column let you scroll through the entries.

Using this panel, move to your home directory, such as /me. This directory is probably already being displayed, as Figure 10.12 shows. Once you're there, type "first", which will appear in the text entry field near the bottom of the panel. You can now either press Return or click on the OK button. The panel will disappear, and the title at the top of the document window will change to "/me/first.wn". Note that WriteNow added the extension ".wn" to the end of your file name; this identifies your document as having been created by WriteNow.

EDITING TEXT

Now that you've saved your first document, let's have you go back and make some changes to the text you typed in. To start, select a single word somewhere in the paragraph. You can do this by moving the cursor over the word and double-clicking on it. Or you can move the cursor to one end of the word, hold the mouse button down, drag the cursor to the other end of the word, and then let the button up. You can tell the word is **selected** because its background—the "paper" behind it—will change from white to light gray. Also, notice that the text insertion cursor has disappeared. Now type a different word. Note that the selected word disappears, and the word you're typing appears in its place, with the text insertion cursor to the right of the characters you're typing. The text following that word shifts and adjusts to accommodate it. Note that repeatedly pressing the Delete key deletes what you've just typed, character by character.

This same method works for changing phrases, sentences, paragraphs, and so on. Find a sentence in the text you've entered. Move the cursor to the start of the first word in the sentence. Hold the mouse button down, and move the cursor to just past the period at the end of sentence, then release the mouse button. Notice that the entire sentence is now selected. If you start typing, that sentence will disappear and be replaced by what you're typing. If you just press Delete, you'll delete the entire sentence. If you click the mouse button once, or if you select text elsewhere in the document, that sentence is now deselected.

If you just need to insert text, you can do so without having to select anything. Just move the arrow cursor to the point where you want to insert text and click the mouse button once. You'll see that the text insertion cursor appears in that spot. If you start typing, the words appear in that spot, with the text to the right of the bar getting pushed aside to make room. Like-wise, if you start pressing Delete, the text to the right of the bar gets deleted.

Saving Changes

It is a good idea to save your work frequently when doing exten-sive editing: adding, deleting, changing, or rearranging the con-tents of your document. That way, should catastrophe strike in the form of a power outage, a program or system crash, or any other abrupt termination of your work session, all your efforts won't have been lost.

To save your work, just use the Window/Save command again or, more simply, press Command-s. Since you've already saved it to disk once, you won't get the File Selection panel again. In fact, all that will happen is that there will be a momentary pause as the revised document is written to disk.

Suppose you want to save a copy of your file under some other name—what do you do? You use the Save As command in the Windows menu. This will bring up a standard file panel just like the one you got when you first used the Save com-mand.

CUTTING, COPYING, AND PASTING

When you are working with text, there are some standard oper-ations you want to perform. You looked at three of them above: inserting, replacing, and deleting. There are three others that add a higher level of functionality: cutting, copying, and pasting. **Cutting** refers to selecting some text—paragraphs, sentences, words, or characters—by any of the usual methods, making a copy of it, and then deleting the original. **Copying** is just cutting without the deletion: selecting and then copying. **Pasting** means taking the text that you've either cut or copied and inserting it somewhere in your text. Or you can paste it "over" some selected text, replacing the selected text with the text you had cut or copied. Using these three actions, you can revise and reorganize your text very quickly.

These actions are always found in the Edit menu of any application, and WriteNow is no exception, as Figure 10.13 shows. WriteNow adds quite a few more functions, some of which you'll learn about later. Note that several of the commands are gray, rather than black. This indicates functions that you can't currently use. For example, Cut and Copy are black, which indicates that some text has been selected; however, Paste is gray, which means that there isn't any text which has been copied or cut yet, and, therefore, there is nothing to paste.

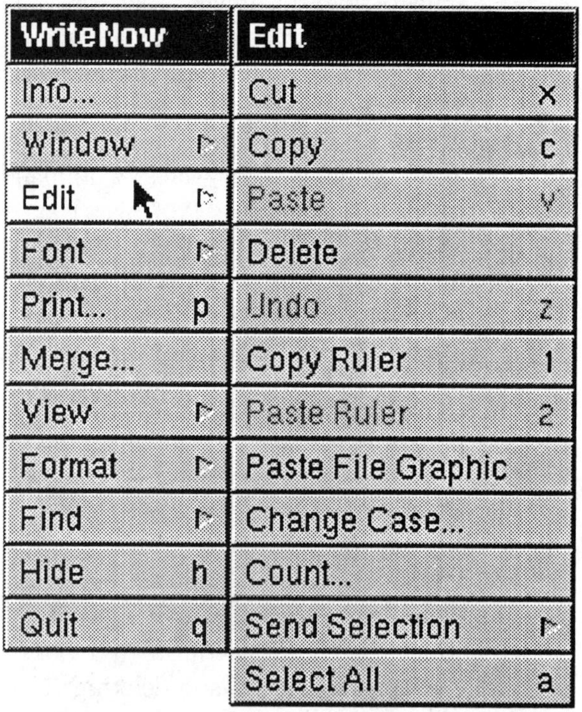

WriteNow		Edit	
Info...		Cut	x
Window	▷	Copy	c
Edit	▷	Paste	v
Font	▷	Delete	
Print...	p	Undo	z
Merge...		Copy Ruler	1
View	▷	Paste Ruler	2
Format	▷	Paste File Graphic	
Find	▷	Change Case...	
Hide	h	Count...	
Quit	q	Send Selection	▷
		Select All	a

Figure 10.13. The Edit submenu of the WriteNow menu

Let's start by having you move the first sentence in your first paragraph so that it's now the last sentence. Select the first sentence; choose Edit/Cut (or press Command-x); move the cursor to the end of the last sentence and click once; choose Edit/Paste (or press Command-v). Press Command-v a few more times; another copy of the sentence is pasted in each time. Figure 10.14 shows this process in three steps: selecting the sentence, cutting it, and then pasting it.

Now select the entire first paragraph, and choose the Edit/Copy command. Note that the paragraph remains intact and selected. Move the cursor to the end of your document and click the mouse button once. Now choose Edit/Paste; a complete copy of the first paragraph (or whatever text you selected and copied) appears.

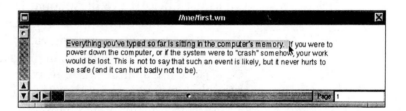

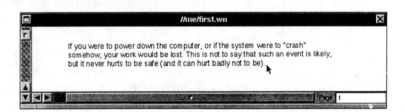

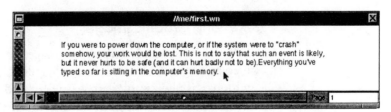

Figure 10.14. Selecting a sentence, cutting it, and then pasting it in elsewhere

Finally, select some text that you want to get rid of and choose the Edit/Delete command. This removes the selected text, but it does not save a copy like the Cut command does. In fact, it leaves alone any text that has been cut or copied. It's equivalent to selecting text and pressing Delete. Practice all these techniques until you become comfortable with them.

PASTING FILE GRAPHICS

WriteNow also lets you put graphical images into your documents. These images must be previously stored in a format known as Encapsulated PostScript (EPS); files containing these images have the extension ".eps". There are commercial collections of EPS clip art images available for the NeXT system, such as the ClickArt EPS Illustrations from T/Maker; there are also utilities bundled with Release 0.9, such as Scene and Preview, that allow you to create and view EPS files, though these programs might not be supported in Release 1.0.

To paste a graphical image in your document, select the Paste File Graphic command in the Edit menu. You'll get a standard File Selection panel, but one that will search specifically for EPS files. It will even treat WriteNow files that contain EPS images as "subdirectories," showing you the images contained within. When you find the image you want, click on its name and press the OK button; the image will then be pasted into your document. For example, Figure 10.15 shows a document with Figure 10.12 pasted into it. Once the image is in your document, you can cut, copy, delete, and paste it, just as you would text.

Resizing Graphic Images

Once you've pasted in a graphic image, you can resize it, scaling it to be larger or smaller. To do this, double-click on the image, which will become faintly highlighted (a thin white band around the inside of the image). You can then move the cursor

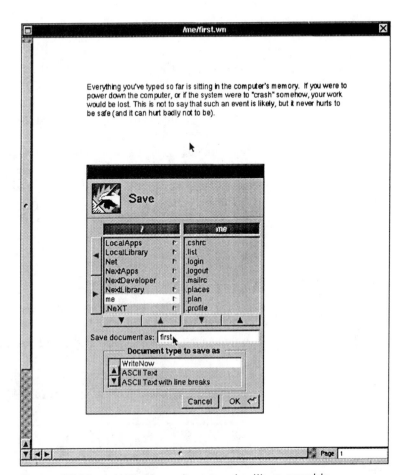

Figure 10.15. A WriteNow document with a graphic
image (Figure 10.12) pasted into it

over the image, hold the mouse button down, and drag the cursor in or out. As you do, a thin gray box will appear, changing size as you move the cursor. At the same time, x- and y-axis scaling values will appear down at the bottom of the window, in the "page" box, indicating the size of the box compared to the original image. When you release the mouse button, the image is resized to fit the box. Because of the scaling properties of PostScript, images tend to scale very well when printed, though they may look a bit odd on the screen.

WORKING WITH FONTS

All the text that you've typed in so far has been in medium 12-point Helvetica font. A font, as you may remember from Chapter 7, is a designed character set—that is, a particular version of the letters, numbers, and symbols that appear as you type. The point size refers to the size of the text; for example, the point size of the title above ("Working With Fonts") is larger than the point size of the text in this paragraph. The term "medium" refers to the text style; other styles include **bold**, *italic*, and even ***bold italic***.

Most applications that involve creating or working with text let you adjust various font attributes for the text involved. For example, with WriteNow you can mix fonts, point sizes, and styles within a document, indeed, within a sentence or a word. And almost all applications that let you adjust fonts use a standard Font menu, much like the one shown in Figure 10.16.

To illustrate how this menu works, let's start by changing the entire document. Click on the Select All item in the Edit submenu (or press Command-a); all the text in your document

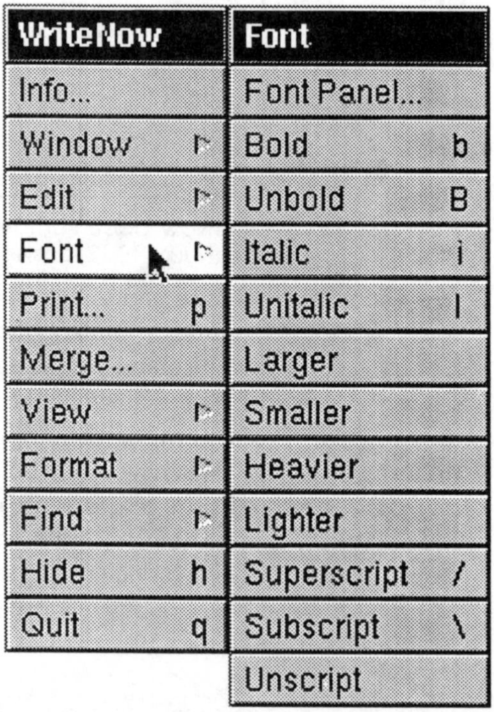

WriteNow		Font	
Info...		Font Panel...	
Window	▷	Bold	b
Edit	▷	Unbold	B
Font	▷	Italic	i
Print...	p	Unitalic	I
Merge...		Larger	
View	▷	Smaller	
Format	▷	Heavier	
Find	▷	Lighter	
Hide	h	Superscript	/
Quit	q	Subscript	\
		Unscript	

Figure 10.16. The WriteNow menu with the Font submenu

is selected. Now, click on the Font item in the WriteNow main menu to bring up the Font submenu. Click on the Bold command (or press Command-b); the text becomes darker and thicker. Clicking on Unbold (or pressing Command-Shift-B) reverses the action. Likewise experiment with Italic/Unitalic, Larger/Smaller, and Heavier/Lighter; the last two have the same effect here as Bold/Unbold because this font (Helvetica) has only two weights, Medium and Bold. Some fonts have additional weights; you can use the Heavier/Lighter commands to step through them.

Figure 10.17 shows a single paragraph repeated several times on a page, with each copy of the paragraph adjusted somehow using the Font submenu. In the case of the Larger and Smaller sections, the corresponding command was used several times on each paragraph for a more visible effect.

Of course, you have additional font controls you can use by way of the standard Font panel, shown in Figure 10.18. To bring this panel up, just click on the Font Panel... command in the Font submenu. It will then reflect the font settings for any text

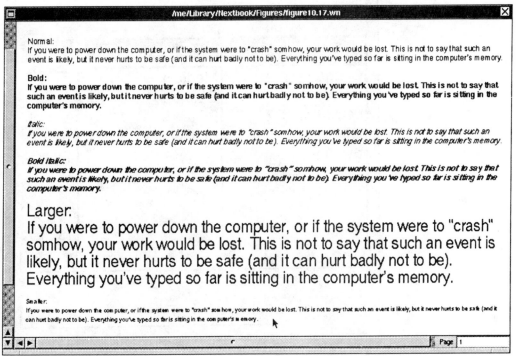

Figure 10.17. A WriteNow document using several effects from the Font menu

you currently have selected in the box at the top of the panel; if no text is selected, then it will reflect the settings for the entire document. In this case, the settings are for Helvetica font, Medium style, 12.0 point size.

The Font panel has three columns, one to select the font itself (Helvetica, Times, etc.), one to select the typeface (medium, bold, etc.), and one to select the point size (9, 10, 11). The buttons below the column let you scroll through its contents in case the column has more items than can fit in it. Also, there is a text field above the size column to allow you to enter sizes not listed; Display PostScript will then do the appropriate scaling to generate that point size.

Select the entire body of text again using Command-a. Bring up the Font panel and click on Helvetica Medium 12.0 pt (if it's not already highlighted), and then click on the set button.

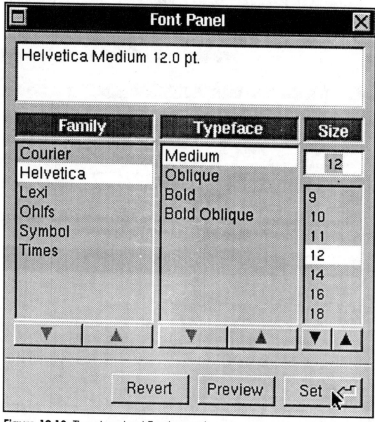

Figure 10.18. The standard Font panel

You've now restored your text back to how it was when you first typed it in. Now select each of the other fonts (Times, Courier, Symbol) and click on the set button. Watch how all the selected text changes to that font, with the document reformatting itself as necessary. Figure 10.19 shows the same paragraph done in these four standard fonts.

Note that Courier is a **non-proportional** font, meaning that each character has the same width. By contrast, Helvetica, Times, and Symbol are all **proportional** fonts, which means that each character is only as wide as it has to be. Helvetica is a **sans serif** ("without serifs") font, meaning that—unlike Times, Courier, and Symbol—its characters have no extra little lines (serifs) at the end of each stroke; compare, for example, a capital "I" in all four fonts. Times, like Helvetica, is a general-purpose font, the main difference being that Times has serifs while Helvetica doesn't. Symbol is a special font that makes available for your use the Greek alphabet, as well as a number of special characters (available using the Alternate key).

As you explore the Font panel, you'll see that each font has various typefaces, such as medium or Roman (normal), bold, and oblique (italic). These represent typefaces that are specifically defined for that font, just as the point sizes listed are those which are specifically available. However, as mentioned, Display PostScript can generate typefaces and point sizes other than those listed.

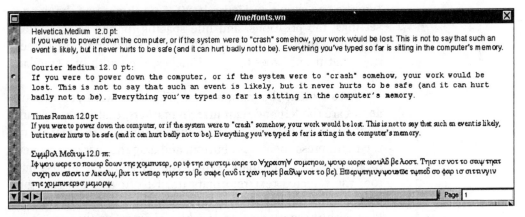

Figure 10.19. The same paragraph done in Helvetica, Courier, Times, and Symbol

While you still have the entire document selected, choose various settings for the text size. Notice that, again, the text is automatically reformatted to accommodate the new text size. Try the extreme sizes, that is, the largest and smallest. As you can see, the smallest text sizes are difficult, if not impossible, to read on the screen; however, those same sizes are very readable when printed out. There are two reasons for the differences: first, the screen image is about 20 percent smaller than the printed version; second, the screen has a resolution of only 94 dots per inch, while the printer uses a resolution of either 300 or 400 dots per inch.

Once you're done with this, try the same steps again, but this time with a smaller text selection: sentences, words, letters. See how the text adjusts to fit your changes. Also note that dramatic variations of font, size, and style within a body of text don't look that wonderful; moderation and consistency are your best guidelines when choosing font, typeface, and point size.

CHANGING MARGINS

Select the entire document again (Edit/Select All, or Command-a), and set it to a single font, size, and style (such as Helvetica Medium 12.0 pt). Now, with all the text still selected, click on the Show Ruler command in the View submenu (or press Command-r). At the top of your document a text ruler will appear, like the one shown in Figure 10.20. This shows you the margin settings, tab positions, and line spacing for the selected text. The ruler itself shows the width of the document in inches; note that it only goes up to 8.5 inches, the width of a standard piece of paper.

Let's look at the margins first. The downward pointing triangles are the **left** and **right margin markers**, that is, the left and right bounds of the text. Move the cursor over the marker on the right, press the mouse button, and drag the marker to a new location, say, the 6" mark. When you let go of the mouse button, the selected text reformats itself to fit this new margin. The same thing happens if you adjust the left margin marker. Play with these markers for a while, then move them to some normal settings, such as 1.25" on the left and 7.25" on the right.

Figure 10.20. A text ruler

The left margin marker has a small box sticking above it. This is actually a separate control, the **paragraph indent marker**, which determines how much the first word of each paragraph is indented. With the entire document still selected, move the cursor over that box and drag it 0.5" or so to the right of the left margin marker. When you release the mouse button, the text is reformatted with the appropriate indentation at the start of each paragraph. Now drag the indent marker to the left of the left margin; the result is a "negative" or "hanging" indent, where the first line of a paragraph overhangs the rest. Finally, move the left margin marker and note how the indent marker "follows" it, maintaining a constant distance. This feature allows you to adjust the left margin without having to adjust the indent as well.

CHANGING JUSTIFICATION

The text you've been typing has all been **left-justified**. This means that all the lines are evenly aligned along the left margin, while the text along the right margin is uneven; because of that, this format is sometimes called **ragged-right**. The four buttons above the ruler, on the left side, are used to select which justification you want for the selected text. The first one, representing left-justification, is white, indicating that it's the current choice.

Select the entire document (Edit/Select All or Command-a), then click on the second button. This is the **dual-justification** button; the result is that the selected text is now evenly aligned down both sides. WriteNow did this by increasing the gap between the words in each line until that line was exactly as wide as the margins. If you alternate between left-justification and dual-justification, you can see how the lines grow and shrink. Figure 10.21 illustrates the difference between left- and dual-justification.

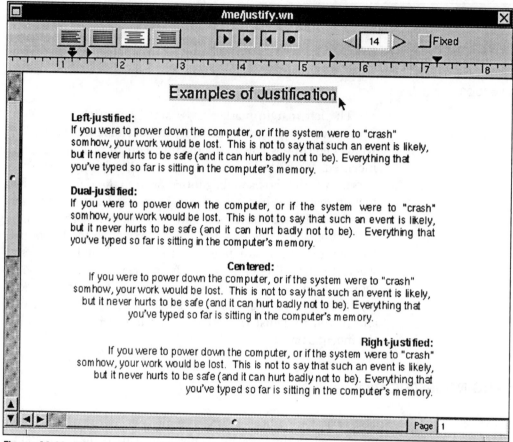

Figure 10.21. Different types of text justification

Click on the next button. This button **centers** the selected text, that is, moves each line over so that its ends are equally distanced from the left and right margins. This is what you use to center titles. For example, reset the text to left-justification, then move the cursor to the start of your text and click once, deselecting the text and making the text insertion cursor appear. Type some title for your document, then press Return a few times to put some space between it and your first paragraph. Select just the text in that title. Bring up the font menu and set the point size of the title a few sizes larger than the rest of the text. Finally, click on the centering button in the ruler. Note that only the currently selected text—the title—is centered; the rest of the document remains unaffected. If you select some other portion of the document, you'll find that the ruler changes to reflect the setting there. You can have multiple rulers within a document, each affecting only the lines in the corresponding text.

The last button performs **right-justification** (ragged-left). Select a paragraph, then click on this button. The selected text is now even along the right margin and "ragged" along the left. This is not a commonly used format, but it's there if you need it.

CHANGING TABS

To the right of the justification buttons are four boxes containing different symbols. These are **tab markers** that you can drag up to the ruler; in fact, there are already two tab markers on the ruler shown in Figure 10.20, one at 1.5", the other at 5.5". The position of a marker shows how far over the cursor will move when you press the Tab key on the keyboard. The shape of the marker indicates how the text will be justified around that marker.

You set tabs on the ruler by dragging one of the appropriate shapes down to some position on the ruler and releasing it. Once it's there, you can shift it left or right as you wish. And if you want to get rid of a tab, you just drag it up off the ruler and release the button.

The first marker, which points to the right, is a **standard tab**. It left-justifies the text at that tab setting; the text you enter continues to the right until it hits the right margin, at which point it wraps around. The second marker, shaped like a diamond, is a **centering tab**; text entered there is centered around the tab setting, until the line fills up or you tab over to another setting. The third marker, pointing left, is a **reverse tab**; text entered there is right-justified. The last marker, round with a dot in the middle, is a **decimal tab**; this is used for aligning columns of numbers along the decimal point in each number.

Here's a quick exercise to demonstrate all four tabs. Go to the bottom of your document, add several blank lines, then select them (the blank lines). Go up to the ruler and get rid of any existing tabs. Set the following tabs: a reverse tab at 2.75"; a standard tab at 3.0"; a centering tab at 4.5"; and a decimal tab at

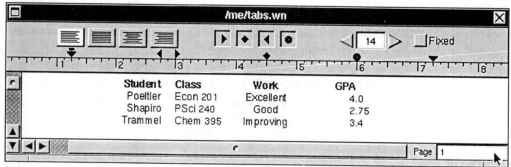

Figure 10.22. Different types of text justification

6.0". Now, click on one of the selected blank lines, and type the following text. ([Tab] and [Return] indicate which key to press; don't type the words "Tab" or "Return.")

```
[Tab] Student [Tab] Class [Tab] Work [Tab] GPA [Return]
[Tab] Poeltler [Tab] Econ 201 [Tab] Excellent [Tab] 4.0 [Return]
[Tab] Shapiro [Tab] PSci 240 [Tab] Good [Tab] 2.75 [Return]
[Tab] Trammel [Tab] Chem 395 [Tab] Improving [Tab] 3.4 [Return]
```

The result will look something like that shown in Figure 10.22. Once you have these lines typed in, select all four lines. Now, shift some of the tabs around, and watch how the table adjusts the columns accordingly.

CHANGING LINE SPACING

One last use for the ruler is to set **line spacing**, that is, how far apart the lines are. The current value is in the text field (white box) to the right of the tab boxes. This value indicates the spacing in terms of points, the same units that measure the text height. The effective lower limit is the text size; attempts to set the line spacing smaller than that won't affect the actual spacing, either on the screen or in printed output.

To change the current setting, select the text desired. You then can edit the value in the box directly, or you can click on the arrow buttons on either side to raise or lower the value. Select a paragraph in your document, and increase the line setting value. Watch how the lines move farther apart as you do so, as shown in Figure 10.23. Now lower the value, and see

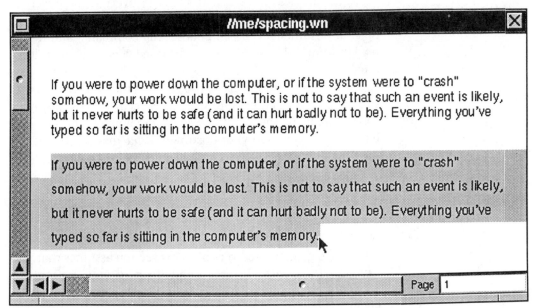

Figure 10.23. Using the line spacing controls

them move closer again. As mentioned, after a certain point, the lines don't get any closer.

UNDO-ING CHANGES

You've learned how to make many changes in your document; you may have found yourself making some changes that you didn't mean to. For example, if you chose Edit/Select All and then typed any key, your entire document would have been replaced by what you typed. Needless to say, such mistakes could be aggravating, if not disastrous.

WriteNow provides two means to recover from such inadvertent slips. The first is the Undo command in the Edit submenu (Command-z). This powerful command will reverse most actions *if* you execute it before taking any other action. For example, if you do select your entire document and then press the spacebar, all your text will disappear; if you then select Edit/Undo, it will reappear. If you select Edit/Undo again, the Undo command will be undone, and the text will disappear.

A second, less immediate form of recovery is the Revert to Saved command in the Window menu. If you really mess things up in a document, you can choose this command, and it will read in from disk the most recently saved version of your document, overwriting whatever you currently have in the window on the screen. To be effective, though, this method requires that you save your document to disk on a regular basis (always a good idea), using the Window/Save command (or Command-s). Note that if you save your document *after* messing things up, then the Revert to Saved command won't help you any.

PRINTING A DOCUMENT

Now that you've created your first document using WriteNow, it's time to get a printed version. This section assumes that you have a NeXT Laser Printer hooked up to your system, or hooked up to another NeXT cube to which you are connected via Ethernet.

The process is simple: click on the Print command in the WriteNow menu. The standard Print panel, shown in Figure 10.24, will appear. You don't need to worry about any of the options provided, so just click on the print button or press Return. For more details on the options and use of the Print panel, see Chapter 4 , The Printer.

If the laser printer hasn't been used up until now, the NeXT cube will send it a "power up" message, and the printer will require a few seconds to warm up. In the meantime, WriteNow has prepared a PostScript description of your document, which it passes on to a special system task running in the background. That task uses the PostScript information to create a bitmapped (dot-by-dot) image of the document, which it sends to the printer. The printer obligingly writes that onto one or more sheets of paper, and you have your printed output.

If you're printing a multipage document, you'll find that WriteNow is smart enough to print your document so that the pages come out facing in the right order. Since pages come from the printer face up, this means that the last page is printed first, then the next to the last, and so on, until the first page is printed.

If the printer runs out of paper while printing, a small panel will appear on the screen, telling you that. You can then refill

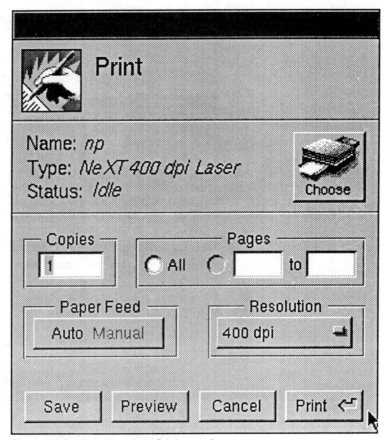

Figure 10.24. The standard Print panel

the paper cartridge (following the instructions in the NeXT documentation), come back, and click the OK button on the panel. Your printing job will resume where it left off. Panels will also appear if other problems occur—a piece of paper gets jammed, the printer runs out of toner, and so on. In each case, refer to the NeXT documentation to determine what action to take.

The Printer application can be of use if you're printing several documents. When launched, it brings up a window, like that shown in Figure 10.25, displaying the status of any documents being printed. You can view the documents being printed; you can also cancel the printing, if desired. It's perfectly all right to launch this application and leave it running as you work; that way, if you need to cancel a print request quickly, it's there and available.

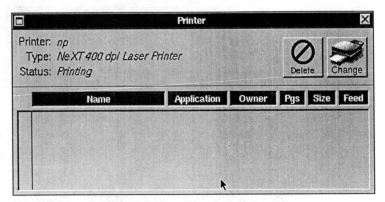

Figure 10.25. The main window of the Printer application

For more details on the uses and options of the Printer application, see Chapter 4, The Printer.

HIDING AND QUITTING AN APPLICATION

What do you do when you're finished using an application? The first thing you should do is to save the document(s) that you've been working on, using the Window/Save command or whatever the application's equivalent is. That way you know that your work won't be lost.

The next thing to do is to decide whether or not you'll be doing more work with that application or even on that particular document later on. If so, then you may want to use the Hide command, found in the main menu of every application. When you click on this command (or press Command-h), then every window, panel, menu, and other screen element associated with that application disappears, save one: the application's icon, which remains at its current location on the screen or in the dock. The application remains hidden until you double-click on its icon, at which point all the windows, panels, menus, etc., reappear just as they were.

The Hide command allows you to have several applications running at the same time without the screen getting cluttered. When you need a particular application, you just click on its icon as you normally would, and it appears instantly. Be aware, though, that these applications are still consuming system resources, such as memory, and that having a lot of applications launched and hidden can slow overall performance some.

When you're truly done using a program—especially if you're getting ready to log out—then you should quit the application, using the Quit command found in its main menu (or by pressing Command-q). If there are any associated documents which haven't been saved, the application should ask you if you want to save them. Once you have handled that, the application releases all its system resources and is purged from memory. If the application's icon has been sitting on the screen, it disappears; if it's in the dock, then the three small dots reappear in the lower-left corner, showing that the application is no longer running. To use the application again, you must go once more through the process of launching it.

LOOKING UP REFERENCES

The NeXT system comes with over 100 megabytes of on-line reference information. This includes *Webster's New Ninth Collegiate Dictionary*, the *Oxford Dictionary of Quotations*, the Oxford edition of the complete works of William Shakespeare, and complete NeXT, Mach, and UNIX documentation. Three applications—Webster, Quotation, and Librarian—let you quickly search these references for the information you need.

USING THE DICTIONARY

Suppose you were using WriteNow to create a department memo, and you wanted to use the word "eclectic" in a sentence. However, you weren't sure if you were using the word correctly. You could reach for the dictionary sitting on your bookshelf. Or you could just select the word (by double-clicking or dragging the cursor across) and then choose the Define command in WriteNow's Edit submenu (or pressing Command-d).

This command launches the Webster application (if it's not already running) and passes the selected word to it. The Webster application window then appears, showing the pronuncia-

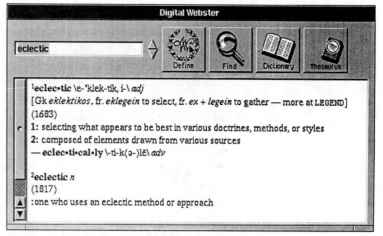

Figure 10.26. The Webster application window, showing the dictionary entry for "eclectic"

tion, etymology (origins), and definitions of the word in question. Figure 10.26 shows the Webster entry for "eclectic."

Suppose you're now convinced that you are using the word correctly, but you want to use a more common word or phrase. You can then use the thesaurus to see if Webster has suggestions. Click on the thesaurus button in the Webster window so that the book displayed appears open, then click on the define button. The same entry appears, but now there is additional information below. Using the scroller, you can bring this into view; the result is shown in Figure 10.27.

You're curious about "catholic" being listed as a synonym for "eclectic," so you want to look up its entry. To do that, just double-click on the word "catholic" in the Webster window; that word now appears in the field at the top of the window, and within a few seconds, its dictionary and thesaurus entries appear. You can continue to do this, skipping from word to word, until you find the one you want.

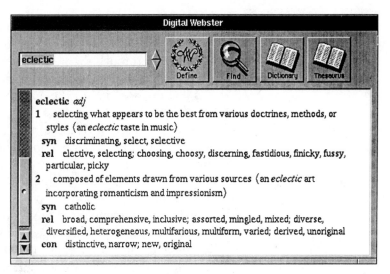

Figure 10.27 The Webster application window, showing the thesaurus entry for "eclectic"

LOOKING UP QUOTATIONS

Having done all that, you decide that you need a nice quotation for your memo, something about the world ending, just to catch everyone's attention. WriteNow has no direct mechanism for calling up the Quotation application, but that's no problem: just use the Directory Browser to find Quotation (which is in /NextApps), and double-click on Quotation when you find it. If there's room in the application dock, you can drag the icon over there first, so that you'll always have it handy.

When you launch Quotation, its window comes up, with the reference area displaying the copyright notice for the *Oxford Dictionary of Quotations.* You want to find all quotations with the words "world" and "end" in them, so click on the text field at the top of the window, type "world end," and click on the search button (or press Return). You are quickly informed of how many quotations were found—in this case, twenty-four—and the text of those quotations is displayed in the reference area, as shown in Figure 10.28. You can use the scroller to read through them, or you can click on the find button to find successive occurrences of the word "world."

As you can see, not all the quotations have to do with the world ending; instead, they each have the words "world" and "end" in them. One likely candidate, though, is the quotation by Robert Browning: "Who knows but the world may end to–night?" To copy it into your document, select it as you would any other text, use the Edit/Copy command (from the Quotation menu), click on your WriteNow document, then use the Edit/Paste command (from the WriteNow menu).

The quotation by Robert Browning intrigues you; you want to see where it came from. So you click on the text field, enter "Browning," click on the quote button (which then becomes the author button), and then click on the search button. The Quotation application finds two authors, Elizabeth Barrett Browning and Robert Browning, and lists all the quotations for each. Click on the text field and type "world", but *don't* press Return. Instead, click on the find button and keep searching through the quotations until you find the one above, as shown

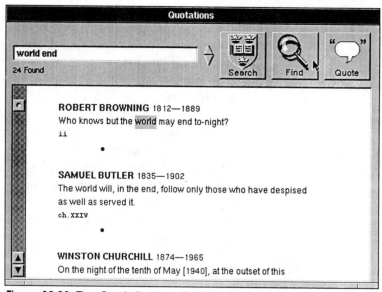

Figure 10.28. The Quotation application window, listing all quotations containing the words "world" and "end"

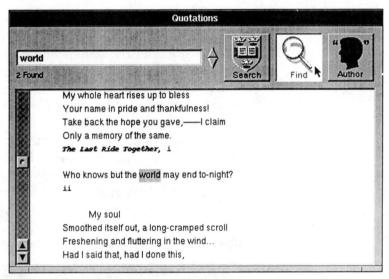

Figure 10.29. The Quotation window, listing quotations by Robert Browning

in Figure 10.29. You can now see that the quotation comes from Browning's poem, "The Last Ride Together."

When finished, choose the Hide command to get Quotation out of the way, or the Quit command to be rid of it altogether.

SEARCHING THROUGH THE DIGITAL LIBRARY

Webster and Quotation are both specific to a given reference work; the Digital Librarian, on the other hand, lets you search through a variety of documents, all at once if you desire. If you followed the instructions at the start of this chapter, you should have moved the Librarian icon over to the dock; if not, do so now. The icon looks like several books on a bookshelf. Launch the Librarian application now by double-clicking on its icon; its window will soon appear.

Since you've been searching in a literary vein, let's continue that for now by looking up references in Shakespeare. Reading the liner notes to an album you bought some time back, you discover that a phrase in one of the songs—"My mistress' eyes are nothing like the sun"—comes from Shakespeare. You're interested to know where it came from. So you click on the Shakespeare icon along the top row, enter the word "sun" in the text field below that row, and click on the search button. Librarian finds fifteen references to "sun" in Shakespeare, listing the works in the document area below the text field, as shown in Figure 10.30. You scroll through this list; sure enough, Sonnet 130 is listed, beginning with that very phrase. You click on that document, and it appears in the viewing area at the bottom of the window.

You want a copy of the sonnet, so you choose the Print command in the Librarian menu. In a matter of seconds, you have a hard copy of Sonnet 130 by William Shakespeare.

Now let's look at something less artistic. Suppose you're interested in hooking up a modem to your NeXT system and want to see what the NeXT and UNIX documents have to say about modems. You could search the sets of documents one at a

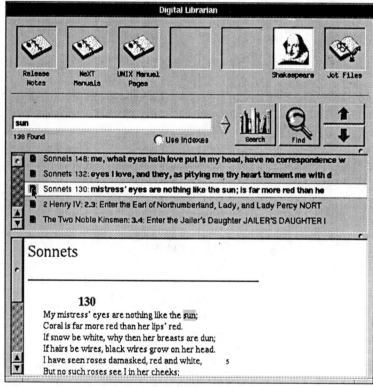

Figure 10.30. The Librarian window, with a reference from Shakespeare

time, but it would be easier to search them all at once. Holding the Shift key down, click on the first three icons: Release Notes, NeXT Manuals, and UNIX Manual Pages. If Shakespeare is still selected, you can deselect it by clicking on it while holding the Shift key down. Now click on the text field, type "modem," and click on the search button (or press Return).

Several documents are listed, and you have several choices as to how to look up information. You can click on each document once and, after it's displayed in the lower view, scroll through it using the scroller. You can do the same thing, then click repeatedly on the find button to look up just those references to "modem" in each document. You can double-click on each document, opening it up for direct reading, most likely under Edit or WriteNow. You can ask Librarian to print the document out.

Librarian is extendible; as other on-line references—**digital books**—become available, you'll be able to search through them using Librarian. What's more, an automatic indexing function is built into Librarian to let you put your own documents on line as well. See your NeXT user documentation for more details.

USING ELECTRONIC MAIL

One of the strengths of the NeXT system is its ability to be easily connected to a computer network, that is, a collection of other computers that are hooked together by various means. If you're hooked up to an Ethernet network and you have had a mail account set up by the system administrator, you can send and receive mail messages using the Mail application. This includes the ability to send voice mail and attach documents and certain types of data files to your mail message.

ON-LINE HELP

The NeXT system comes with extensive, well-written on-line documentation covering all the different aspects of using Mail. When you click on the Help... command in the Mail main menu, a small Directory Browser window will appear, showing you the subdirectories and files containing the Mail documen-

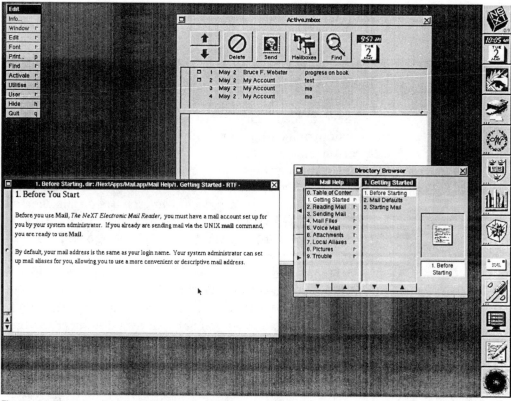

Figure 10.31. Using the on-line help for Mail

tation. To bring up the document covering a given topic, just double-click on its entry or icon in the browser. This launches the Edit application (if it's not already running) and opens a window containing that document, as seen in Figure 10.31. You can then read it (using the scroller to move through the document) or print it out.

Rather than duplicate the rather thorough on-line documentation, this section will just give some basic instructions on using Mail, along with pointers to some of the more advanced features.

SENDING MAIL

Sending mail is quite simple. To create your message, launch the Mail application and click on the send button; the resulting

window will look like the one shown in Figure 10.32. You now
have three fields to fill in:

> **To:** the IDs of the person(s) you want the message to go to.
> These IDs are usually the user login IDs (jdow, bob-
> smith); if there are multiple IDs in this line, then they
> are separated by commas. It's possible to set up **aliases**,
> so that you could (for example) enter "Joanne" instead
> of "jdow."

> **Subject:** a brief description of the message's subject.

> **cc:** the IDs of other people who should get a copy of this
> message, but for whom it isn't directly indended.

Of the three, only "To:" has to have anything in it, though
you should put something in "Subject:" as a matter of courtesy.

Once you've filled in the appropriate fields, enter the text of
the message in the lower section (the **message view**). This area
works just like a normal NeXT editor: you can cut, copy, paste,
and delete; you can use the Font menu and panel to selectively
change any portion of the message; you can copy text in from
other applications (such as WriteNow and Edit), and so on.

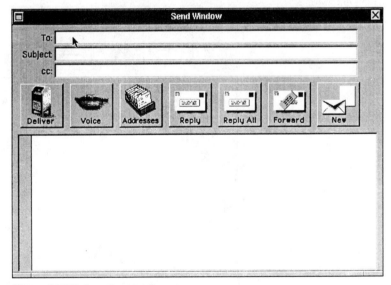

Figure 10.32. Sending mail

Attaching Files

Mail makes it very convenient to send files along with your mail messages. All you have to do is to drag the file's icon from a directory window or browser into the message view, as shown in Figure 10.33. The icon just becomes another item in the message view; you can insert text before and after it, and you can remove it by selecting and deleting it.

Generally, you should only use this technique when sending files to users on NeXT systems, since other UNIX users may have no way of correctly accessing the files you send. Also, if your mail is going to be routed over phone lines between network sites, you may want to be careful about sending large files.

Attaching Voice Mail

If you have a microphone plugged into the back of your MegaPixel Display, you can also send voice mail to other NeXT users. To do this, just set up the address fields as if you were

Figure 10.33. Attaching files to a Mail message

sending a regular mail message, then click on the voice button. The Lip Service panel will come up, as shown in Figure 10.34. When you're ready to record, click on the record button and speak into the microphone; click on the same button (now named "stop") when you're done.

You can play back your recording by clicking on the play button and erase it by clicking on the erase button. More importantly, you can edit it by clicking on the edit button, which will bring up the Sound Editor panel, shown in Figure 10.35. Using this panel, you can play back and re-record selected portions of your voice message. You can also cut, copy, paste, and delete sections using the Edit submenu of the Mail menu: just select the segment by dragging the cursor over it, then use the appropriate command. When you have your message just the way you want it, click on the OK button to get back to the Lip Service panel.

Figure 10.34. The Lip Service panel

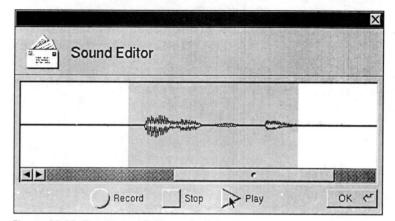

Figure 10.35. The Sound Editor panel

When you're all done, click on the close box on the Lip Service panel. Your voice message will then show up as an icon in the message view. Note: digitized sound takes up a lot of space, so don't send lengthy messages as a rule. Also, if the recipient doesn't have a NeXT system, he or she won't be able to listen to the voice mail.

READING MAIL

No new mail

New mail waiting

Figure10. 36. The Mail icon

Reading mail is simple. The mail icon signals you when you have mail by showing extra letters; Figure 10.36 shows how the icon changes.

When you launch Mail, it checks your mailbox and lists all your messages, as shown in Figure 10.37. Unread messages are indicated by a round marker; attached files and voice messages are indicated by a small icon. You can read each message by double-clicking on its entry; the text of the message is displayed in the message view below.

If there are attached files, their icons will appear in the message view; the files themselves will be automatically added to your home directory. You can open an attached file from within Mail by double-clicking on its (the file's) icon in the message view.

If there is voice mail attached, it will show up in the message view as an envelope icon with a pair of lips on it. When you double-click on that icon, the Lip Service panel appears. You can then listen to the voice message by pressing the play button.

Once you're done reading a message, you have several options. You can just leave it in place, so that you can go back and read it later. If you want a printed copy of it, you can select the Print... option in the main menu and send it to the printer. And if you have no more use for it, you can delete it by reading it and then clicking on the delete button in the main window.

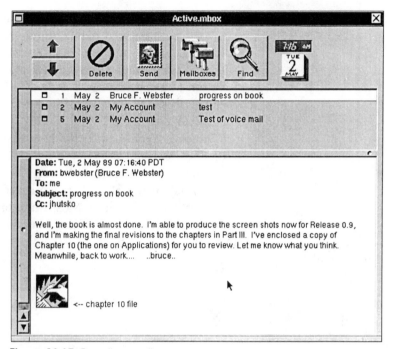

Figure 10.37. Reading mail

There is much that hasn't been covered here—multiple mailboxes, address books, and the Find submenu for searching through lengthy mail messages—but you can learn more about that using the on-line documentation. Now you know enough to get started and to use Mail to communicate with other users on your network and—with proper connections—around the world.

COMMENTARY

Obviously, this chapter doesn't cover all the applications that come with the NeXT system. A few, such as Mathematica, Allegro Common Lisp, and the NeXT SQL Database Server, were still under development while this was being written and so won't be described here. Others, such as Shell, Terminal, Interface Builder, and Edit, are described in the chapters that follow. And the ones described here may well change slightly in function and appearance by Release 1.0. In short, this chapter isn't a substitute for the printed and on-line documentation that NeXT provides.

However, you now know how easy it is to sit down at a NeXT system and do something useful. And having learned how these basic functions work in these applications, you know much of how the others work, reducing the learning time for any other applications. Most importantly, you've broken the ice and now know how to get real work done on a NeXT system. The rest is up to you.

11

Exploring the Shell

```
                          Shell 0.9 (ttyp1)                            X
ls -l
total 1252
drwxr-xr-x  2 root        1024 Apr 29 17:44 LocalApps/
drwxr-xr-x  4 root        1024 Apr 29 14:56 LocalLibrary/
lrwxrwxrwx  1 root          11 Apr 26 16:33 Net@ -> private/Net/
drwxr-xr-x  6 root        1024 Apr  7 19:39 NextApps/
drwxr-xr-x  5 root        1024 Apr 14 15:33 NextDeveloper/
drwxr-xr-x 10 root        1024 Apr 26 17:46 NextLibrary/
drwxr-xr-x  2 root        2048 Apr  7 23:22 bin/
drwxr-xr-x  3 root        1024 Apr 26 15:43 clients/
lrwxrwxrwx  1 root          11 Apr 26 16:33 dev@ -> private/dev/
lrwxrwxrwx  1 root          11 Apr 26 16:33 etc@ -> private/etc/
drwxr-xr-x  3 root        1024 Apr  7 23:22 lib/
drwxr-xr-x  2 root        8192 Apr 26 15:42 lost+found/
lrwxrwxrwx  1 root           9 Apr 26 15:44 mach@ -> $BOOTFILE*
drwxr-xr-x  7 me          1024 May  9 01:04 me/
-r-xr-xr-x  2 root      619879 Apr  7 00:09 odmach*
drwxrwxr-x 11 root        1024 Mar 22 23:31 private/
-r-xr-xr-x  2 root      619879 Apr  7 00:09 sdmach*
lrwxrwxrwx  1 root          11 Apr 26 16:33 tmp@ -> private/tmp/
drwxr-xr-x 13 root        1024 Apr 26 16:33 usr/
lrwxrwxrwx  1 root           4 Apr 26 15:44 vmunix@ -> mach*
localhost> cd /me
localhost> ls
Active.mbox      Apps/           Mailboxes/
Active.mbox-TOC  Library/        Programming/
localhost>
```

Underneath Workspace Manager, behind all of its applications, lies Mach, a multitasking, virtual memory operating system. Mach, as implemented on the NeXT computer, is UNIX-compatible, meaning that it provides the same features and utilities as the BSD 4.3 UNIX implementation. This also means that you can directly interact with Mach, bypassing Workspace Manager. As it turns out, there are some cases where you have to interact with Mach, because Workspace Manager just doesn't provide the functionality. To do this, you use **the shell**, a program that provides a direct user interface to Mach; the purpose of this chapter is to teach you how and when to use that program.

LOOKING IN THE MANUAL

Entire books have been written on how to use the UNIX shell; space limits this chapter to a simple introduction. However, the NeXT system has a substantial amount of on-line documentation concerning Mach, UNIX, and the shell. To use it, launch Digital Librarian, select the NeXT and UNIX manuals, and do a search on "Shell." Two of the documents listed that are well worth reading are "An Introduction to the C Shell" and "An Introduction to the UNIX Shell."

Information specific to each shell command can be found quickly using the man (manual page) command within the shell. Just type "man [command]" at the shell prompt, where [command] is the name of the command. The UNIX manual information about that command will be printed in the shell window. If there's more information than can fit on the screen at once, man will pause after so many lines (21 is the default), then give you a --More--[xx%] prompt, where [xx%] shows how much of the entry has been displayed so far. You can respond by pressing Return (to show one more line), the spacebar (to show another page), or "q" (to quit).

If you want a nice printout of the manual page information for a given command, then use the -t option. For example, to get complete information about the ls (list contents of directory) command, you would type:

```
localhost>man -t ls
```

Within a minute or so, you'll have a nicely formatted, laser-printed copy of the UNIX manual entry for ls.

SHELL VERSUS TERMINAL

NeXT provides two different applications to let you use the Mach shell: Shell and Terminal. Terminal, shown in Figure 11.1, is designed to emulate a VT-100 computer terminal, that is, it accepts the same screen commands as a VT-100. This means that you can use it with standard UNIX applications that make use of direct cursor addressing, such as vi (a screen-oriented editor). Like other NeXT applications, it does have a menu, but only with the bare minimum of commands: Info, Hide, and Quit. Text scrolling off the top of the Terminal win-

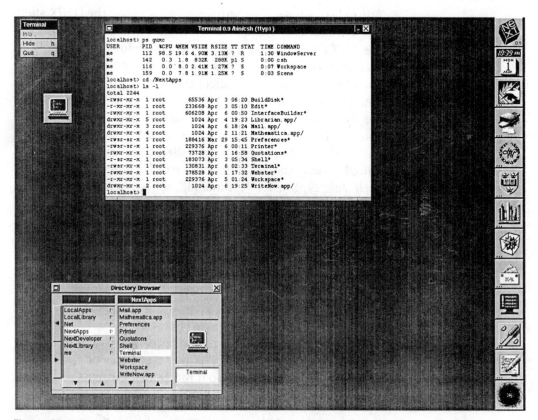

Figure 11.1. The Terminal application

dow is lost, just like on a real terminal; however, you can adjust the window size using the resize bar at the bottom.

Shell, shown in Figure 11.2, is more like a regular NeXT application. It gives you a typical NeXT window, with a vertical scroller, a resize bar, and a miniaturize button. As text scrolls off the top of the window, it is saved, so that you can always go back (using the scroller) and see what was done before. It also has copy and paste facilities, making it easy to save output into other files. Several Find commands let you quickly search through the entire contents of the window, while Jump to Bottom and Empty commands let you easily control your position and contents.

Shell will also open up multiple windows for you, if you desire; just use the Window/New command. Each window works independently from the others, so you can have active tasks running in each one.

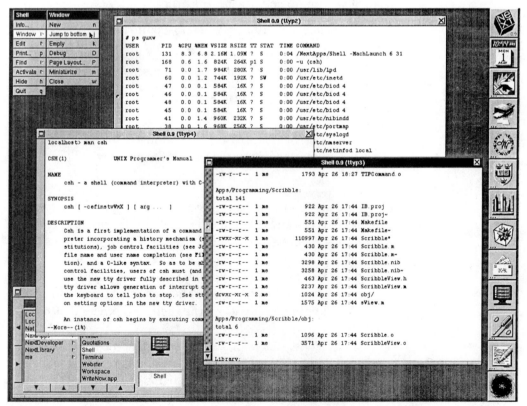

Figure 11.2. The Shell application

If you want, you can have both Shell and Terminal open and running at the same time; in fact, you can even have multiple copies of each. Which of the two you use is, of course, up to you and your needs. However, unless you are using an application that requires the VT-100 emulation, then you'll probably be best served by Shell.

The rest of this chapter talks about the shell, referring to the Mach user interface. Whether you access the shell using Shell or using Terminal is largely irrelevant, and no presumption is made that you are using one or the other.

USING THE SHELL

The shell creates a command-line interface within the Shell or Terminal window. This interface is oriented toward text and keyboard input, and it works like this:

1. The shell prompts you for a command

2. You type the command in, along with any **arguments** (options and other specifications, such as file names)

3. You press Return, signaling that you want Mach to execute the command

4. The shell processes the command, often resulting in output being printed within the window

5. You get prompted for the next command

This type of interface was designed originally for systems with teletypes and text-only displays, and it remains prevalent on minicomputers and mainframes, as well as older microcomputers (such as IBM compatibles using MS-DOS). And while it may seem a bit arcane and awkward compared to graphical interfaces, such as Workspace Manager, there are some tasks you can do more easily using the shell, and others that require you to use it.

Like Workspace Manager, the command-line interface used in Shell and Terminal is actually just another program running under Mach, one with the cryptic name of csh (for "C shell"). csh reads in the command line that you type, then parses it, that is, breaks it up into the individual elements: the command itself, options, file names, and so on. It then handles the commands, either by doing the work itself or, more commonly, by asking Mach to load and run another program, passing the arguments on to that program.

All you need to know to use the shell, then, is the format for each command: its name, what options you can select from, and what other information you might need. As mentioned, this information is available using the man command, though you need to know the command name first. The rest of this chapter will introduce you to some commonly used commands; you can investigate the rest on your own.

One important note: the shell is **case sensitive**. In other words, it considers "man" and "Man" to be different commands, just as it considers "-r" and "-R" to be different options, or "MyDisk" and "mydisk" to be different directory names. If things don't seem to be working, make sure that you've got your case right.

NAVIGATING THROUGH DIRECTORIES

You've already learned in Chapter 9 about how files and directories are organized under Mach, and how you can examine and traverse them using Workspace Manager. When you're using the Mach shell, you naturally have access to all the same files and directories—you just use a different approach.

At any point during your use of the shell, you are "working" in a given directory. To see what directory that is, enter the command pwd (print working directory) at the prompt; the shell will echo back the current working directory, like this:

```
localhost>pwd
/me
```

This represents the default directory for any Mach commands you might enter. For example, if you were to now type the command ls (list contents of directory), you might get a display like this:

```
localhost>ls
Active.mbox       Active.mbox~      Library/
Active.mbox-TOC   Apps/             Mailboxes/
```

These are the files and directories found in /me, the directories being distinguished by the slash ("/") at the end. If you wanted to get more information about these entries, you could use the -l (for "long") option in the ls command:

```
localhost>ls -l
total 13
-rw-r--r-- 1 me      660 Jun  4 12:05 Active.mbox
-rw-r--r-- 1 me       90 Jun  4 12:05 Active.mbox-TOC
-rw-r--r-- 1 me      658 Jun  4 12:05 Active.mbox~
drwxrwxr-x 3 me     1024 May 19 18:42 Apps/
drwxrwxr-x 6 me     1024 Jun 26 18:42 Library/
drwxrwxr-x 2 me     1024 Jun 26 18:42 Mailboxes/
```

If this display looks familiar, that's because it's very similar to the directory windows that you can bring up under Workspace Manager. It shows the entry type ("-" means a plain file, "d" means a directory), access privileges (read/write/execute for you, for members of your group, and for everyone else), the number of links to other files or directories, the owner (in this case, you), the size of the file or directory header in bytes, the date of creating or last modification, and the name of the file or directory.

CHANGING THE WORKING DIRECTORY

Well, so far you know how to find out what the current working directory is and how to list the files and directories it contains. What if you want to change the working directory? The command to do this is cd (change directory). Without any arguments after it, cd will change to your **home directory**, that is, the private directory that's created for you when your account is set up. The examples above assume that you've logged in under the predefined user ID "me" and show the corresponding home directory, /me. If your user ID were something else, such as "jdow", then your home directory would be /jdow, and a directory listing would show jdow as owner of the files and directories found there.

Since you're starting out in your home directory, you'll want to use cd to change to another directory. The syntax is simple: type cd, followed by the name of the new working directory. This can be an absolute path name or a relative path name. An **absolute path name** gives the full path, from the root (topmost) directory on down; because of that, it always starts with a slash ("/"), which is the name of the root directory. For example, to make Apps/ the working directory, you could type:

```
localhost>cd /me/Apps
localhost>pwd
/me/Apps
```

Note that you don't need to follow the `cd` command with the `pwd` command; this was done above just to show you the change in the working directory.

As you might guess, your home directory is one that you refer to often. Because of this, the shell recognizes a tilde character ("~") as equivalent to the absolute path name of your home directory. This means that you could have typed the commands above as:

```
localhost>cd ~/Apps
localhost>pwd
/me/Apps
```

This is a welcome short cut for referencing your home directory, but what about referencing other directories? Obviously, typing the full path name each time could get tedious—which is why the shell accepts relative path names. A **relative path name** is just that: a path name relative to the current working directory. It differs from an absolute path name in that it doesn't start with a slash; when the shell sees that, it automatically appends the current working directory to the front of the path name (with a slash in between as a separator). Consider the following set of commands:

```
localhost>pwd
/me
localhost>cd Apps
localhost>pwd
/me/Apps
```

As you can see, this command had the same effect as the one previously shown, namely, to change the working directory from /me to /me/Apps. The example above just involved less typing, and thus less chance for a typing mistake.

This approach is fine for moving down into subdirectories, but what if you wanted to move the other way, such as from /me/Apps to /me? As it turns out, there is a predefined "directory" named ".." in each directory that refers to the enclosing directory; in other words, the path name /me/Apps/.. is equivalent to /me. You can use this directory name in a relative path name, as the following sequence shows:

```
localhost>pwd
/me/Apps
localhost>cd ..
localhost>pwd
/me
```

You can change as many levels as you wish going in either direction—provided, of course, that you don't run out of levels. Assuming that the directory /me/Apps has two other subdirectories, Alpha and Beta, you could type in the commands shown below, with the indicated results:

```
localhost>pwd
/me
localhost>cd Apps/Alpha
localhost>pwd
/me/Apps/Alpha
localhost>cd ../Beta
localhost>pwd
/me/Apps/Beta
localhost>cd ../../..
localhost>pwd
/
```

CREATING NEW DIRECTORIES

That last example assumes that the subdirectories Alpha and Beta already exist in /me/Apps, but, of course, they don't unless you or someone else has created them. You learned back in Chapter 9 how to create new directories using Workspace Manager; you can achieve the same thing using the shell with the mkdir (make directory) command. Consider the following sequence of commands:

```
localhost>pwd
/me
localhost>cd Apps
localhost>mkdir Alpha
localhost>mkdir Beta
localhost>ls -l
total 2
```

```
drwxr-xr-x 2 me      1024 Jun 5 14:20 Alpha/
drwxr-xr-x 2 me      1024 Jun 5 14:20 Beta/
```

Using this, you've created two new directories—Alpha and Beta—both of which are found in /me/Apps. Note that you can use either absolute and relative path names with `mkdir`; the following sequence of commands produces the same results as the previous one:

```
localhost>pwd
/me
localhost>mkdir Apps/Alpha
localhost>mkdir/me/Apps/Beta
localhost>ls -l Apps
total 2
drwxr-xr-x 2 me      1024 Jun 5 14:20 Alpha/
drwxr-xr-x 2 me  ·   1024 Jun 5 14:20 Beta/
```

Note that you used a relative path name for the `ls` command as well. The `ls` command defaults to the current working directory, but you can specify which directory you want listed, giving either an absolute or a relative path name.

DELETING DIRECTORIES

Just as you can create directories, you can also delete them. The shell, at least for this command, requires that the directory be empty first. In other words, you have to delete all the enclosed files and directories first.

Once a directory is empty, you delete it with the `rmdir` (remove directory) command. As with related commands, you can use absolute or relative path names. For example, suppose that you had created the Alpha and Beta directories as described above, then decided to get rid of them (before putting anything into them or after deleting everything in them). The following command sequence would achieve that:

```
localhost>cd
localhost>pwd
/me
localhost>rmdir Apps/Alpha
localhost>rmdir Apps/Beta
```

As you may remember, the `cd` command with no arguments returns you to your home directory. You could have just as easily changed to the Apps directory and then removed Alpha and Beta without having to put "Apps/" in front of each.

WORKING WITH FILES

Directories, of course, exist to organize files, the actual programs, documents, and collections of information stored on the disk. It comes as no surprise, then, that most shell commands are designed to operate on files. Here are some of the commands to perform basic operations: listing, moving, copying, and deleting files.

LISTING FILES

You've learned how to list all the files in a directory, using the `ls` command. As it turns out, `ls` has a long list of **options** (eighteen, according to the manual) and that you can give a **file specification** that determines which files you want to see.

All options appear in a single string following a hyphen, for example, "`ls -lRsa filespec`". Some commonly used options include:

- `l`: long format; shows a lot of information about each file
- `t`: sort by time modified
- `a`: show all entries (including those beginning with ".")
- `R`: recursively list subdirectories

The file specification, if left empty, defaults to the current working directory; as mentioned, you can also put in an absolute or a relative path name, and it will give a listing for that directory. But you can narrow it down even more using certain **wildcard** symbols to ask for just those files matching a given pattern. Suppose that you had a directory /me/Library/Docs in which you kept any documents that you created for editing. If you wanted to see just the WriteNow files (which have a .wn suffix) in that file, you'd use the following command (assuming you're in your home directory):

```
localhost>ls -l Library/Docs/*.wn
```

The expression "*.wn" says "match all files whose names end with the sequence ".wn". In other words, the "*" character will match any number of characters in the file name—hence being called a wildcard.

In a similar fashion, the wildcard character "?" will match any single character. For example, if you wanted to see all the WriteNow files with five-letter names that start with "a" and end with "n," you'd use the following command:

```
localhost>ls -l Library/Docs/a???n.wn
```

Finally, you can narrow down even more by defining a set of characters that can appear in a given spot. To do this, you enclose the list of acceptable characters in brackets, such as "[aeiou]" For example, if you wanted to list just the WriteNow files with five-letter names that start with "a," end with "n," and have the letter "q," "p," or "r" in the third position, you'd use the following command:

```
localhost>ls -l Library/Docs/a?[pqr]?n.wn
```

As you might guess, these wildcards don't apply to just the ls command; instead, they can be used with many commands that reference files, including the next few that you'll learn about.

MOVING FILES

In Chapter 9, you learned how to move files (and entire directories) from one location to another by opening two directory windows and dragging the icons. The shell lets you accomplish the same task, and lets you use wildcards while you're at it. The command is mv (move), and it has the following basic forms:

```
mv [-if] filespec filespec2
mv [-if] filespec directory
```

The brackets around the options means that they're optional; you don't actually put the brackets around the options when using them. *Filespec* is just as you've learned it: an absolute or relative path name, optionally followed by a file name. The first version requires that *filespec* name a specific file (no wildcards); *filespec2* gives the new file name, preceded by the path name of its current or new location. The second form just requires an absolute or relative path name (*directory*) and can also use wildcards if a file name is given; it moves all the files that match *filespec* into the given directory. Note that this command deletes the files being moved from their current location.

The -i (interactive) option prompts you to verify overwriting an existing file, while the -f (force) option causes an overwrite even if the existing file is write-protected.

Suppose that you wanted to move all the WriteNow documents that had five-letter names starting with "a" and ending with "n" from the directory /me/Library/Docs over to the directory /me/Library/Test (which, we'll assume, already exists). You also wanted to move the file "mylist.wn" from Docs to Test, renaming it to "oldlist.wn" in the process, but you want to be able to cancel the move if "oldlist.wn" already exists. Here's one way of getting that done (assuming that you're already at the directory /me):

```
localhost>mv Library/Docs/a???n.wn Library/Test
localhost>mv -i Library/Docs/mylist.wn Library/Test/oldlist.wn
```

The first mv command moves all the "a???n.wn" files into Library/Test, deleting them from the Library/Docs directory. The second one moves the file "mylist.wn" into Library/Test, renaming it to "oldlist.wn"; however, if "oldlist.wn" already exists in Library/Test, you'll have an interaction like this (assuming you choose not to overwrite the existing file):

```
localhost>mv -i Library/Docs/mylist.wn Library/Test/oldlist.wn
remove Library/Test/oldlist.wn? n
localhost>
```

COPYING FILES

Under Workspace Manager, copying files or directories was a bit involved: you first had to duplicate the file or directory, drag it over to its destination, and then rename it. The shell does this for you all at once, with the cp (copy) command. This works much like `mv` and has the following formats:

```
cp [-ip] filespec filespec2
cp [-ipr] filespec directory
```

Unlike `mv`, `cp` leaves the original files or directories (*filespec*) alone. The first version copies a single file (*filespec*) to another specific file (*filespec2*), optionally renaming it in the process. The second version copies the indicated files (wildcards are allowed) or directories into the indicated destination (*directory*). The `-i` (interactive) option verifies any file overwrites, while the `-p` (preserve) option attempts to copy the file status information (for example, modification time) into the new file, even if it's overwriting an existing file. The `-r` (recursive) option does a recursive copy of any subdirectories found in *filespec*, creating them in *directory*, if necessary. This allows you to easily make a copy of an entire directory, including all its subdirectories.

Going back to the previous example, suppose that you just wanted to copy the various WriteNow files into the Test directory, leaving the originals in the Docs directory. Your commands would now be:

```
localhost>cp Library/Docs/a???n.wn Library/Test
localhost>cp Library/Docs/mylist.wn Library/Test/oldlist.wn
```

You'll see an example of the `-r` option later on.

DELETING FILES

When you delete files under Workspace Manager by moving them into the Black Hole icon, all you are really doing is moving them to another directory (.NeXT/.NeXTtrash, located off of your home directory). There they sit until you ask for them to be destroyed using the Utilities submenu in the WM menu. The shell allows you more direct action, with the `rm` (remove) command—but it also means that your deletions are largely irreversible. So you need to be careful when using `rm`, because if you remove files that you wanted, you won't be able to get them back.

The rm command has the following format:

```
rm [-ifr] filespec filespec...
```

You can list several file specifications, each consisting of an absolute or relative path name followed by a file name, using wildcards, if desired. rm will then delete all files matching each specification. If you just use the "*" wildcard, rm will delete all files in that directory, but will leave untouched any subdirectories and their contents. You can use the -i (interactive) option to have it prompt for each file before deleting it, while the -f (force) option overrides write-protection. Drawing on the previous example, if you wanted to delete all the files in the Test directory that fit the pattern "an??t.wn", but wanted to verify each deletion, you could do so with the following command (assuming, as always, that you're at /me):

```
localhost>rm -i Library/Test/an??t.wn
```

The -r (recursive) option is both powerful and dangerous. When you use it with rm, it will delete any matching subdirectories and their contents. With this option, each *filespec* can be just a directory name; in that case, the directory and its entire contents (including all subdirectories) are deleted. For example, to delete the Test directory and all its contents, you could just type:

```
localhost>rm -r Library/Test
```

This would delete the entire contents of Test, including all its files and subdirectories, and then delete Test itself.

Needless to say, this option should be used with great caution, and you should be sure you know what you're deleting. In fact, it's probably a good idea to use the -i (interactive) option along with this option; the little extra time and effort of verifying each deletion is worth avoiding that awful sinking feeling that comes when you realize that you've deleted an irreplaceable file. So, a better version of the command above would be:

```
localhost>rm -ir Library/Test
```

This would delete the directory Test and all its contents, but it would prompt you file by file, so that if you discovered a file you didn't want deleted, you could preserve it.

RUNNING PROGRAMS

You launch NeXT applications from the shell just as you would invoke any command: you type its name at the prompt (remembering that the shell is case sensitive), then press Return. For example, if you are using the shell and want to launch WriteNow, just type the following:

```
localhost>WriteNow
```

This launches WriteNow just as if you had double-clicked on its icon, with one exception: if WriteNow is already running, this launches a second copy of WriteNow. This is something you can't do by double-clicking on the icon of an already running application. The new copy of WriteNow has its own icon, which will probably appear down at the bottom of the screen.

EXECUTION PATHS

When you typed the command to launch WriteNow above, the current working directory was probably your home directory. Obviously, you don't have a copy of the WriteNow application in your home directory, so how did the shell know where to find it?

As it turns out, the shell has a predefined set of **execution paths** that tell it where to look for any programs (or, for that matter, commands) that you want to run. If you want, you can see what those paths are by entering the following command:

```
localhost>echo $PATH
.:/me/Unix/bin:/usr/local/bin:/bin:/usr/usb:/usr/bin:/me/Apps:/LocalApps:
/NeXTApps
```

The echo command echoes its arguments to the screen and is used most often in shell script files (which won't be covered here). Its argument here, $PATH, is a shell variable that contains all the current execution paths, separated by colons (":") and listed in the order in which they are searched. Finally, the directory "." always refers to the current working directory, much as ".." always refers to the enclosing directory.

When you type a command or program name, the shell first checks to see if it's a **built-in command**, that is, one that the csh program can handle itself. If not, then it starts searching each of the directories in $PATH in the order listed. As you can see, the first place searched is the current working directory, so that any programs or commands local to that directory have priority. After that, the shell searches the directories that contain the standard UNIX commands and utilities. Finally, it looks in the application directories, including your own private Apps directory.

SPAWNING PROGRAMS

If you've launched WriteNow (or any other application) from the shell, you may have noticed something: the shell is tied up until you quit that application, at which point the shell considers the "command" to be finished and puts up the next prompt. Obviously, this may cause problems if you want to launch a program or application from the shell and continue to use the shell itself. There is a solution: by putting an ampersand ("&") as the last character on the line before pressing Return, the shell will launch that program as a separate task and immediately return with a prompt. So, if you typed this:

```
localhost>WriteNow&
[1] 147
```

then WriteNow would be launched; the shell responds by telling you how many spawned programs (or **tasks**) are currently running—the number in brackets—and the process ID of this program.

Note that this technique allows you to bring up multiple copies of the Shell and Terminal applications. For example, if you launched Terminal by double-clicking on its icon, and then typed the following at the prompt inside the Terminal window:

```
localhost>Terminal&
[1] 145
localhost>Shell&
[2] 146
```

you would then have two Terminal applications and one Shell application, all running at the same time.

CHECKING PROGRAM STATUS

At any given moment, Mach is running any number of processes. A **process** is a general term for an executing program or task; a running application or a program is a process, and if you launch multiple copies of a given application, each one is a separate process.

You can use the shell to look at what processes are running, how much CPU time they're using, and so on, using the ps (process status) command. All the various details of the ps command won't be given here, but here are some suggestions.

First, when you use it, use the options guxc (which, unlike those used with most shell commands, don't have to be preceded by a "-"). The g option prints all "interesting" processes; the u option makes the printout "user oriented"; the x option includes all processes without a "terminal" (shell); and the c option gives just the command name in the last column, instead of the full path and command arguments.

The command, and its results, look something like this:

```
localhost>ps guxc
USER       PID%CPU %MEM    VSIZE RSIZE  TT  STAT TIME   COMMAND
me         119 16.2 14.9   3.68M 2.38M  ?   R    4:00   WindowServer
me         151  2.0  7.6   1.84M 1.22M  ?   S    0:06   WriteNow
me         138  1.7  1.7    824K  280K  p2  S    0:00   csh
me         135  0.0  8.1   2.38M 1.30M  ?   S    0:12   Workspace
me         124  0.0  1.7    824M  280K  p1  S    0:01   csh
```

Here's a quick explanation of the various columns:

- PID: process ID (unique for each currently running process)

- %CPU: percentage of CPU time being used by that process

- %MEM: percentage of "real" memory being used by that process

- VSIZE: Size of the process in terms of virtual memory

- RSIZE: Amount of "real" memory being used by the process .

- TT: Terminal process is attached to (? = no terminal)

- STAT: Process status (R=running, S=sleeping)

- TIME: Total CPU time used by the process so far (minutes:seconds)

More details can be found by looking up the `ps` entry in the UNIX manual (to do this, type "`man ps`" at the shell prompt).

KILLING PROGRAMS

You can also use the shell to "kill" (halt) programs or processes that are currently running. You normally wouldn't do this; instead, you'd just use a Quit command or whatever other mechanism the program uses to halt itself. But there are cases when a program might **hang**, that is, stop responding to user input or otherwise refuse to quit. In that case, you can use the shell to kill the program directly.

The command to do this is, not surprisingly, `kill`. It expects one of two types of parameters: either the process ID or the command used to launch the process (preceded by a "%" character). You can find either one using the `ps` command described above, but the second method works only if you launched it from the shell. Suppose you launched the WriteNow application from the shell as follows:

```
localhost>WriteNow&
[1] 145
```

You could then kill it with either of the two following commands:

```
localhost>kill 145
```

or

```
localhost>kill %WriteNow
```

Once the shell has actually killed the process (which may take a few seconds), it will print out a message that looks something like this:

```
[1] Terminated WriteNow
```

At that point, a check with the `ps` command will show you that the task no longer exists.

COMMENTARY

The shell is an arcane, and somewhat archaic, means of interfacing with a sophisticated computer like the NeXT system. It's also a bit dangerous, in that it's easy to make things disappear without realizing until later that they're gone. And it lacks the visual metaphor that makes Workspace Manager easy to learn and simple to use.

Even so, you should gain a basic proficiency in using the shell for two reasons. First, the shell is powerful. As you've seen in this chapter, there are many tasks to which the shell is better suited than Workspace Manager, and some tasks you cannot accomplish at all without the shell; for example, Appendix B explains how to perform system administration using the shell. There are other capabilities of the shell that haven't been mentioned here, such as piping, I/O redirection, and scripts. There are also many utilities and commands, common to UNIX implementations everywhere, that are available to you. All that is waiting to be used.

Second, the more you use and understand the shell, the more you'll understand Mach and, ultimately, the NeXT system itself. A simple command like `ps` can tell you more about what's going on in the computer than all the windows and icons floating around the screen.

So go out and get yourself a good beginner's guide to UNIX. Sit down at the NeXT system, open up the Shell window, and start exploring. You might be surprised by what you find.

12
Creating Programs

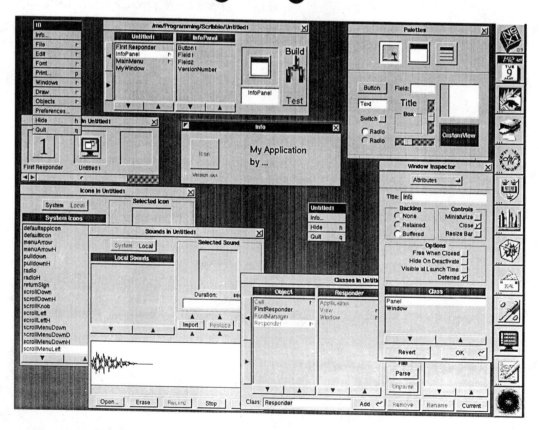

While the NeXT system offers a variety of bundled applications, it can't anticipate your every need. Furthermore, many of those needs are going to be so specific that independent software firms are unlikely to meet them, either. This means that you'll either have to find someone who can write the program for you, or write the program yourself.

The subject of writing programs for the NeXT computer is far too extensive for a complete discussion here. It is worthy of an entire book on its own, and in, fact, Addison-Wesley will be publishing one such book, *Scientific Applications for the NeXT Computer*, by Richard Crandall and Marianne Colgrove. The NeXT technical documentation, which discusses all the factors involved in programming, takes up three thick volumes in Release 0.9 and will be expanded even more by Release 1.0.

This chapter does make a few assumptions. It assumes that you've read the previous three chapters in this section, so that you know how to drag icons, launch applications, select menu commands, edit text, and use the Mach shell. For the second half of the chapter, which involves writing code in Objective C, you really need know enough about programming, particularly about the C programming languages, to know what a variable is, know what a function (procedure, subroutine) is, and be able to scan a short program listing and pretty much follow or guess what's going on.

While the topic of creating programs may be complex, the basic concepts are simple. Applications can be created using Interface Builder, Objective C, or (most commonly) a combination of the two. These tools work on an **object-oriented approach**: your application consists of a series of objects (windows, menus, controls, views) sending messages to one another in response to certain events (key presses, mouse movements, button clicks). The Application Kit, an extensive library of predefined objects, does most of the work for you. All you need to do is to define the additional information and behavior required for your application, usually by creating new types of objects derived from existing ones found in the Application Kit.

The aim of this chapter is to introduce those concepts. It does this by helping you to create a working application—a program we'll call "Scribble"—on the NeXT system, using

Interface Builder and Objective C. The instructions are step by step, with enough theory and discussion along the way to help you understand what's happening, and why. When you are done, you'll not only have a complete program, you'll have the setting and information to be able to go back and experiment, adding new features or changing old ones. But let's start at the beginning.

DESIGNING THE PROGRAM

Before you create a program on the NeXT—or any other—computer, you need to **design** it, that is, determine what it's going to do and how it's going to do it. Few contractors would dream of starting to build a house without a detailed set of blueprints, but programmers are notorious for sitting down at a computer and typing in a program without a lot of planning. They get away with it, because programs—unlike houses—can easily be modified, reorganized, or even thrown away and rebuilt from the ground up. Still, numerous studies (and common sense) indicate that time taken at the start for thoughtful design pays off tremendously later on.

The first step in designing a program is determining just what you want it to do. That's seems obvious, but many programmers—including professional ones—often launch into a project with only a vague or general idea as to what the program is supposed to accomplish. Unfortunately, this approach, born out of a desire to complete something quickly, usually leads to long delays and lots of backtracking. It really is best to begin with the end clearly in mind.

So, let's start the program design by describing what we want the Scribble program to do; that is, what should happen during a typical session using the Scribble program:

1. On launching the program, a window appears.

2. To draw, you move the cursor into the window, hold the left mouse button down, and then move the cursor; as you do so, a black line is drawn inside the window, following the cursor.

3. You can use some kind of controls to change the color and thickness of the line being drawn, as well as the color of the background it's being drawn against.

4. When you're done, the window goes away, and the application stops running.

You now have an idea what the program does, but the details aren't clear. Here are some additional questions to ask yourself, along with the correct answers for the Scribble program:

- *What does the window look like?* Rectangular, with the title "Scribble window."

- *Does it have any controls?* Yes, a miniaturize button (to turn the window into an icon) and a close button (to make the window go away).

- *How much of the window can you draw in?* Only the section below the title bar, with a slight border around the drawing area.

- *How does the drawing area look?* It's white, and the lines that are drawn are black.

- *Can you change those settings?* Yes, using three sliders below the drawing area: one for pen color, one for pen width, and one for background color.

- *How does the pen color control work?* It sets the drawing color from black (0.0) to white (1.0); it doesn't change what's already drawn, just what drawing occurs next.

- *How does the pen width control work?* Just like the pen color control, but it ranges from 0.0 (thinnest possible line) to 10.0 (however fat that is).

- *How does the background color control work?* It also ranges from black (0.0) to white (1.0), but only has an effect when you clear the drawing area.

- *Does the program have a menu?* Yes, every NeXT application should have a menu.

- *What commands are in the menu?* At least three: Info, Hide, and Quit.

- *Does the program have an info panel, then?* Yes.

- *What does the info panel look like?* It has the words "About Scribble" in the title bar and my name (the "author" of the program's name) in the panel itself; it also has a close button to make it go away.

- *Do you want to be able to clear the drawing window and start over?* Yes; it should also reset the drawing area to the color specified by the background color slider.

- *How are you going to do that?* With a Clear command in the menu.

- *Do you want to be able to print drawings or save them out to disk?* No, at least, not in this version.

- *How do you exit the program?* By clicking on the close button of the drawing window, or by selecting the Quit command in the menu.

Having gone through these questions, you now have a much better idea of how the program will look and act. There are others you could ask, but these cover the two major points: how the interface looks, and how the program behaves.

DEFINING THE OBJECTS

As mentioned above, the NeXT system uses an object-oriented approach in its software architecture. That is, a program can be thought of as a collection of visible objects and views, as well as nonvisible objects. These objects send messages back and forth to each other; as mentioned, a menu item might send a message to a view to clear itself. All objects of a particular type belong to the same **class**; for example, all window objects belong to the object class Window. Each actual window is then considered an instance—a working copy—of the class Window.

Now that you know how the Scribble program will work, you can sit down and define the objects that you'll use. The Application Kit provides some thirty or so objects that are already defined for you; you can use these as they are, or you can **subclass** them—that is, create new types of objects that are derived from existing ones.

The three most obvious objects in the Scribble program are the window, the panel, and the menu. You need a single window (in the parlance, "a single instance of the Window class") that has a close button, a miniaturize button, and the title "Scribble window." The window's actual size will be determined later. The window's behavior will be standard—it won't do anything unusual—so you can use the regular Window class from the Application Kit. Initially, the window will be visible.

You can't draw in a window or a panel per se, so you need another object inside the window: a View object. However, a View object has no inherent drawing behavior, so you'll have to define a View subclass, which you'll call PaintView, and then create an instance of that class, that is, a PaintView object. This object will have to know how to clear itself and how to draw lines when you move the cursor over it with the left mouse button down. This accounts for the only Objective C programming that you'll have to do.

The panel will have a close button and the title "About Scribble"; again, size will be determined later. It will have inside of it the text, "Written by," followed by your name. This is actually a separate object—a TextField—which is "attached" to the panel. The panel's behavior (as well as that of the TextField) is all standard, so no extra work will be required. Also, initially, the panel will be invisible.

The menu will have four items, each a separate object, though tightly associated with the menu. Clicking on the "Info..." item will send a "show yourself" message to the panel. Clicking on the Clear item will send the "clear yourself" message to the PaintView object. But what happens when you click on the Hide and Quit items? They send messages, but to what object?

As it turns out, you need another object: an Application object. This is the object that gets the hide and quit messages from the last two menu items. It also passes events (clicking, dragging, etc.) to the appropriate objects (menu, window, panel) to be handled.

Finally, there are three more objects, all of the same class: the three sliders that control pen color and width, and background color. Each time you adjust one, it needs to send a message to the PaintView object to let it know that things have changed. The PaintView object can then interrogate the slider to find out what its new setting is.

All this talk about objects and messages may seem a bit overwhelming, but most of the work is going to be done for you in Interface Builder. And that's exactly what you need to do next: build the interface.

BUILDING THE INTERFACE

At this point, in most programming environments, you would start writing the code to bring up all of the **user interface** elements described above: the window, the info panel, and the menu. In fact, you'd find that most of your time and coding effort went toward implementing the user interface, and that relatively little code was needed to do the actual drawing. This imbalance has become more and more pronounced as personal computers (and their user interfaces) have gotten more sophisticated. The real challenge in programming on systems such as the Macintosh, the Amiga, the Atari ST, the IBM PC (using Windows or Presentation Manager), and UNIX workstations (using X-Window and similar systems) is the time and effort required to support the user interface and other aspects of the operating system.

As mentioned in Chapter 7, NeXT has made an effort to reduce that challenge and to let you focus more on solving problems than on creating user interfaces. Interface Builder, written by Jean-Marie Hullot and Lee Boynton, is a large step in that direction. It allows you to build the user interface for your program directly, not by writing program code, but by actually moving the elements (windows, panels, menus, buttons, sliders, text fields, and so on) around the screen. As you put the elements together, you can adjust their sizes, their relative positions, and various other factors. This way, you can quickly determine just how the program will look when it's on the screen.

It's hard to overstate what a help this is in designing and creating programs, especially when the program has graphical elements such as windows, buttons, and menus. The alternative is to estimate the sizes and positions, write a program that displays them, then go back and "tweak" the values until the program looks the way you want it to. The cycle of change-and-run, change-and-run gets tedious, and the result is often a sloppily laid out program. So Interface Builder makes a significant contribution in cutting down the time required for that task, as well as the actual program code required.

Another important feature of Interface Builder is that it allows you to define **relationships** between the objects, that is, how the objects interact with each other. For example, you can "connect" a button with a window, so that the button asks the window to disappear each time the button is pushed. You can connect a slider with a textfield, so that the value displayed in the field changes as you move the slider. Or, as you'll see in the program you're creating, you can connect a menu item with a View (drawing) object, so that the view gets a message to clear itself when you select the menu item.

CREATING A PROGRAMMING DIRECTORY

Your first step is to create a directory where you can save all your work in one spot. Since you probably will want to work on several programming projects, you should create a "Programming" subdirectory within your home directory. To do this, select the Directory Browser window, find the entry for

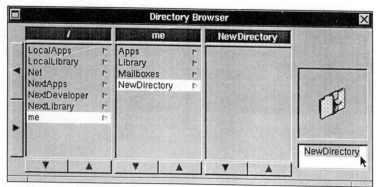

Figure 12.1. Creating a new directory within your home directory

your home directory (such as /me), and click on it. Then, with that directory highlighted, click on the Files/New Directory command in the WM menu (or press Command-n). A new directory (named NewDirectory) will appear inside your home directory. Select its name underneath its icon, as shown in Figure 12.1, type in its new name (Programming), and press Return.

Now, you need to go through the process again. Each program being developed must have its own subdirectory, in order to keep the project and object files separate from each other. So, with Programming still selected, use the New Directory command again, and name this new directory "Scribble". Your browser window should now look like the one shown in Figure 12.2. With this taken care of, you're ready to start building your interface.

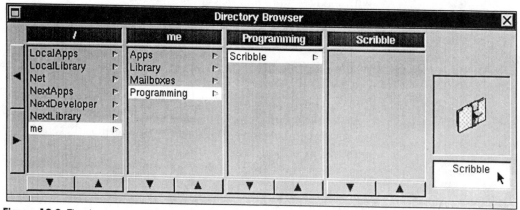

Figure 12.2. The browser with both the Programming and Scribble directories created

LAUNCHING INTERFACE BUILDER

Your next step, then, is to launch Interface Builder (IB). It is located in the directory /NextApps, which you can examine using the browser. Since you're going to be using Interface Builder a lot, you should probably drag its icon over to the application dock. While you're at it, you should also drag the icons for Shell and Edit over to the dock; you'll be using them later on, too.

Now that you've got its icon over in the dock, you can launch Interface Builder just by double-clicking on its icon. After a few seconds, you'll get the IB menu, a project browser showing your project organization, and a panel, labeled "Palettes," containing objects that you can use. You're now ready to create the user interface for the Scribble program.

To start a new project, select the Project item in the IB menu; when the Project submenu appears, select the New Application command, or press Command-n. Your display will now look something like Figure 12.3. Interface Builder has created a window (labeled "My Window") for you and a menu ("Untitled1") with three commands: Info..., Hide, and Quit. It has also created an info panel for you, though that panel isn't visible right now. In short, a large portion of your interface is already done; it's just up to you to make it look the way you want it to.

CUSTOMIZING THE WINDOW

Let's start with the window. You wanted it to have a specific title ("Scribble Window") and to have controls for closing and miniaturizing. To change these things, you are going to use the **Inspector**, a panel that shows you the current settings for a given object. First, you need to select the window, either by clicking on it, or by going to the project browser and clicking on "MyWindow." Next, bring up the Inspector by selecting the Windows command in the IB menu, then selecting the Inspector... command in the Windows submenu; as a short cut, you can bypass the menu completely and just press Command-2. The Inspector for MyWindow will now appear. Figure 12.4 shows the changes to be made.

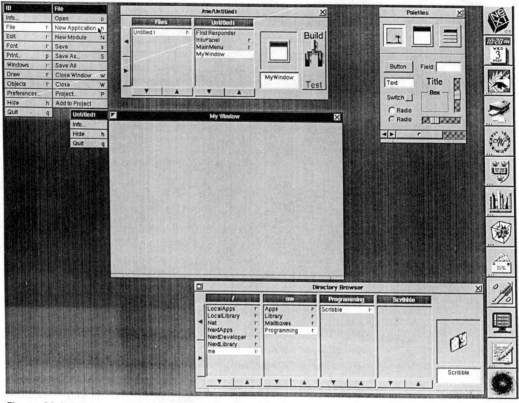

Figure 12.3. Interface Builder, showing a brand-new project

To change the window title, just edit the text in the "Title:" field at the top of the Inspector. The area labeled "Controls" shows the three controls a window can have: miniature and close buttons and a resize bar. All three are selected by default for a window; click on the "Resize Bar" switch to make the checkmark go away, so that your window won't have a resize bar. Leave the other options as they are, and click on the OK button to make the necessary changes.

You'll notice that the window title has changed, and that the resize bar has disappeared. However, there is a small button at the left end of the title bar that's a special resize button. When you click on this button, a resize bar appears in the window. That's because you still may need to adjust the initial size of the window. The bar goes away as soon as you either resize the window or click on something (including that win-

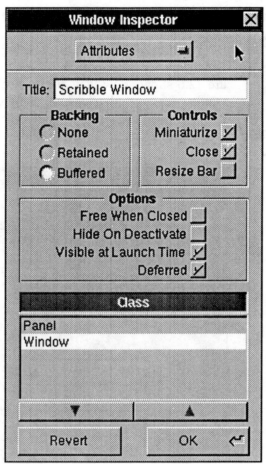

Figure 12.4. The Inspector window, showing the attributes for MyWindow

dow). Also, there is no miniaturize button yet, because you don't need or want it until you're testing the interface—and it will appear when you start testing.

Inspecting the Inspector

There's a lot more to the Inspector window than meets the eye. If your eyes are sharp, you may have noticed that the top control in the Inspector is a pop-up list. When you move the cursor over it and hold the mouse button down, you get a list like the one shown in Figure 12.5. You can then select (by moving

Figure 12.5. The pop-up list on the Inspector window

the cursor up and down) any one of these five aspects for the Inspector.

You'll be seeing most of these aspects, either for the main window or for other objects, as you proceed. For example, Figure 12.6 shows how you can precisely adjust the size of the window (or any other object), using direct coordinates. We'll discuss the other aspects when it's appropriate.

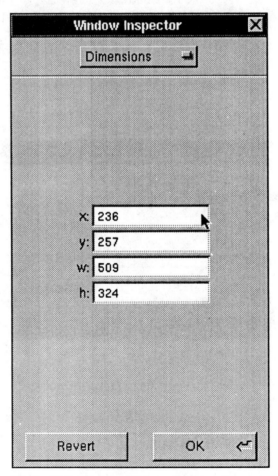

Figure 12.6. The Inspector window, showing absolute window dimensions

STARTING A PROJECT

Before you go any further, you should save the work you have and, at the same time, give your project a name. To do this, go to the File submenu of the IB menu, and click on the Save command (or press Command-s). You'll get a standard File Selection panel; click through the subdirectories until you get to Scribble; then type Scribble as the name of your file, too. The panel should look like that in Figure 12.7. Click on the OK button (or press Return), and your interface will be saved as "Scribble.nib" (the ".nib" is added for you).

Notice, by the way, that both the main menu and the project name in the interface browser have changed to "Scribble". This happened when you saved the interface file to disk.

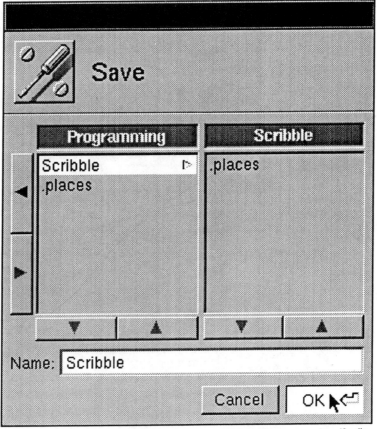

Figure 12.7. Saving the interface out as "/me/Programming/Scribble/Scribble.nib"

Now you need to start up a **project**, that is, the complete collection of text and data files that will make up your new application. Select the Files/Project... command. Since no project yet exists, you'll be asked if you want to create one; click on the yes button (or press Return). You'll then get the Project window. This window has two aspects, controlled by the Attributes/Files button at the top; clicking on this button switches between the two aspects. Figure 12.8 shows the attributes aspect, which you use to set the application's name,

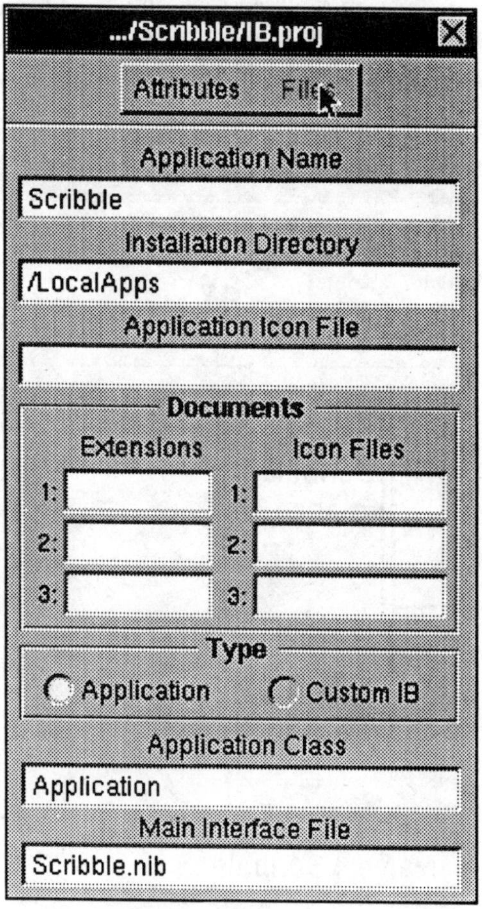

Figure 12.8. The Project window, showing the project's attributes

where it will be installed, where its icons are located, the file name extensions and file icons associated with its documents, and so on. Leave these settings as they are; there's nothing here you need to change for the purpose of this project.

CUSTOMIZING THE MENU

It's now time to work on the menu. There really isn't much to be done, other than to add a "Clear" item. To create one, go over to the window labeled "Palettes." This window has three icons across the top, the rightmost of which looks like a menu. Click on it, and it will change to look as it does in Figure 12.9.

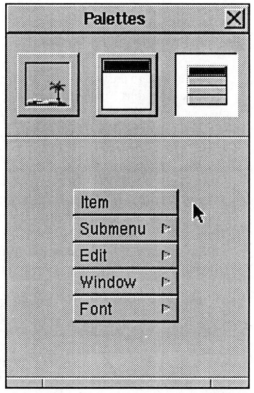

Figure 12.9. The Palettes window, showing the available menu components

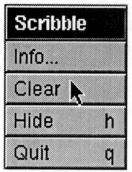

Figure 12.10. Your
application's menu
with the new menu
item renamed to
"Clear"

Move the cursor over the item labeled "Item," hold the mouse button down, and drag that item over to your Scribble menu. Position it on the border between the "Info..." and "Hide" items, and then release the mouse button. The item snaps into place between the other two. To change its name, double-click on "Item," which will then be selected; now type in "Clear" and press Return. Your menu should now look like the one in Figure 12.10.

This is a good point at which to save your work again. Select the Save command from the Files submenu (or press Command-s). You should do this periodically to make sure that your work is saved to disk.

CUSTOMIZING THE PANEL

Now it's time to customize the information panel, so you need to make it visible. To do that, go up to the project browser and click once on the project name, which should now be "Scribble"; you may have to use the buttons on the left side of the browser first to scroll back to the Files column. Several items will be listed in the next column over, one of which should be "InfoPanel." Click on that once, and the corresponding icon will appear in the browser's icon box. Double-click on that icon, and the info panel itself will appear, looking something like the one shown in Figure 12.11.

Let's completely redesign the info panel. It currently has four objects in it: a button (faintly labeled "icon") and three

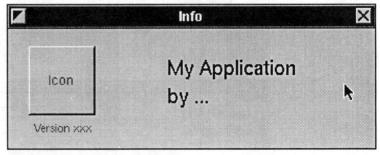

Figure 12.11. Default info panel

TextField objects, one each for version number, program name, and author. Remove each one by clicking on it and then selecting the Cut command from IB's Edit submenu (or pressing Command-x). You can also select all four at once by either holding the Shift key down while clicking on each, or by moving the cursor to the upper-left corner of the panel's content area, holding the mouse button down, dragging the cursor to the lower-right corner, and then releasing the mouse button. With all four selected, a single Cut command will remove them all. Notice that as you cut them, they also disappear from the project browser.

Now go to the Palettes window and click on the leftmost icon. You'll get the same assortment of objects you had when you first launched IB. Note the scroller and the resize bar at the bottom; to get rid of both, and to see all the available objects at once, use the resize bar to make the Palettes window larger. It should now look as it does in Figure 12.12.

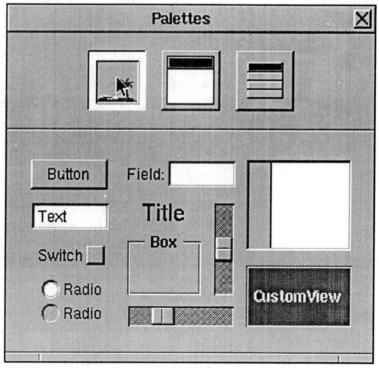

Figure 12.12. Palettes window showing controls

You'll be using several of these objects in building your application, and the first one will be the text field (shown as the word "Title" in a larger Helvetica font).

Editing Text Fields

Go over to the Palettes window, select a Title (text field) object, drag it over to the info panel, and release it. Note that little control points appear at each corner and along each side. Use these to resize the text field so that it's almost as large as the panel itself; you do this by moving the cursor over a control point, holding the mouse button down, and then dragging the point in the desired direction. If you need or want to shift the box's location, move the cursor in the middle of the box itself, hold the mouse button down, and drag the box to where you want it. If you want to make the info panel itself larger, use the resize control in the panel's title bar.

At this point, you should have a large text field with the word "Title" sitting up at the top center. Double-click on "Title" to select it, then type *Scribble*, press Return, type *by*, press Return, and then type your name. Unless you've made the info panel much smaller, this text still won't fill the text field. So bring up the Font submenu and panel, and experiment with different fonts and font sizes. Note that, if necessary, the text field expands to hold the text. Adjust the text font and size, the size of the text field, and the size of the info panel until it all looks the way you want it to.

Once you're satisfied, click on the text field (to make sure it's selected) and then click on the Inspector window. The TextField inspector will appear, as shown in Figure 12.13.

Create a border by clicking on the rightmost border button, then clicking on the OK button to apply your changes. Note that the text field in the info panel changes to reflect your choice. Likewise, you can select the text color, the background color, and the text alignment. Play with all these elements until you're satisfied with how it looks; Figure 12.14 shows one possible arrangement. Select the File/Save command (Command-s) to save what you've done so far. Finally, make the info panel disappear for now by clicking on its close button.

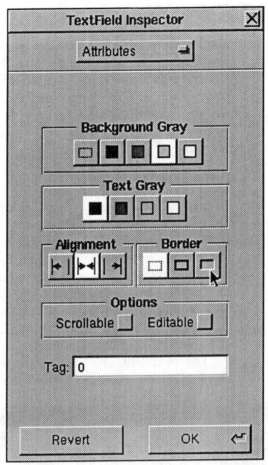

Figure 12.13. The Inspector panel, showing TextField information

Figure 12.14. A customized info panel

CREATING A NEW CLASS: PAINTVIEW

You are about one-third done at this point. You've got the window, the menu, and the info panel, but you still don't have anywhere to draw. That's because a program can't draw in a window. It can, however, draw in a View object contained within a window. So your next task is to create a custom View object type—PaintView—and then place such a View object in the window.

Defining the New Class

To create a new type of object within Interface Builder, you need to bring up the Classes window using the Windows submenu. This is a class browser that lets you look through some of the hierarchy of object classes in the Application Kit, and to add new classes of your own. When the panel comes up, search for the View object (Object -> Responder -> View), and click on its entry. Now, type in the name PaintView, and click on the add button (or press Return). This creates a new view object type called PaintView, as shown in Figure 12.15.

The next step is to define the **outlets** for a PaintView object. Outlets don't necessarily have to do with output;

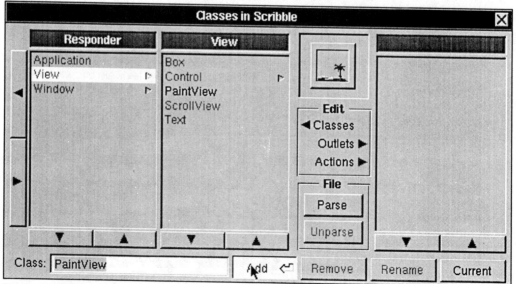

Figure 12.15. The Classes window, after creating the View-derived object class, PaintView

they're just other objects that a PaintView object will want to know about. In this case, you want three outlets, one for each of the sliders that will control the drawing parameters.

To add the outlets, click first on the outlets button within the edit box in the Classes window. Now type in the names of the three outlets, one at a time, clicking on Add or pressing Return after each. Let's call them `penColorCtrl`, `pen-WidthCtrl`, and `backColorCtrl`. The Classes window should now look like it does in Figure 12.16.

Now you need to define the **actions** that can be requested of a PaintView object. The PaintView class will inherit most of its behavior from the View class, but there are four actions which will be requested by other objects in the interface you've built, to wit:

- `clearView:`, sent by the Clear item in the menu

- `setPenColor:`, sent by the pen color slider

- `setPenWidth:`, sent by the pen width slider

- `setBackColor:`, sent by the background color slider

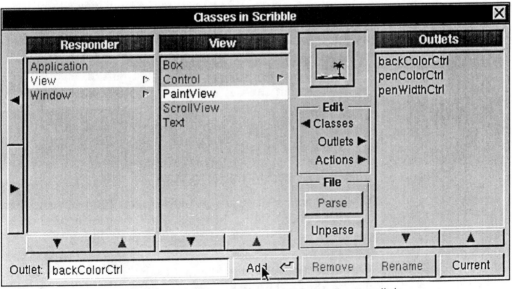

Figure 12.16. The Classes window, after creating PaintView's three outlets

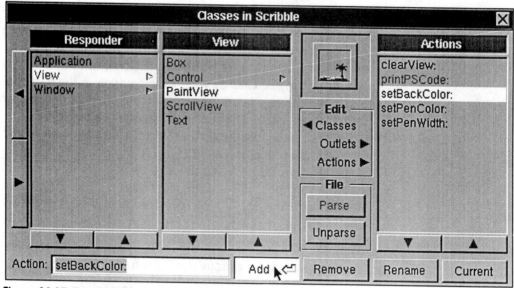

Figure 12.17. The Classes window, after creating PaintView's new actions

The names above aren't the only ones allowable, but they are selected according to certain NeXT conventions. The phrase "sent by" simply means that when you interact with one of these objects—click on them, slide them, whatever—it will send the appropriate message to the PaintView object.

To add these actions, click on the actions button within the edit box in the Classes window. Now type each of the names above, one at a time, complete with colon, and then either press Return or click on the add button. Figure 12.17 shows you what the Classes window should look like when you're done. (Ignore the predefined `printPSCode:` action that's already there; it's not of importance at this time.) When you're all done, press Command-s to save your work so far.

Generating and Integrating Source Code

Now that you've defined your new object, you need to create the source code files for it, which you'll be editing later on in this chapter. To do this, click on the unparse button in the Classes window. An attention panel will appear, asking if you want to create the files "PaintView.h" and "PaintView.m"; click on the OK button or press Return.

Your next step is to add those files to your project, so find the Project window (if it's closed, select the Add to Project command in the File submenu) and bring up the Files display by clicking on the button at the top of the window. You'll see a pop-up list (most likely labeled "Interface Files") and a column showing exactly one file: "Scribble.nib". What you want to

Figure 12.18. The Project window showing the only class file added to the Scribble project

add are some source code files, so select the Class Files option from the pop-up list.

Now click on the Add... button at the bottom. A standard file select will come up; select "PaintView.m"; and click on the OK button (or press Return). Your project window should now look like the one in Figure 12.18.

Once again, this is a good time to press Command-s and save your work.

Adding an Instance of an Object

All you've done so far has been to create a new class of objects, namely PaintView. What you really want to have is a PaintView object on your main window. To do this, go over to the Palettes window, grab a CustomView object, drag it over to the Scribble window, and release it. As you did with the text field in the info panel, resize the custom view to take up as much space as you wish for drawing, leaving, however, some space at the bottom for the three sliders.

While it's still selected (that is, while its resizing control points are still visible), click on the Inspector window. Using the Attributes aspect, you'll see a scrollable list of View-derived objects, including PaintView. Click on "PaintView" and then click on the OK button (or press Return). Note that

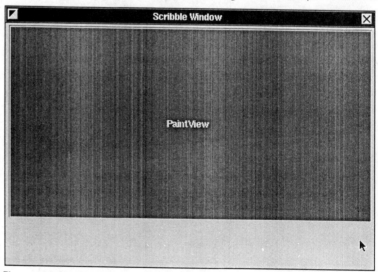

Figure 12.19. Scribble's main window, with the PaintView object in place

the object name in the middle of the custom view has just changed to "PaintView." The window should now look something like Figure 12.19.

INTERMISSION: CLOSING AND OPENING PROJECTS

Time to take a break, and learn about how to close and open projects. Go to the File submenu and select the Save option to save out all your work so far. Now select the Close option. The Scribble menu and main window disappear, the project browser clears, and the PaintView class vanishes from the Classes window. Select the Quit command from the IB main menu, and watch everything else disappear. Now get up and walk around a bit. Get a drink of water. Make a phone call. Come back when you feel ready to continue.

Now that you're back, relaunch Interface Builder by double-clicking on its icon. Go to the File menu and select the Open command (or press Command-o). A standard File Selection panel will appear; use it to look in your Programming/Scribble directory for "Scribble.nib". Once you've selected that file, click on the OK button or press Return. Presto! You're right back to where you were, though a few of the windows (Inspector, Classes, etc.) you had opened are closed again. Don't worry about them for now; first you're going to add some controls to your application.

ADDING CONTROLS

You're going to have three controls along the bottom of the window, all three of which are going to be sliders. Grab a horizontal (left to right) slider and drag it over to the Scribble window, placing it near the left side of the area below the PaintView object. As with other objects, the slider now has resizing "knobs" around it. Grab one on the right end and pull it right a bit; the slider grows larger to accommodate your design.

Next, release the mouse button, hold down the Alternate key and, while holding it down, grab one of the right knobs on the slider and drag it toward the right edge of the window. As you do, other sliders—identical in length and appearance to the first—appear within the bounded area. Do this until you have three sliders altogether, then release the mouse button.

One last trick: hold down the Command key, grab a right knob again, and drag it right again. This time, the left slider stays put, and all three stay their starting length, but they become spaced apart more. The result should look something like Figure 12.20.

You now have three sliders, all of the same length and of equal spacing. What's more, all three will move as a single object, remaining aligned and equally spaced, if any one of the three is moved. This collection of identical objects is called a **matrix**, which is itself an object class in the Application Kit. Each item in the matrix is a **cell** (yet another object class), and each cell contains a slider control. When you click on any of the sliders, or the space between them, you select the entire matrix; when you double-click on the sliders themselves, you select them. This is an important distinction, as you'll see in a while.

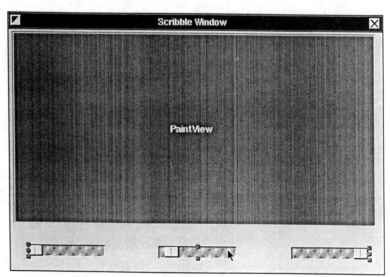

Figure 12.20. Scribble's main window, with the sliders in place

Using Boxes

The last thing you need to do to set these sliders up is to label them. You could do this with text objects ("Title"), but let's try something new. Grab one of the items labled "box" and drag it over to the Scribble window, placing it so that its left edge lines up with the PaintView's left edge. Resize the box, using its knobs, until it covers the left slider.

Now, with the box selected, bring up the Draw submenu, and click on Send To Back. The left slider appears within the box, and you can now adjust its position to your satisfaction. However, there is a problem: the connection between the sliders appears to be causing a section to disappear out of the right side of the box. You can see this rather plainly if you move the entire matrix up and down. What's going on here, and how do you fix it?

The answer to both questions is found in the Inspector window, which you should open again (using the Windows submenu). Once the Inspector is open, click once on the matrix to select it. You'll see that a matrix has a background color; in this case, light gray is selected, and it's overwriting the box edge. Select each of the other background shades, clicking on OK after each, to see how they look. The leftmost shade—"invisible"—solves your problem.

With that done, click on the box. The Inspector window changes immediately to show various box attributes. Play with the different settings until you're satisfied. Then double-click on the box's title ("Box"). Type the new title ("Pen Color"), and press Return.

Copying, Pasting, and Aligning Objects

When you're happy with how the box looks, select it (by clicking on it once) and use the Edit/Copy command (or press Command-c). Then press Command-v (Edit/Paste). A second copy of the box will appear right over the first. Grab it with the mouse and drag it over the middle slider. Before going any further, press Command-v again. Drag the third copy of the box over the rightmost slider. Click on each of these and select the Draw/Send To Back command. Make any desired adjustments to the size and position of the boxes and of the slider matrix.

Also, double-click on the other boxes' titles and change them to "Pen Width" and "Background Color."

Chances are, you'd like the three boxes to be nicely aligned. To do this, bring up the Align submenu (from the Draw submenu), and the Preferences... panel from the Align submenu. In the Align Preferences panel, click on the top radio button (Left Edges/Bottom Edges).

Now, deselect anything else by clicking on some unused portion of the Scribble window. Next, hold the Shift key down and click on all three boxes; all three should now be selected. Finally, click on the Make Row command in the Align submenu, or press Command-Shift-R. All three boxes are finished.

If you're feeling very ambitious, you can drag down some text objects from the Palettes window to make upper and lower limits for each of the controllers. Figure 12.21 gives you an idea of how it might look.

You have one last task here: you must define the range of values and inital settings for each slider. To do this, bring up the Inspector window in its Attributes aspect, and double click on the Pen Color slider. The display should look like that in

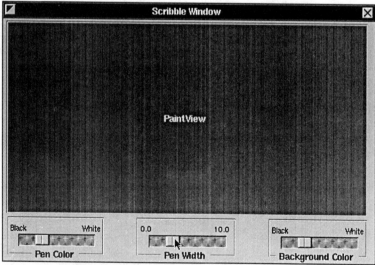

Figure 12.21. Scribble's main window, with the boxes and labels for each slider

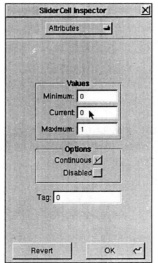

Figure 12.22. The Inspector window, showing attributes for the Pen Color slider

Figure 12.22. The minimum and maximum values are fine as they stand—black is 0.0, and white is 1.0—but you're going to start out drawing with a "black" pen, so set the Current field to 0. Leave the other settings as they are, and click on the OK button (or press Return).

With the Inspector still up, double-click on the Pen Width slider. Set the Maximum field to 10 and the Current field to 1, then click OK. Finally, double-click on the Background Color slider. Since you want this to start out white, set the Current field to 1, and click OK. Notice, by the way, that the buttons in the sliders move to reflect the values in the Current field.

MAKING CONNECTIONS

Your last task to perform within Interface Builder is to make connections between the various objects. Specifically, you need to connect:

- The menu's Clear item with the PaintView's `clearView:` action

- The PenColor slider as the PaintView's `PenColorCtrl` outlet; also with the `setPenColor:` action

- The Pen Width slider as the PaintView's `PenWidthCtrl` outlet; also with the `setPenWidth:` action

- The Background Color slider as the PaintView's `BackColorCtrl` outlet; also with the `setBackColor:` action

To make these connections, you need to bring up the Inspector window (if it isn't visible already). You'll connect actions first. Use the pop-up list on the Inspector to bring up its Target/Action aspect, which will start out blank.

Target/Action Connections

Here's how you make **target/action connections**, which is when manipulating one object sends an action message to another. Locate the Control key on the keyboard (between Tab and Shift, on the left end). Hold the Control key down. While holding it down, move the cursor over the Clear item in the Scribble menu, and press the mouse button down. Now, while holding both the Control key and the mouse button down, drag the cursor over to the PaintView object in the Scribble window. As you drag, a black line will follow the cursor, growing from the Clear item. When you move the cursor over the PaintView object, let go of the mouse button (and the Control key). You'll see the black line form a box around the PaintView object, and a list of the PaintView actions will appear in the Inspector. Click on the appropriate action (`clearView:`). Your screen should look something like Figure 12.23.

You're now going to do this three more times, once for each slider. Start with the Pen Color slider. As you did above, double-click on the slider itself, so that it's selected. Now hold the Control key down, move the cursor over the slider, press the mouse button down, and drag the cursor—and accompanying black line—up to the PaintView object. When you let go, the PaintView actions will again appear in the Inspector window; click on the `setPenColor:` action. You've now made another connection.

Repeat this process for the other two sliders, connecting the Pen Width slider with the `setPenWidth:` action, and the Background Color slider with the `setBackColor:` action. Then select File/Save (or press Command-s) to save your work so far.

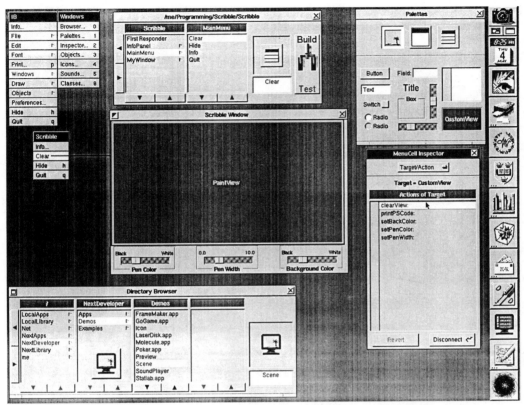

Figure 12.23. Connecting the Clear item with the PaintView's clearView: action

Outlet Connections

Your last task is to make the **outlet connections**, associating specific objects with the outlet fields of other objects. In this case, the only outlets are the three you defined for PaintView. Strictly speaking, these are a bit redundant, but they could come in handy for future enhancements to your program.

To make these connections, select the Outlets aspect of the Inspector window, and then click on the PaintView object in the Scribble window. The three outlets will appear in the Inspector. Click on the first one, `backColorCtrl`. Now go over to the PaintView window and drag a connection from the PaintView object to the Background Color slider—the same actions you performed before, but now going from view to slider. The connection will form, and a connector symbol will appear across from `backColorCtrl`, indicating that the outlet has been identified with an object. Note that if you accidental-

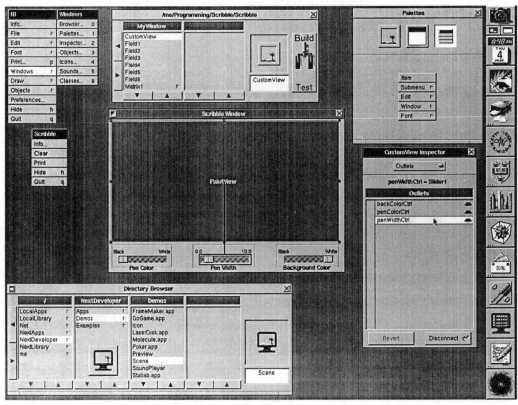

Figure 12.24. Connecting outlets with other variables

ly make a wrong connection, you can use the disconnect button at the bottom to sever the link.

Repeat the process for `penColorCtrl` and `penWidthCtrl`, using them to link PaintView with the Pen Color and Pen Width sliders. Your screen should now look something like Figure 12.24.

Before you go any further, use the File/Save command or press Command-s, so that you save all your work so far. This is another good spot to take a short break.

TESTING THE INTERFACE

Having done all this work, you can now test your interface. After saving your project as suggested above, click on the "Build/Test" switch in the project browser. The switch will

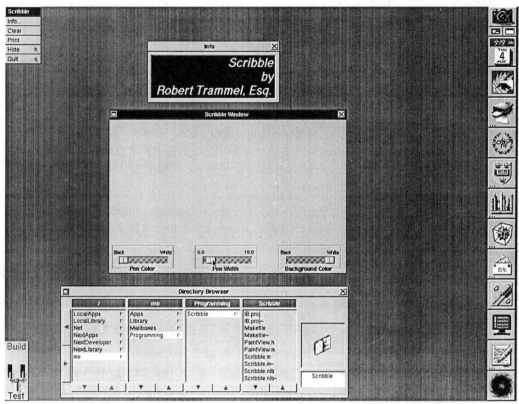

Figure 12.25. Your sample program being tested under Interface Builder

move to the "test" position, and all the Interface Builder menus and panels will disappear; all that remains is your interface and a "Build/Test" switch, as shown in Figure 12.25.

Make sure that the miniaturize and close buttons on the window work, that the Info command in the menu does bring up the info panel, that the sliders do slide, and that the Hide command hides both the interface and the project browser (which can be restored by double-clicking on the Interface Builder icon). To get out of "test" mode, you can either select the Quit command in your program's menu, or you can click again on the "Build/Test" switch in the lower-left corner of the screen.

You might also notice that you can't draw in the window, and that the Clear command has no effect. This is because you still need to define how the PaintView object works. You can't do that within Interface Builder; you need to write some program routines to accomplish that, which is your next task.

Save your work out one last time, then select the Quit command from the Interface Builder main menu.

PROJECT AND SOURCE FILES

As you've been working with Interface Builder, it has been creating and maintaining a set of files for you. Bring up the Directory Browser and browse through to the Programming/Scribble subdirectory. Here is a list of the files you'll find and what they contain:

- IB.proj—the Interface Builder project file, which contains all the information found in the Project window under IB

- "Scribble.nib"—the interface information created by Interface Builder; this file is linked in when your program is compiled

- Scribble.m—the main body of your Objective C program

- PaintView.h—the header (interface) file for PaintView, the View object that you defined in Interface Builder

- PaintView.m—the body (implementation) file for the PaintView object

- Makefile—the instructions to the Objective C compiler, telling it what files to compile and link

Most of these files are very small, except for "Scribble.nib," and even it isn't terribly big. That's because this program doesn't do much; it just creates the various objects and establishes a few connections between them. You're going to add in the real work a little later.

COMPILING THE PROGRAM

You can actually compile and run the program at this point. To do this, launch either the Terminal or the Shell application. When you get the Mach prompt, change to your Scribble directory by typing the following command (followed by Return):

```
localhost>cd /username/Programming/Scribble
```

where *username* is the user ID that you use to log on to the NeXT system (such as "me"). You can verify that you're at the right place by typing "`ls -l`" at the prompt and pressing Return; this should list the names of the files mentioned above.

To compile the program, just type "`make`" at the system prompt, and press Return. This invokes a UNIX utility called `make` which will look for a file called "Makefile" and follow the instructions in that file. Interface Builder has created "Makefile" already, giving instructions on how to build Scribble. You'll see the commands that `make` uses to create Scribble echoed to the screen; basically, it compiles each of the Objective C source code files, then links them all together into an executable program called Scribble. Note that "Makefile" will create a subdirectory within Scribble named "objs", in which it will store the **object** (machine code) **files** created by the compilation.

RUNNING THE PROGRAM

When `make` is finished and you get the system prompt again, type "`Scribble`" (sans quotes) and press Return. This will run your program, which will act just as it did when you tested it under Interface Builder. The only difference is that it now has its own icon. If you select the Hide command in the Scribble menu, you'll have to double click on that icon (instead of on the Interface Builder icon) to make the menu and window reappear.

WORKING IN OBJECTIVE C

At this point, you're half done. You've designed the program and defined the object to be used. You've created the entire user interface using Interface Builder. You've established the relationships between the various objects. You've generated the necessary source code files for the interface. You've compiled that code, resulting in a stand-alone version of the interface. But you still can't draw. To do that, you'll need to add some code to the PaintView files, which means that it's time to switch from Interface Builder to Objective C.

EDITING THE PROGRAM

You should now take time to look at the files created by Interface Builder. Most don't require any changes and, in fact, should not be modified by you at this time. However, two of them—"PaintView.h" and "PaintView.m"—are going to require substantial additional material typed in. To do this, you're going to use the Edit application.

Edit is a text editor designed primarily for writing programs and similar document preparation tasks. It lets you have multiple documents open at the same time; offers cutting, copying, and pasting, both within a document and between documents; and lets you access on-line utilities (including issuing shell commands and looking up UNIX manual pages) without having to switch to another application.

The simplest way to edit one of these files is to find it using the Directory Browser, and then double-click on its name or icon. This will automatically launch Edit (if it's not already running) and open a document window for that file. You should do that now for "PaintView.h" and "PaintView.m" and get ready to make the changes described below.

CREATING AN OBJECT CLASS

When you create a new object class, there are four things you can define: the superclass, instance variables, factory methods, and instance methods. The first is mandatory, the other three are optional. Let's look at each.

The **superclass** is the object class from which a given class is derived. Every class has a superclass, except for the predefined object type Object, from which all other classes are derived. For example, the class PaintView that you defined in Interface Builder has as its superclass the class View, which in turn is derived from Responder, which is itself derived from Object. A class inherits all of its superclass's instance variables and methods, including those that the superclass inherited from its superclass, and so on back to the class Object.

Instance variables contain the information associated with each instance of a particular object class. They are declared very much like you would declare regular variables in a C program, that is, with a data type and a name for each one. Every time you create a new instance of a given class—in other words, a new object—it gets a complete set of its class's instance variables. For example, each View object has eight instance variables, including two rectangles defining its frame and its bounds, a set of flags containing information about the view instance, four pointers to other objects (one pointer variable is inherited from the class Responder) and a structure containing low-level information (inherited from the class Object). You defined three additional instance variables from within Interface Builder: `penColorCtrl`, `penWidthCtrl`, and `backColorCtrl`. You'll define a few more before you're through.

Methods (or actions) are how you get objects or object classes to perform work. They are sets of instructions—functions or subroutines, if you're already familiar with programming—that get called when you send a message to an object or an object class (the "target"). In your objective C programs, these messages take the general format:

```
[target method1:parameter];
```

Some methods have no parameters, in which case the messages look like this:

```
[target method2];
```

while others can have multiple parameters, which are handled by having a colon ("`:`"), along with an optional additional name, in front of each parameter:

```
[target method3:parm1 name2:parm2 :parm3];
```

In all cases, the colons are part of the method's name and must always be used when referring to the method, even in Interface Builder. For example, the names of the methods above would be "`method1:`", "`method2:`", and "`method3:name2::`". You defined several methods within Interface Builder, such as `clearView:` and `setPenColor:`.

Factory methods define messages sent to object classes (such as Object, Window, View), rather than to the objects themselves. Most factory methods are used to create instances of a given object class, that is, working copies of a given object type, hence the name. For example, the method `newFrame:` is used to create a new View object. Other factory methods are used to get information about objects of a given class without having to actually create any. When you declare a factory method in an Objective C program, you indicate that it is a factory method by preceding its name with a plus sign ("`+`").

Instance methods define messages sent to actual objects— that is, instances of a given object class that have already been created. For example, the method `display` is used to tell a View object to go draw itself. Most methods defined in the Application Kit are instance methods; the same will probably be true in your programs. When you declare an instance method in an Objective C program, you precede its name by a minus sign ("`-`").

Interface

A class definition in Objective C has two parts, usually in separate files: the interface and the implementation. The **interface** states the object's superclass, lists the instance variables, and has a declaration for each method, giving its name and parameter types. The general format for the interface is shown in Listing 12.1, where NewClass is the name of the new object class and SuperClass is the name of its superclass.

Let's look at the object class you're creating, PaintView. Listing 12.2 shows a suggested interface file for PaintView.

This example adds three instance variables (backColor, pen-Color, penWidth), one factory method (newFrame:), and two instance methods (mouseDown:, drawSelf::). The double slash ("//") indicates the start of a comment, that is, some note or remark about that particular line (or the program in general) that you want to remember.

```
#import <appkit/appkit.h>
#import <appkit/SuperClass.h>
@interface NewClass:SuperClass
{
  instance variables
}
declarations of methods
@end
```
Listing 12.1. General format for an object class interface file

```
#import <appkit/appkit.h>
#import <appkit/View.h>
@interface PaintView:View
{
 id      penColorCtrl;  // outlets def'd in IB
 id      penWidthCtrl;  // point to the three
 id      backColorCtrl; // slider controls
 float   backColor;     // background color
 float   penColor;      // pen (writing) color
 float   penWidth;      // pen width
}
- setPenColorCtrl:anObject; // called at start
- setPenWidthCtrl:anObject; // of execution to
- setBackColorCtrl:anObject;// link sliders
- setPenColor:sender;  // called when one of the
- setPenWidth:sender;  // sliders is moved; sender
- setBackColor:sender; // is pointer to slider
- clearView:sender;    // called when Clear is used
+ newFrame:(NXRect *)nf;  // creates new PaintView
- mouseDown:(NXEvent *)ptr; // handles drawing
- drawSelf:(NXRect *)list :(int)count; // redraws view
@end
```
Listing 12.2. Suggested interface file for the object class PaintView

The three instance variables are going to hold the three major values that will determine how your drawing will look: the background color of the PaintView, the color of the lines drawn by the pen, and the width of the lines drawn by the pen. These three values will get initialized in `newFrame:`; modified in `setPenColor:`, `setPenWidth`, and `setBackcolor`; and used in `mouseDown:` and `drawSelf::`.

The first three methods (`setPenColorCtrl:`, etc.) were automatically added by Interface Builder. They are called when your program first starts running, assigning the pointer being passed (an object) to the appropriate instance variable. These are completely functional and don't need to be modfied or added to.

The next three methods (`setPenColor:`, etc.) are ones you created. They are called any time you adjust one of the sliders. Likewise, the `clearView:` method is called when you click on the clear button in the menu. These were all automatically generated for you in "PaintView.m," but only as empty methods; it's up to you to put the "brains" into them. The other three methods—`newFrame:`, `mouseDown:`, and `drawSelf:` —are redefinitions of standard methods inherited from the View class.

Implementation

The object class **implementation** actually defines how the methods work. It contains all the methods declared in the interface. It can also contain other methods, as well as standard C functions; these won't be "visible" to any other object, though, since they weren't listed in the interface. The general format for an implementation is shown in Listing 12.3.

```
#import "NewClass.h"
@implementation NewClass
methods and C functions
@end
```

Listing 12.3. General format for an object class implementation

Each method looks very much like a C function; the only real difference is that the method header uses the same syntax (format) as the method declarations in the interface. You can declare local variables within a method and can use any and all standard C statements, functions, and operators, as well as sending methods to other objects (including the object receiving the method).

The only real differences are that the predefined variable "self" acts as a pointer to the actual instance of the object that got the message, and that the instance variables for that object can be referenced directly. For example, consider Listing 12.4, which shows one possible implementation of the methods you defined in Interface Builder (such as `setPenColor:`). The PaintView object receiving this message sends a message to "sender", the object which sent the message in the first place, asking what it's current float value is. It then sets the appropriate instance variable (such as `penColor`) to that value. Note that the method returns a value, `self`, that is, a pointer to the object that received the message. This is a standard practice for those cases where a method doesn't need to return an explicit value.

The method `clearView:`, also in Listing 12.4, works a bit differently. It requests that the PaintView object be redrawn by sending itself the message `display`. This will ultimately result in the method `drawSelf::` (described below) being called.

```
- setPenColor:sender
{
  penColor = [sender floatValue];
  return self;
}
- setPenWidth:sender
{
  penWidth = [sender floatValue];
  return self;
}
- setBackColor:sender
{
  backColor = [sender floatValue];
  return self;
```

continues

Listing 12.4. The `setPenColor:` method for the class PaintView

```
}
- clearView:sender
{
  [self display];
  return self;
}
```

Listing 12.4. *continued*

Initialization

When your program starts executing, the initialization code created by Interface Builder sends the PaintView class a message with the factory method `newFrame:`, shown in Listing 12.5. This method is responsible for creating a new PaintView object, which is simply a View object with whatever additional instance variables have been defined. It does this by sending the `newFrame:` method on to its superclass, assigning the View object returned to `self`, and then assigning values to the PaintView-specific instance variables.

```
+ newFrame:(NXRect *)nf // create a new PaintView object
{
  self = [super newFrame:nf]; // create a new View object
  backColor = 1.0;   // background is white
  penColor = 0.0;   // pen is black
  penWidth = 1.0;   // line width = 1 unit (1 pixel)
  return self;    // return pointer to new PaintView
}
```

Listing 12.5. The `newFrame:` method for the class PaintView

After newFrame: is called, the methods `setPenColor-Ctrl:`, `setPenWidthCtrl:`, and `setBackColorCtrl:` will also be called. This is not because of any inherent property, but because these were created by Interface Builder to establish the outlet connections between the PaintView object and the appropriate controls.

A few notes on drawing with Display PostScript. The "color" of a shape or a line is given as a value from 0.0 to 1.0. The NeXT system supports four pure shades: black (0.0), dark gray (0.333), light gray (0.667), and white (1.0). If you pick values others than these—say, 0.5—then the gray shade used will be a

dithered or **halftone pattern**, that is, a mixture of shades (in this case, dark and light gray) that approximates the desired level. Also, pen width is expressed in local coordinates, which by default map to the pixels on the screen; in other words, a pen width of 1.0 means that the lines drawn will be 1 pixel wide.

Redrawing

After `newFrame:` is called, the window sends the PaintView object a message with the `display` method, telling it (the object) to display itself. After all the proper setting up, the `drawSelf::` method, shown in Listing 12.6, is called. This is a predefined View method that is called when a View is first created, or when it needs to be redrawn (for example, because of resizing). It gets passed two parameters—a list of the areas to be redrawn and a counter telling how many there are. But for this program, you'll just redraw the entire PaintView object each time.

```
- drawSelf:(NXRect *)list :(int)count // redraw a PaintView
{
    [self lockFocus];  // lock into local coordinates
    PSsetgray(backColor); // use defined background color
    NXRectFill(&bounds); // fill entire PaintView object
    [self unlockFocus]; // unlock coordinates
    return self;   // as usual, return pointer
}
```

Listing 12.6. The `drawSelf::` method for the class PaintView

This method is set up so that it sets the entire PaintView to the current background color. It does this in four steps. First, it sends the `lockFocus` message to itself, which sets up things with the Window Server so that you can draw in the PaintView object using its local coordinate system. It then calls a PostScript function, `PSsetgray()`, which sets the gray shade to be used for any drawing. Then it calls `NXRectFill()`, passing it the `bounds` instance variable (inherited from the View class), a rectangle defining the drawing area of the PaintView object; as you might guess, `NXRectFill()` fills it with the current drawing color. Finally, it sends the `unlockFocus` message to itself, freeing PostScript to draw elsewhere on the screen.

HANDLING EVENTS: THE mouseDown: METHOD

The last method to be implemented is mouseDown: , shown in Listing 12.7. Like newFrame: and drawSelf::, this method is already defined for the View class; you're redefining it because you want it to work differently than the View version. As you can see, it's longer and more involved than the other methods you've looked at. Let's look at it a piece at a time.

```
- mouseDown:(NXEvent *)ptr // handle mouseDown event
{
  NXPoint   mLoc,oldLoc;   // mouse locations
  NXEvent  *nextEvent;     // event record
  BOOL    looping = YES;   // control drawing loop
  int       oldMask;     // old event mask
  int      checkMask;     // mask for events in loop

   oldMask = [window eventMask]; // get current event mask
  checkMask = NX_MOUSEUPMASK | NX_MOUSEDRAGGEDMASK;
         // set up mask for inside loop
  [window setEventMask:(oldMask|checkMask)];
         // add mouseDragged, mouseUp events
  [self lockFocus];     // lock into local coordinates
  oldLoc = ptr->location;  // get mouse location at event
  [self convertPoint:&oldLoc fromView:nil];
         // convert to local coordinates
  PSsetgray(penColor);    // use defined drawing color
  PSsetlinewidth(penWidth);  // use defined line width
  while (looping) {    // do while mouse button is down
     nextEvent = [NXApp getNextEvent:checkMask];
        // get any mouseUp, mouseDragged events
     looping = (nextEvent->type != NX_MOUSEUP);
        // check if user released button
     if (looping) {     // if not, then keep drawing line
        mLoc = nextEvent->location; // get new mouse location
        [self convertPoint:&mLoc fromView:nil]; // convert
        if ((mLoc.x <> oldLoc.x) | (mLoc.y <> oldLoc.y)) {
           // if mouse has moved, then draw
           PSnewpath();     // start new path
```

continues

Listing 12.7. The mouseDown: method for the class PaintView

```
         PSmoveto(oldLoc.x,oldLoc.y); // draw from old location

         PSlineto(mLoc.x,mLoc.y);  // to new location
         PSclosepath();    // end of new path
         PSstroke();    // draw path as a line
         [window flushWindow];   // update screen image
         oldLoc = mLoc;    // remember new location
      }
    }
  }


  [self unlockFocus];   // unlock coordinates
  [window setEventMask:oldMask]; // restore old event mask
  return self;    // as usual, return pointer
}
```

Listing 12.7. *continued*

Programs that are created to use the Application Kit and Display PostScript are **event driven**. This means that they respond to events, such as moving the mouse, pressing a key on the keyboard, clicking the mouse buttons, and so on. One of the advantages of the Application Kit is that most of this event handling is done for you automatically; you handle just those events that you need to.

When an event does occur, an **event record** is created and passed along to the appropriate object or objects to be handled. This event record is a data structure (a C `struct` variable) that has a number of fields containing information, such as the type of event, where it occurred, and so on. A number of predefined constants (such as NX_MOUSEUP) can be used to determine what the event was. In a similar fashion, you can use other constants (such as NX_MOUSEUPMASK) to create an **event mask**, a collection of bits that determines which events get passed to a particular object.

Stepping through mouseDown:

Here's a general overview of how this version of mouseDown: works. When you press the left mouse button while the cursor is over the PaintView object (inside your Scribble window), a "mouse down" event occurs, and an event record with that information is created and passed to the Scribble window. The window, recognizing that it occurred within the PaintView object, passes it (or, technically, a pointer to it) on to the `mouseDown:` method given above. This method then does the following:

1. Modifies the window's event mask so that it will also get mouseDragged (moving the mouse with the left button still held down) and mouseUp (releasing the left mouse button) events

2. Goes into a loop that checks only for mouseDragged and mouseUp events; if a mouseDragged event occurs and the mouse has moved, it draws a line from the mouse's old position to the new one

3. When a mouseUp event occurs, it leaves the loop, restores the window's old event mask, and then exits

When `mouseDown:` is called, it gets passed a single parameter, a pointer to an `NXEvent` data structure (the event record). In addition, it declares several local variables. `mLoc` and `old-Loc` are data structures that contain the X and Y coordinates of where the mouseDown and mouseDragged events occur. `nextEvent` is an event record data structure used within the loop to retrieve mouseDragged and mouseUp events. `looping` is a boolean (true or false) variable that determines when the loop is done; it's initially set to "yes" (true), then gets reset each time through the loop based on the type of event received. `oldMask` is used to hold the event mask for the Scribble window, while `checkMask` is used to screen out all but the mouse-Dragged and mouseUp events.

Analyzing the Code

Now let's examine the code, line by line. The first statement sends the `eventMask` message to `window`, a View instance variable pointing to the enclosing (Scribble) window. This method returns the window's current event mask, which gets stored into `oldMask`. The variable `checkMask` gets set to a value allowing mouseUp and mouseDragged events (the "|" character is the C operator for bitwise logical OR). The third statement then modifies the window's event mask by including those two events in the list of events accepted by the window.

The `lockFocus` method has already been discussed; again, it's used here to tell PostScript to set everything up to the PaintView object's local coordinate system. `oldLoc` gets assigned the window coordinates of where the mouseDown event occurred; the call to the `convertPoint:fromView:` method changes those to PaintView coordinates. The calls to `PSsetgray()` and `PSsetlinewidth()`, as you might guess, set the color and pen width for the lines that are going to be drawn.

Next comes the loop. The first thing that happens is that the `getNextEvent:` message is sent to NXApp (the program's Application object; more on this later), asking for any mouse-Dragged or mouseUp events. The variable `looping` is then set false if the event is mouseUp, true otherwise. If `looping` is true, then the mouse location for that event is saved into `mLoc` and then converted to local coordinates. It's compared against `oldLoc` to see if the mouse has been moved; if so, then drawing takes place.

This drawing code illustrates some aspects of Display PostScript. As you may remember from Chapter 7, drawing in PostScript is done using **paths**. The path defines the image to be used; you can then trace it with lines, fill it, or do other things. To start a path, you call `PSnewpath()`. You then call all the drawing routines to create the image itself, here done by moving to the old mouse coordinates and then drawing a line to the new ones. You then signal the end of the path with a call to `PSclosepath()`. Once done, you draw the path with the appropriate routine; in this case, `PSstroke()`.

All this drawing is taking place in an off-screen buffer. To **flush** it to the window on the screen, that is, to cause it to be drawn on the screen display, you need to send the "`flushWin-dow`" message to the window itself. You then set the old mouse location equal to the new one, and then start over again.

Once you release the mouse button, and the loop exits, only a few things remain to be done: unlocking the coordinate system, restoring the old event mask, and (as usual) returning a pointer to the PaintView object. At which point the method is done, having handled the events specific to it and having left all others alone.

That completes the implementation of the PaintView object class. Having written this, you could now go back into Interface Builder and create a different application that used one or more PaintView objects, and you would already have this code ready to use. Or you could go back and add methods to this implementation, allowing you, for example, to modify the `backColor`, `penColor`, and `penWidth` values with controls, such as sliders, buttons, or text fields.

THE REST OF THE PROGRAM

You've now completed the other half of your task: you've written (or, at least, typed in) the Objective C code that puts the "brains" behind the interface you created with Interface Builder. This went into the files "PaintView.h" and "PaintView.m", which should now be safely saved to disk. But before you compile it all together, let's take a look at the other files that Interface Builder generated.

THE MAIN PROGRAM: Scribble.m

For your program to run, it needs to create an instance of the Application object, load in the "Scribble.nib" interface produced by Interface Builder, and then tell the Application object to run. This is done in the `main()` function, which is the main body of any traditional C program. Objective C is no exception: the "Scribble.m" file created by Interface Builder has a `main()` function that does just what is required, as shown in Listing 12.8.

```
#import <appkit/Application.h>
#import <soundkit/soundkit.h>
#import <appkit/Slider.h>
main(argc,argv)
int     argc;
char    *argv[];
{
  NXLinkUnreferencedClasses(Sound);
  NXLinkUnreferencedClasses(Slider);
  NXApp = [Application new];
  [NXApp setAppName:"Scribble"];
  [NXApp loadNibSection:"Scribble.nib" owner:NXApp];
  [NXApp run];
  [NXApp free];
}
```

Listing 12.8. The "Scribble.m" file created by Interface Builder

The file has just the one function in it, `main()`, which has the standard C parameters: `argc` (argument count) and `argv` (list of argument strings). These apply principally if you run the program from the Mach shell; that is, if you type the name "Scribble" at a Mach system prompt, follow it with additional parameters, and then press Return. In that case, `argc` has the number of "arguments" (separate words or strings) on the line, and `argv` has the arguments themselves, as separate strings.

`main()` itself has just seven statements. The first two, which may not be generated by future versions of Interface Builder, call `NXLinkUnreferencedClasses()`. This function doesn't actually do anything; the call is placed here by Interface Builder to force the Objective C compiler to link in from the Application Kit the code implementing each of these classes (Sound and Slider objects).

The next statement invokes the factory method `new` for the class Application, creating a new instance of that object and assigning it to `NXApp`. `NXApp` is a predefined global variable that should point to the program's Application object (which you've just created). The next statement loads the "Scribble.nib" code created by Interface Builder and linked into the Scribble code file. By loading this section, it links all the code and data there with the Application object pointed to by

NXApp. The next statement simply sends the Run command to NXApp, which will then start handling events and continue to do so until its `terminate:` method is invoked. After that, the free message tells NXApp to release any memory it might have left around.

MAKING IT RUN

Having made the indicated changes to the "PaintView.h" and "PaintView.m" files, you're now ready to compile your program again and to run it. Make sure you save these changes out, then get into the Shell (or Terminal) application again, make sure that you're in the right spot (type "`ls -l`" at the prompt to see all the files), and then type "`make`", pressing Return afterward (as with all Mach commands). Note that since you made no changes to the "Scribble.m" file, it is not recompiled; only "PaintView.m" is.

HANDLING ERRORS

You may get some errors during compilation. If you do, chances are they are due to one of the following problems:

1. You have the capitalization wrong on the name of a method, variable, or other identifier. Objective C, like standard C, is case-sensitive; in other words, it considers "PaintView," "Paintview," and "paintview" to be three different names.

2. You inserted an unnecessary colon (":") into, or left a necessary one out of, a method name. There should be one colon for each parameter passed to a method; methods with no parameters should have no colons in their name.

3. The names of instance variables and methods given in the interface file ("PaintView.h") don't match exactly the names used in the implementation

("PaintView.m"). This is really just a rehash of points number 1 and 2, but it indicates where the problem may exist.

In any case, if there are errors you will get an error message in the Shell window telling the type of error and giving the line number where it occurred. If you get back into Edit, you can use the Find/Line Number command to jump to a specific line. When you've corrected the errors, save the file to disk, get back into the shell, and compile again.

Once the recompilation is successful, enter "Scribble" at the system prompt. This will bring up your Scribble program. You can click on its window to make it the active application, and then start drawing. You should also be able to use the Clear command in the menu to clear the drawing area. Test out Info, Hide, and (last, of course) Quit as well.

Congratulations. If you followed these steps, you should have created your first working NeXT application.

COMMENTARY

Object-oriented programming has been around for some time, and it certainly is not unique to the NeXT system. Its benefits are reflected by Apple's growing support for C++ and MacApp, IBM's licensing of NextStep, and Microsoft's commitment to an object-oriented programming environment for Presentation Manager. Likewise, prototyping software packages for these various systems are becoming more popular and more sophisticated. What is unique is NeXT's commitment to object-oriented programming as the standard development approach, and the way that commitment is reflected in all levels of the system software. Bundling a complete object-oriented development system with every NeXT computer is also unprecedented, though it does follow the UNIX tradition of including development tools with the operating system.

One of the classic pitfalls in program development is the communication gap between the person requesting the program and the programmer developing it. With Interface

Builder, a nonprogramming designer can actually create the desired user interface, establishing not only the detailed layout but also the connections between various objects. A programmer can then take the resulting files and make them work, that is, add the required functionality. If the designer decides to change the interface, especially in terms of the layout, the programmer may not have to change a line of code and might not even have to recompile. And as of Release 0.9, the programmer will be able to create new objects which the designer can then use and test within Interface Builder. The result: a significant division between interface and function, allowing each task to be handled by that person who can do it best. If the designer and the programmer happen to be the same person, development time is decreased that much more. The results may be more far-reaching than anyone expects.

Appendix A: SOFTWARE AND HARDWARE PROUCTS

The NeXT system is a powerful hardware platform and comes with a significant amount of useful software. Even so, the system as it comes from the box may not meet all your needs. It doesn't need to; there are many third-party companies developing products for the NeXT system. Some of these products are already available, others will be appearing in the coming months or years.

The purpose of this chapter to is give you a look at what's available or under development, so you can know whom to contact for your particular needs. Most of the information here is based on press releases, so little evaluation or comparison is given, because of lack of first-hand experience. Future editions of this book will contain hands-on information and assessment of products, but for now, *caveat emptor*. If you're interested in a given product, be sure to check with the corresponding company about actual features, pricing, and availability.

SOFTWARE

The NeXT computer forms a bridge between personal computers and UNIX workstations, and the software being developed reflects that position. Some of the products are already available on personal computers, such as the Apple Macintosh; others have been available previously on Sun, DEC, and Apollo work-stations. And, of course, some are being developed for the first time on the NeXT system itself.

DESKTOP PUBLISHING

Given its use of Display PostScript for both screen and printer imaging, its high-resolution display and its standard laser print-er, the NeXT system is a good candidate for **desktop publishing** (DTP), that is, the use of a personal workstation for document layout, preparation, and production. A number of the products currently being developed for the NeXT system are designed to be used in desktop publishing; here are some of the ones which should be available soon.

Adobe Illustrator/Adobe Type Library

Adobe Systems, Inc., is one of the better known companies in the DTP marketplace. They are, of course, the firm that devel-oped the PostScript language and that, with NeXT, developed Display PostScript. It's not surprising, then, that they are devel-oping products for the NeXT system.

Adobe Illustrator, initially developed for the Macintosh and since brought up on MS-DOS systems, is being developed for the NeXT system as well. It is a graphic design and illustration program, which allows you to create images from scratch or to process scanned images (though there are no scanners currently announced for the NeXT system).

The NeXT system comes with four basic fonts: Helvetica, Times, Courier, and Symbol. These four obviously may not meet all your needs. Because of that, Adobe also plans to offer their Adobe Type Libraries, sets of fonts which you can then use in all your applications and documents. Adobe has some 400-plus fonts available, which will be marketed in a variety of combinations.

For pricing and availability information, contact Adobe Sys-tems, Inc., 15875 Charleston Road, Mountain View, CA 94039, or call (415) 961-4400.

Artisan and Pres•To

Artisan is a graphics creation (painting) package that has been available on various UNIX workstations (Sun, HP, Silicon Graphics, Sony) for the last few years. Its creator, Media Logic Incorporated, is developing a version for the NeXT system as well. Announced features in the NeXT version of Artisan include support of 8-bit grayscale images (with dithered representations on the NeXT system), a variety of image and text manipulation abilities, compositing of images (including 8-bit alpha channel support), and various paint and drawing tools.

Media Logic is also developing Pres•to, a new program designed for doing single-page layouts. According to company literature, Pres•to will combine text processing, object-based graphics, and continuous tone painting.

The announced price for Artisan is $695; that for Pres•to is $795, with discounts for quantity and for educational institutions. Announced availability for both products is July 1989. For more information, contact Media Logic Incorporated, 2501 Colorado Avenue, Suite 350, Santa Monica, CA 90404, or call (213) 453-7744.

ClickArt EPS Business/EPS Illustrations

The Macintosh made popular computerized libraries of **clip art**, scanned or drawn images which you can incorporate into whatever documents you prepare. T/Maker Company, well-known in the Macintosh market for its ClickArt libraries on disk, is offering two of their libraries—EPS Business Art and EPS Illustrations—on a single optical disk. This collection comprises some 400 illustrations in Encapsulated PostScript (EPS) format, with a variety of topics (both business and general) covered.

According to T/Maker literature, this product is already available and has an announced introductory price of $295. For more information, contact T/Maker Company, 1390 Villa Street, Mountain View, CA 94041, or call (415) 962-0195.

FrameMaker 2.0

FrameMaker 2.0 is a well-known DTP package for UNIX workstations from Frame Technology Corporation. It incorporates a

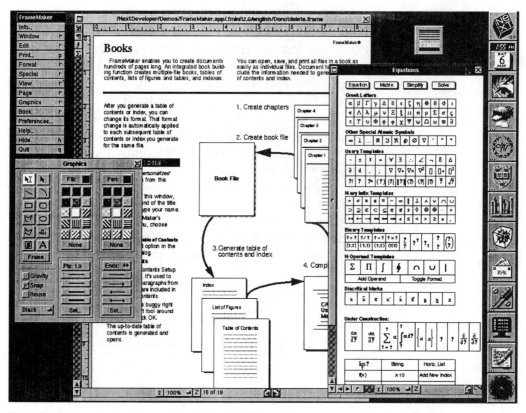

Figure A.1. A pre-release version of FrameMaker 2.0

long list of features, including page layout, word processing, layout of equations and formulæ, simple graphics creation, integration of text and graphics, capture and inclusion of screen images, and book-generation tools, such as index generation, pagination, headers and footers, and so on. Figure A.1 shows a screen shot generated using an early pre-release version of this software.

The announced price for FrameMaker 2.0 for the NeXT is $995, with substantial discounts (up to 50%) for quantity purchases. For availability information, contact Frame Technology Corporation, 2911 Zanker Road, San Jose, CA 95134, or call (408) 433-3311.

BUSINESS AND PRODUCTIVITY

The announcement in April 1989 about the NeXT/Business-land deal caught a lot of people by surprise, including a lot of software companies who had postponed doing development on the NeXT system because they felt their expertise was in business, not in education. Because of that, there isn't a long list of announced products, though quite a few of those firms have since started NeXT development. Even so, here's a list of what's known to be under development.

Knowledge Retrieval System

KnowledgeSet has announced plans to bring up a version of its Knowledge Retrieval System (KRS) for the NeXT system. This software is designed to allow the user to rapidly search through large bodies of text and graphics for specific items or references. Searching can be linear or hierarchical, and hypertext-like cross-referencing is available. KRS is already available for UNIX, Macintosh, and MS-DOS systems.

For pricing and availability information, contact KnowledgeSet, Inc., 888 Villa Street, Suite 500, Mountain View, CA 94041, or call (415) 968-9888.

NEXPERT *OBJECT*

Neuron Data is in the business of making expert system software—NEXPERT *OBJECT*—for PCs and workstations. They have separate development and run-time platforms with object-code compatibility, so that you can, for example, develop the expert system database on a Macintosh and use that database on an IBM PC or a Sun workstation. Features include a hybrid rule-and-object-based approach, ability to embed expert systems within conventional programs, ability to access command database and spreadsheet formats from within the expert system, and so on. Neuron Data has already ported its run-time package to the NeXT computer; it is unclear whether the development package will be ported, but you can do development on other computers (Macintosh, Sun, etc.) for the NeXT system.

For pricing and availability, contact Neuron Data, 444 High Street, Palo Alto, CA 94301, or call (415) 321-4488.

DeskPad

Foundation Publishing is developing DeskPad, a personal productivity package designed (according to press releases) to help you get more functionality out of your NeXT system without having to buy a variety of different software packages. DeskPad is especially designed to aid users familiar with personal computer systems in making the transition to the NeXT system. Planned features include access to key UNIX utilties via the NeXT user interface, system management functions, and several helpful utilities.

For pricing and availability, contact Foundation Publishing, 5100 Eden Avenue, Edina, MN 55436, or call (612) 925-6027.

DEVELOPMENT

The NeXT computer comes with a complete development system, including Interface Builder, Objective C, Allegro Common Lisp, Edit, and the standard UNIX utilities (though not the usual UNIX compilers). Even so, there are often compelling reasons to look for additional development software, depending upon your needs and circumstances. Here are some of the products known to be under development.

Absoft FORTRAN 77 Compiler

Absoft has developed its globally optimizing FORTRAN compiler for a number of 68000-based systems. They plan to release their compiler for the NeXT system with object-oriented syntax extensions to give you full access to the Application, Array Processing, Music, and Sound kits.

The announced price is $750 for universities. For availability and other information, contact Absoft Corporation, 2781 Bond Street, Rochester Hills, MI 48309, or call (313) 853-0050.

BUG-56

One of the NeXT system's more unusual features is the Motorola DSP56001 digital signal processor chip, support in software by the Music Kit, the AP Kit, and the use of dspwraps within Objective C programs. BUG-56, from Ariel Corporation, is a symbolic debugger for the DSP56001, allowing you to develop low-level 56001 code in an interactive NeXT environment.

For pricing and availability information, contact Ariel Corporation, 433 River Road, Highland Park, NJ 08904, or call (201) 249-2900.

Displaytalk

Display PostScript is a complete programming language in and of itself. Personal Displaytalk, from Emerald City Software, is designed to help you learn and develop code in Display PostScript, using an interactive NeXT-based environment. This includes on-line tutorial help, observation of PostScript stacks and variables, and display of generated images. Professional Displaytalk also provides interactive source-level debugging (with tracing and breakpoints), multi-window editing, and a Display PostScript dictionary browser. Figure A.2 shows a beta version of Displaytalk in action.

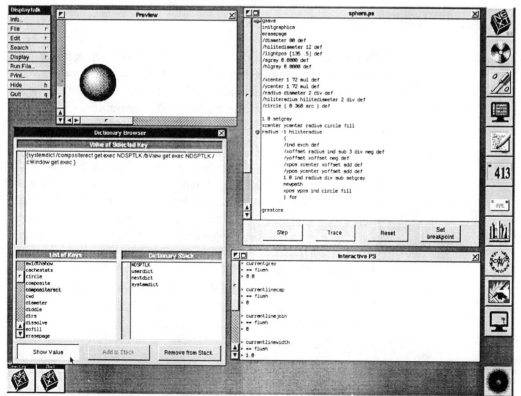

Figure A.2. A beta version of Professional Displaytalk

The announced price is $595 for Personal Displaytalk, $995 for Professional Displaytalk. For availability information, contact Emerald City Software, 800 Menlo Avenue, Suite 102, Menlo Park, CA 94025, or call (415) 324-8080.

DSP5600 SIMULATOR AND CROSS ASSEMBLER

Motorola, manufacturers of the DSP56001 digital signal processing chip, have their own development software for the 56001. One package is a DSP simulator that allows you write and test 56001 code on other systems. The other package is a cross-assembler that produces 56001 assembly language code. Both packages run on a variety of computers, including MS-DOS and Macintosh systems.

For pricing and availability information, contact Motorola, Inc., Digital Signal Processors Group, 6501 William Cannon Drive West, Austin, TX 78735-8598, or call (512) 891-2030.

MUSIC AND SOUND

The NeXT system is known for its music output; a major part of the NeXT introduction in October 1988 was a duet between a professional violinist and a NeXT system. Expect to see a lot of music-oriented software for the NeXT computer.

Performer

Mark of the Unicorn is another firm well known for its music software on the Macintosh. One of their products, Performer, is a MIDI sequencing package, allowing you to record performances on electronic instruments, and then edit, transform, and merge those performances using the NeXT system. You can use Performer to play back the resulting performance on your electronic instruments.

For pricing and availability information, contact Mark of the Unicorn, 222 Third Street, Cambridge, MA 02142, or call (617) 576-2760.

EDUCATION

Many different universities are currently developing software for teaching and research for the NeXT system, including Brown University (foreign languages), the University of Michigan (multi-media performance), Dartmouth University (medical research, foreign languages), and Carnegie-Mellon University (speech recognition).

MATLAB

MATLAB, from The MathWorks, is an interactive system for numerical computations, including polynomial evaluation, statistics, signal processing, and linear algebra. It is (according to press releases) widely used for research and classroom teaching, running on MS-DOS systems, Macintoshes, Sun and Apollo workstations, and VAX minicomputers; The MathWorks is now developing a version for the NeXT system. Since a copy of the product was not available at press time, there is no easy way of telling how it stacks up to Mathematica (which comes free with the NeXT system).

For pricing and availability, contact The MathWorks, Inc., 21 Eliot Street, South Natick, MA 01760, or call (508) 653-1415.

COMMUNICATIONS

While the NeXT system comes with Ethernet hardware and software, there is little communications software for serial and modem channels. Expect to see some telecommunications packages available soon. In the meantime, here's what's been announced.

DEC Terminal Emulators

White Pine Software has several software packages out for the Macintosh computer that allow it to emulate certain text and graphics terminals manufactured by Digital Equipment Corporation (DEC). They are in the process of making one or more of these products available on the NeXT system. Using such a product, you can use the NeXT system as a DEC terminal hooked up to DEC mainframes and minicomputers.

For pricing and availability information, contact White Pine Software, P.O. Box 1108, Amherst, NH 03031, or call (603) 886-9050.

HARDWARE

Because of its use of Macintosh-compatible SCSI and serial ports, the NeXT system already has a large number of hardware products available for it. For example, you can connect most modems or other serial devices, using the appropriate cables; you can use most Mac-compatible SCSI hard disks; and you can hook it up to various PostScript laser printers, such as the Apple LaserWriter II. The purpose of this section is to point out hardware products that are specifically adapted for the NeXT system.

MASS STORAGE AND BACKUP

The NeXT motherboard has an internal SCSI adapter identical to that found on the Apple Macintosh computers. This means that you can purchase hard disks designed for use with Macintoshes and plug them into your NeXT system. Ads for such disk drives can be found in periodicals such as *Macworld*, *MacUser*, and *MacWeek*. Other SCSI-based mass storage devices should also be easily configurable for the NeXT system; however, you will most likely have to wait for the manufacturers to provide the necessary device drivers before buying and using such devices.

JETSTREAM Tape Backup System

One such device is the JETSTREAM tape backup system from Personal Computer Peripherals Corporation (PCPC). This system allows you to back up your hard disks and/or optical disks to 8mm video tape, storing up to 2.3 gigabytes on a single tape. Press releases claim transfer rates of up to 14.4 megabytes/minute.

The announced price for this system is $5995; availability is planned to coincide with Release 1.0 of the NeXT system software. For more information, contact PCPC, 4710 Eisenhower Blvd., Building A4, Tampa, FL 33634, or call (813) 884-3092.

NETWORKING AND COMMUNICATIONS

The NeXT system comes with the hardware and software necessary to attach it to a standard Ethernet network, as well as having serial ports for modems. Even so, there may still be needs for special hardware to fit special circumstances. Here's a look at some of the products being developed.

DaynaFILE

Dayna Communications is the manufacturer of DaynaFILE, an MS-DOS-compatible floppy disk drive for the Macintosh. They are now developing an external SCSI floppy disk drive to allow you to read from and write to MS-DOS and UNIX format 3.5" floppy disks.

For availability and pricing, contact Dayna Communications, Inc., 50 S. Main Street, Fifth Floor, Salt Lake City, UT 84144, or call (801) 531-0600.

Ethernet PhoneNET

A standard Ethernet network is build using special Ethernet coaxial cabling. Farallon Computing, Inc., has developed a widely-used product, PhoneNET, which allows Ethernet nodes to communicate using standard twisted-pair telephone cabling. They plan to adapt their product for the NeXT computer, allowing NeXT systems to be networked using telephone cabling and to be hooked up to existing PhoneNET networks.

For pricing and availability, contact Farallon Computing, Inc., 2201 Dwight Way, Berkeley, CA 94704, or call (415) 849-2331.

GatorBox

The GatorBox from Cayman Systems is a "gateway" box designed to connect Ethernet networks (such as the NeXT system uses) with LocalTalk networks (such as the Apple Macintosh uses). The result is that you can share files between NeXT and Macintosh systems, within certain limitations based on file content and format. It also means that you can use a NeXT system as a file server for a LocalTalk network. Cayman also plans to introduce software to allow electronic mail between NeXT and Macintosh systems.

The GatorBox is currently available. For pricing and other information, contact Cayman Systems, Inc., 25 Landsdowne Street, Cambridge, MA 02139, or call (617) 494-1999.

LARGE-SCREEN DISPLAYS

While the MegaPixel Display is crisp and clear, it is not designed for presentations or lecturing. For that, you need a larger screen display or a projection system. No specific product is currently announced for the NeXT system; however, there is one announced product that will let you connect an assortment of screens to a NeXT computer.

RGB 111 NeXT Computer Interface

This device, from Extron Electronics, attaches between the MegaPixel Display and the NeXT motherboard. It transforms the NeXT video signal into red, green, blue and composite sync signals, generating a true grayscale image for external monitors and projection displays. Those displays must have a horizontal scan frequency of at least 63 KHz; a list of compatible displays is available from Extron.

The announced price is $370. For availability and other information, contact Extron Electronics, 13554 Larwin Circle, Santa Fe Springs, CA 90670, or call (213) 802-8804.

MUSIC AND SOUND

The inclusion of the DSP56001 digital signal processor, as well as built-in stereo output and digitizing monaural input, makes the NeXT system a natural one for applications dealing with music and sound. Several of the hardware products under development for the NeXT reflect that strength.

Digital Ears

The MegaPixel Display has an 8-bit, 8 kHz CODEC digitizer built into it: good enough for voice and casual sampling, but not sufficient for high-quality input. Metaresearch, Inc., is developing Digital Ears, a CD-quality digitizer that connects to the NeXT system via the DSP port on the motherboard. This allows for 16-bit, 44.1 kHz stereo input (or 88.2 monoaural kHz input). Software bundled with Digital Ears includes Digital Ears Recorder (see Figure A.3) and Monster Scope.

The announced price is $825, with immediate availability. For more information, contact Metaresearch, Incorporated, 516 SE Morrison, Suite M-1, Portland, OR 97214, or call (503) 238-5728.

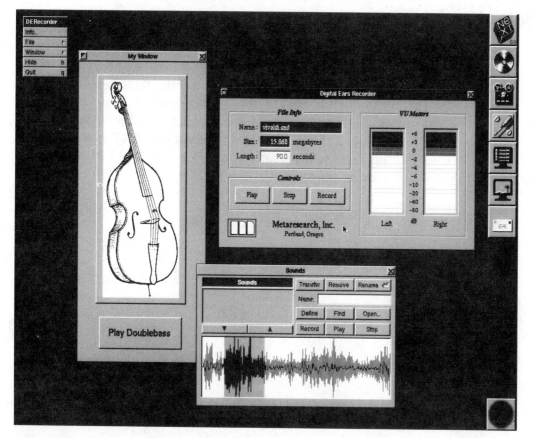

Figure A.3. A pre-release version of Digital Ears Recorder

NeXT MIDI Adapter

Release 1.0 of the NeXT system software will include support (in the Music Kit) for MIDI encoding and decoding of musical performance information. However, you still need to have some way of connecting the NeXT system to MIDI devices. Opcode Systems, manufacturers of MIDI software and hardware for the Macintosh, has developed a MIDI interface for the NeXT computer, allowing you to hook up MIDI cables via one of the serial ports.

For pricing and availability information, contact Opcode Systems, Inc., 1024 Hamilton Court, Menlo Park, CA 94025, or call (415) 321-8977.

FUTURE PRODUCTS

The products listed above represent only a fraction of those actually under development. Major firms such as Lotus Development Corporation (makers of 1-2-3), Informix (WingZ), Ashton-Tate (dBASE IV), Hayes (modems), Cricket Software (Cricket Draw, Cricket Graph), and Autodesk (AutoCAD) all have development teams working on NeXT projects. What products will actually come to market, and in what form, remains to be seen.

Appendix B:
SYSTEM ADMINISTRATION (RELEASE 0.9)

The Mach/UNIX environment underlying Workspace Manager provides a rich, complex operating system capable of supporting multiple users, network interactions, and various hardware devices. Of course, this means that someone—a **system administrator**—has to look after those things. Some of these tasks are built into Workspace Manager. But there are still some tasks you'll have to handle using the UNIX shell (see Chapter 11).

There are entire books about UNIX system administration; this, obviously, isn't one of them. Instead, what this appendix covers are a few key tasks you may have to deal with that aren't handled directly in Release 0.9.

IMPORTANT NOTE: the methods described in this chapter are valid only for Release 0.9. They may not be handled as described here in Release 1.0; if you have Release 1.0, follow directions in your NeXT documentation.

NETINFO

The NetInfo application is designed to make it easy for you to integrate your NeXT system into a network. NetInfo won't be discussed here—for details on how to use it, see your NeXT documentation—but it's still important. That's because NetInfo keeps much of the system information in a special file. This includes information about users and groups. If you want to update this information, you must follow three steps:

- Extract it from the NetInfo file
- Do the appropriate updating
- Save it back into the NetInfo file

The first and last steps are handled via two special commands, `nidump` and `niload`, which you can use from the shell. These commands extract and save NetInfo information, respectively. For example, if you type the following shell command:

```
localhost>nidump group .
```

the current group information will be dumped to the screen. Likewise, if you were to type the command

```
localhost>niload group .
```

the shell would expect you to sit and enter in all the group information, line by line, followed by a Control-d to signal end of input. For more information on these commands, use the `man` command at the shell prompt (i.e., "`man niload`" and "`man nidump`").

INPUT/OUTPUT REDIRECTION

Obviously, these commands are not much use as they stand. However, you can use a special feature of the shell, called **redirection**, to make these commands more useful. This is the ability to have output that normally would appear on the screen redirected to a file instead. Likewise, you can have the contents of a file used in place of input that you would type in. This is a simple, yet powerful facility, and one that has implications far beyond what you're learning here.

Here's an example of redirection. If you wanted to capture the group information used by NetInfo into a file named "groupStuff", you could use the following command:

```
localhost>nidump group . >groupStuff
```

The greater-than symbol (">") tells the shell to send all output generated by the `nidump` command to the file "groupStuff." If you were to then edit "groupStuff", you could save those changes to the NetInfo file with the command

```
localhost>niload group . <groupStuff
```

As you probably guessed, the less-than symbol ("<") tells the shell to read the contents of "groupStuff" and send it, line by line, to `niload` as if you were typing it in.

To learn more about redirection and how to use it with the UNIX shell, consult the UNIX books listed in the bibliography.

USER VERSUS SUPERUSER

As a user on a NeXT system, you have your own account, with a user ID, a password, your own directory, and certain privileges. Something you'll quickly learn is that there are limits to those privileges. There are commands that you won't be allowed to use, data you can't change, even files you can't read. The purpose of this, as explained in Chapter 9, is to provide security for each user and to protect the system files from being damaged or otherwise modified by users.

Obviously, though, there may be cases when you want or need to have greater privileges than your regular account gives you. In such a case, you'll want to become a **superuser**, that is, someone who has the authority to read, modify, search, or (where applicable) execute any file or directory.

To do this, you'll need to log on as "`root`", a predefined superuser account. You can do this one of two ways. First, you can just type "`root`" as your user ID when you log on to the NeXT system, then give the appropriate password. You can tell that you're now a superuser, because the shell will give you a "#" prompt instead of a ">" prompt. When you first install the NeXT system software, "`root`" (like "`me`") doesn't have a password; if a number of people are going to be using a given NeXT computer, you'll probably want to log on as "`root`" and use the `passwd` command to set up a password. If you do so, *be sure to write that password down!* You could find it very frustrating (not to mention embarrassing) to have everyone (yourself included) unable to log in as "`root`".

There is a second, more convenient way to log on as "`root`": the `su` (substitute user) command. This command lets you log on as another user without having to log off first. The format is "su *userID*", where *userID* is the user login ID of the account you want to log on as. If a password is required, you'll be prompted for it; you'll then be logged on as that user, with all the corresponding privileges. To log off as that user, just type "exit" at the shell prompt; you'll then continue as you were before using su.

As you might guess, you can use su to log on as "root", and, in fact, if you omit the user ID, "root" is assumed. If "root" has a password, you'll be asked for it. Once you're logged on as "root", the prompt changes to "#", as mentioned above, and you've got complete authority.

CHANGING GROUPS

Not all users can use su to log on as "root," even if they know the password. They have to belong to a certain **user group** known as "wheel". (Groups were discussed in Chapter 8.) To get into this group, your user ID has to be placed in the group information within the NetInfo file. To edit this information, you have to have superuser privileges, so log into the NeXT system as "root", launch the Shell or Terminal application, and type the following command:

```
localhost#nidump group . >/etc/group
```

The file "/etc/group" is the one which would hold this information in a regular UNIX system, so that's the one we'll use to make the updates.

Now, use the Directory Browser to find "/etc/group," and double-click on its name or icon (which will bring up Edit). One of the lines will look something like this:

```
wheel:*:0:root,me
```

Type in your user ID after "me" (with a comma in between), save the file to disk, and get out of Edit. Your last step is to save the revised group information back into the NetInfo file. To do this, type the following command:

```
localhost#niload group . </etc/group
```

Note that this time, you are using "/etc/group" as input. Once this is done, log out, then log back on under your regular user

ID. You should now be able to use the su command within Shell or Terminal to log on as "root."

One last word about being a superuser: be very, very, very careful about deleting files, especially about using any kind of wildcard character or the -r (recursive) option. As a superuser, you could literally wipe out the entire system. A good rule of thumb is to never use wildcard characters in a deletion as a superuser—or, if you must, to use the -i option so that it asks you to verify the deletion for each file.

CREATING AND UPDATING USER ACCOUNTS

If you are going to have several users on your NeXT system, you'll probably want to set up an account for each one. This gives a degree of privacy and protection for each user, and also protects the system itself from unauthorized (or even authorized) users. This section will show you how to create new user accounts, modify existing accounts, and delete accounts you no longer want.

User account information, like group information, is stored in the NetInfo file. However, that file is updated automatically for you as you use the commands below to create, modify, and delete accounts.

SETTING UP A NEW USER ACCOUNT

As you might expect, it takes superuser status to create a new user account. The command nu (new user), with the -a (add) option, lets you do this. You invoke it like this:

```
localhost>su root
Password:
localhost#nu -a
<answer all the questions>
localhost#exit
localhost>
```

The section labeled <answer all the questions> is where all the work gets done. nu will prompt you for each of the following items of information, offering defaults for the last four. (You can accept a default by pressing Return.)

- Login: the user ID which the person will use when logging in. This is usually all lowercase and derived from the person's first and last names (`ezra`, `jdow`, `jerryp`). It's up to 8 characters long, all alphanumeric (letters and numbers).

- Password: the password the person will use when logging in. This should be at least 6 characters long, and can include any printable character (letters, digits, punctuation, etc.).

- Name: The user's actual name ("Ezra Shapiro", "Joanne Dow", "Dr. J. E. Pournelle").

- Userid: The user's ID number, a unique integer used to identify the user. The system will prompt with an available value; unless you have some reason for doing otherwise, accept what it offers.

- Groupid: The group to which the user belongs. There are a number of such groups; unless you know what you're doing, take the default.

- Login dir: The home directory for the user. The default is the one you'll probably want to use; it'll be created automatically for you.

- Login sh: The shell to be used; just take the default.

Once you're all done, your choices will be presented to you, and you'll have the chance to make any changes. If you're satisfied, you'll be asked if you want to add more users; you can either do so, or you can quit.

MODIFYING AN EXISTING ACCOUNT

You may have to make changes to an existing account, most notably if the user has forgotten his or her password. To do this, use the `nu` command with the -m (modify) option:

```
localhost>su root
Password:
localhost#nu -a
<answer all the questions>
```

```
localhost#exit
localhost>
```

You'll be asked for the user's login name or user ID number, presented with the current settings, and given the chance to modify any or all of them. After each change, you are given the option of selecting another setting to modify, discarding (throwing away) all the changes made to that user's account, or accepting the changes made. When you're all done, the system files are updated accordingly.

DELETING A USER ACCOUNT

Finally, you may want to delete an existing account, either for security reasons or because the user is no longer using the system. There are two ways of doing this. The "safer" way is to use the nu command with the -d (delete) option:

```
localhost>su root
Password:
localhost#nu -d
<answer the question 'y' or 'n'>
localhost#exit
localhost>
```

You'll be prompted for the user's login name or user ID number, shown with the current settings, and asked if you want to delete this account. Note: If you answer "y", nu will delete the user's home directory and all its subdirectories (using the command rm -rf /bootdisk/Homes/login), so if there are any files to be saved, be sure that they've been copied or moved elsewhere first. Also, the user's ID is left in the system files, preventing the ID from being reassigned.

If you're sure you want to do this, there is a short cut of sorts: use the -k (kill) option, followed by the user's login name or user ID number. For example, to delete the account belonging to "jdow", you could do this:

```
localhost>su root
Password:
localhost#nu -k jdow
<some information is printed here>
localhost#exit
localhost>
```

The effects are the same as the −d option, including the deletion of the user's home directory and all the files and subdirectories it encloses. In addition, the user's entry is deleted from the password file, allowing the login ID to be reassigned.

A NOTE ON CHANGING PASSWORDS

If you're familiar with UNIX, you probably know that you can change passwords using the passwd command in the shell. You should not use this command on the NeXT system, because it doesn't properly update the NetInfo file. If you want to change passwords, the best approach is to use the Password panel of the Preferences application (see Chapter 10). You can also use nu −m to change passwords, but it's a lot more work.

MOUNTING AND UNMOUNTING THE HARD DISK

If you're using a hard-disk-based NeXT system, you may go for long periods without booting from an optical disk. This makes sense; the hard disk has greater storage and much better performance. Having booted from the hard disk, you can easily mount and unmount the optical disk using the Workspace Manager menu (see Chapter 9). That way, you can keep the system files on the hard disk, and use your optical disks for backup and storage.

However, there may be rare instances when you want or need to be able to boot from an optical disk and still access the hard disk. For example, some sort of file damage may prevent you from booting off the hard disk, yet you still want to be able to get at the files that are already there. This section will tell you how to do that.

MOUNTING THE HARD DISK

Mach (and UNIX) talks about **mounting** devices or volumes; this means to "attach" them to the system file hierarchy so that they can be accessed. This implies that you have a place to attach them, so the first step (usually done just once) is to create a directory for them. You can then refer to that directory when mounting, accessing, or unmounting the volume.

To access the hard disk, you must first mount it; to mount it, you must have created a directory for it. Here are the commands which will help you to do just that:

```
localhost>cd /
localhost>mkdir hda
localhost>mkdir hdb
```

As it turns out, the typical NeXT hard disk is divided into two partitions or volumes; one contains all the standard applications, data files, and documents; the other is a largely unused volume set aside for additional use and expansion. Each can be mounted or unmounted separately. For that reason, you have now created two new directories (hda, hdb), one for each volume (/dev/sd0a, /dev/sd0b). In most cases, you'll find that you only need or want to mount /dev/sd0a, but it doesn't hurt to be prepared.

To do the actual mounting, using the mount command, you need to have superuser privileges (see the section on that earlier in this appendix). If you're logged on as "root", then you're all set; if you're logged on as "me" (or on another account that has the proper privilege), then use the su (substitute user) command to log on as "root":

```
localhost>su root
Password:
localhost#
```

You'll be prompted for the password only if you've set one for the "root" account; also, remember that you can omit "root" and su will assume that. Also, notice that the prompt changes to a "#" character. You're now ready to mount the volume(s):

```
localhost#mount /dev/sd0a /hda
localhost#mount /dev/sd0b /hdb
localhost#exit
localhost>
```

That's it. You'll now find that you have access to the optical disk through the directories /hda and /hdb, both through the shell and through Workspace Manager (though you might check to see if you need to do a Window/Update command to make it visible through the Directory Browser or a directory window).

That last command above, exit, was used to log off as "root". Note that the prompt changed back to a ">" character. If you were to type "exit" again, you wouldn't log off the NeXT system, but you would close the Shell or Terminal application that you were using, just as if you had select the Quit command from its main menu.

UNMOUNTING THE HARD DISK

When you're done with the hard disk, you can unmount it to prevent any accidental (or deliberate) modification or deletion of files. The command syntax is even simpler: umount *directory*, where *directory* is the directory where the volume was mounted. Again, you need to be a superuser, so you'd probably use the following sequence of commands:

```
localhost>su root
Password:
localhost#umount /hda
localhost#umount /hdb
localhost#exit
localhost>
```

This logs you on as "root," performs the dismounting, and then logs you back off.

If you get a "Device busy" message after attempting to dismount a volume, it means that some application is still making use of that volume. Most likely, you're still logged onto one of the directories on the hard disk, either as the current working directory for the shell, or with a directory window or browser under Workspace Manager. For the shell, just type "cd" with no parameters to switch back over to your home directory on the optical disk. For Workspace Manager, close all directory windows and browsers except for the main one (which won't close), then log that one to /. Once you're done with all that, go back to the shell and attempt to unmount the hard disk volume again.

GLOSSARY

address bus A set of address lines used to select a particular address within memory. Each line represents a bit in a binary value, so that N address lines result in 2^N different addresses (0 through $2^N - 1$).

address line An electrical line found within an address bus; each line has a value of 0 or 1.

application dock The area along the right edge of the screen where you can "park" application icons.

Application Kit The NeXT library of objects used to implement the NeXT user interface.

attention panel A panel which you must react to before you can do further work for a given application.

binary Having to do with base-2 numbers (0, 1, 10, 11, 100...). Used heavily within computer systems because of the on/off nature of computer logic.

bit The basic unit of information; short for binary digit. A bit has one of two values, which can be thought of as 0 or 1, OFF or ON, FALSE or TRUE, etc.

Black Hole An icon always visible on the desktop. You delete files and directories by dragging their icons over this one and then releasing them.

boot device The device from which the operating system is loaded in when you boot the computer. On the NeXT system, this device is the optical disk, the internal hard disk, or another system connected via Ethernet.

bootstrap code The set of instructions (usually stored in ROM and on the boot device) that executes when you first turn on the power; the bootstrap code in ROM loads in the bootstrap code from the boot device.

Brightness keys Two keys to the right of the Power key which you can use to adjust the screen brightness.

buffer A section of memory used to hold information being transferred.

bundling The practice of including software with a computer system.

bus A set of address or data lines used to transfer information between different components within a computer (memory, processors, slots, etc.).

button A small graphical image that you "press" on, using the cursor, to initiate some action.

byte A unit of information. On most micro- and minicomputers, it consists of eight (8) bits, which means that it can hold $2^8 = 256$ different values. Typically, each character (letter, digit, etc.) in a document takes up exactly one byte.

cache A small section of memory used by a processor to hold the contents of recently accessed locations in main memory. When those locations need to be accessed again, the processor can read from the cache instead of from main memory.

clicking Moving the cursor over an image (such as an icon) and clicking the mouse button once.

close button The button found at the right end of the title bar in windows, panels, and submenus; by clicking on the close button, you can make the window disappear.

control One of a set of graphical objects (buttons, sliders, scrollers) that you manipulate directly using the mouse.

cursor An image (usually an arrow or I-beam) on the screen that you move with the mouse in order to select and manipulate images on the screen.

database A collection of information, usually in computer-readable form (that is, stored in one or more files on a mass storage device).

database server A program (or series of programs) that allows you to access a database, either directly or through other applications.

data bus A set of data lines used to read information from or write it to memory. Each line represents a bit in a binary value, so that N data lines result in 2^N different values (0 through $2^N - 1$).

data lines An electrical line found within a data bus; each line has a value of 0 or 1.

decimal Having to do with base-10 numbers (0, 1, 2, 3, 4, 5, 6, 7, 8, 9, 10, 11, 12 ...). Used heavily by most humans because of the number of fingers we have.

desktop publishing The use of a personal workstation for document layout, preparation, and production; abbreviated DTP.

device drivers Small programs used by the operating system to communicate with external hardware devices (hard disk drives, scanners, etc.).

digital signal processor A processor designed to perform certain signal processing tasks; abbreviated DSP.

direct memory access The ability of hardware devices to directly transfer information to and from memory without involving the CPU; abbreviated DMA.

Display PostScript The graphical imaging system used to create images for both the screen and the laser printer.

DMA See **direct memory access.**

dock See **application dock.**

double-buffering The technique of using two buffers so that one buffer can be filled with incoming data while the other buffer is being read.

double-clicking Moving the cursor over an image (such as an icon) and clicking the mouse button twice in rapid succession.

dragging Moving the cursor over an image (such as an icon), holding the mouse button down, and moving the cursor, causing the image to move as well.

DSP See **digital signal processor.**

DTP See **desktop publishing.**

Encapsulated PostScript Files with an ".eps" extension contain graphical images stored as a series of PostScript commands; abbreviated EPS.

EPS See **Encapsulated PostScript.**

floating point   Having to do with real numbers (3.14, -982.32×10^{20}, 0.0).

floating point unit   A processor designed to carry out operations on floating-point numbers; abbreviated FPU.

font   A selectable text style. The NeXT system comes with several fonts, including Helvetica, Times, Courier, and Symbol.

FPU   See **floating point unit.**

GB   See **gigabyte.**

gigabyte   1,073,741,824 (2^{30}) bytes; abbreviated GB.

icon   A small graphical image on the screen, used most often to represent a file or directory.

ICP   See **Integrated Channel Processor.**

integer   Having to do with whole numbers (42, -78832, 0).

Integrated Channel Processor   The custom chip on the NeXT motherboard that implements the 12 I/O channels; abbreviated ICP.

Interface Builder   The NeXT application that allows you to build graphical user interfaces for applications.

KB   See **kilobyte.**

key window   The window that is currently dealing with any keys that you might press; distinguished by having a black title bar.

kilobyte   1024 (2^{10}) bytes; abbreviated KB.

log in   Gaining access to the NeXT system by giving it your login ID and password.

login ID   A short (4 to 8 character) unique identifer for each user on a NeXT system. Used to log into the system; also used in the "owner" field for any file or directory you create.

log out   Ending your work session on the NeXT; the computer is then left in a "locked" state until you or someone else logs in again.

main menu   The principal menu of a given application. When you are working with an application, its main menu is always visible.

main window   The principal window of the application you're working with. This is usually the key window also, but not always; for example, the main window could hold a document you're working on, while a panel (such as the Font panel) could be the key window.

MB See **megabyte.**

megabyte 1,048,576 (2^{20}) bytes; abbreviated MB.

memory Semiconductor chips used to hold information and programs while they are being accessed by the computer's processors. The two basic types are random access memory (RAM) and read-only memory (ROM).

memory management unit Special hardware circuitry to help implement virtual memory and multitasking; abbreviated MMU.

menu A list of commands associated with a particular application, appearing as a column of buttons in a window.

miniaturize button A button in the title bar of windows; when you click on it, the window turns into an icon (known as a miniwindow).

miniwindow An icon that represents a window that has been miniaturized. Clicking on a miniwindow opens it again.

MMU See **memory management unit.**

modal A condition in which your actions are limited because the program you are using is in a given mode.

multiplexed Some computer systems use the same set of lines for address lines and data lines; that is, they use one bus as both the data and address buses. In that case, those buses are referred to as being multiplexed.

multitasking The ability of an operating system to run several programs or tasks simultaneously.

Optical Storage Processor The custom chip on the NeXT motherboard that implements the controller for the optical disk drive, as well as the logic for the internal and external SCSI ports; abbreviated OSP.

OSP See **Optical Storage Processor.**

page fault When a task requires a page that isn't currently in memory, a page fault occurs; the operating system then suspends execution of the task, loads the required page in from the swapping file, and lets the task continue.

pages Sections of memory (usually of equal size) allocated to tasks by the operating system.

panel A window, usually small, and usually containing controls and other information.

parameter RAM The small amount of RAM in a computer system whose contents are maintained by a battery even when the power is shut off.

password A "secret code" which you give to the computer when logging in.

physical memory The actual memory found in a computer system. Tasks can appear to have more memory than is available by use of virtual memory techniques.

pipelining Some processors can fetch the next instruction while decoding the current one; this is called pipelining.

pressing Moving the cursor over an image (such as a control) and holding the mouse button down.

print queue The list of documents waiting to be printed.

RAM See **random access memory.**

random access memory Any memory that can be directly read from and written to; abbreviated RAM. Most RAM loses its contents when the power is turned off (however, see parameter RAM).

read-only memory Memory that can only be read from, but which maintains its contents even when the power is turned off; abbreviated ROM.

record A collection of related information; a database usually consists of one or more records.

resize button A button found in the title bar of windows and panels; it is used to resize them.

Rich Text Format A method of describing complex documents (with multiple fonts, sizes, and styles) using simple ASCII text; abbreviated RTF.

ROM See **read-only memory.**

RTF See **Rich Text Format.**

scroller A control used to move (horizontally or vertically) through a document that is too big to fit within the view displaying it.

SIMM See **Surface-mount In-line Memory Modules.**

slider A control that lets you move a button back and forth, selecting discrete values.

submenu A menu that appears when a command in a menu is selected.

Surface-mount In-line Memory Modules These hold 1 MB of RAM each and snap in to the NeXT motherboard; abbreviated SIMM.

swapped out Data or code that is currently being stored out on disk instead of residing in memory.

swapping file A special file used by the operating system to hold all the pages belonging to a given task that aren't currently in memory.

switch A button that you can select between an "on" and "off" setting.

system build Formatting and transferring information onto a mass storage device (optical or hard disk) so that you can boot from that device.

task A program, application, or other utility that has been loaded into memory for execution.

TB See **terabyte.**

terabyte 1,099,511,627,776 (2^{40}) bytes; abbreviated TB.

text field A control used to display and enter text (strings, numbers, and so on).

thesaurus A reference work that groups together words that are similar (or opposite) in meaning.

title bar The area across the top of a window or menu that allows you to drag the window or menu around the screen.

user interface The collection of techniques and images that allow the user to control the computer.

virtual memory The memory that a task thinks it has (as opposed to the physical memory actually assigned to the task). Virtual memory is implemented by an operating system using pages and a swapping file.

Volume keys The two keys to the left of the Power key; they allow you to adjust the volume of the speaker in the MegaPixel Display.

window   A rectangular box presenting information on the screen.

Window Server   The NeXT process that passes events to applications and handles drawing commands from those applications.

word processing   The process of creating, editing, and printing text.

Workspace Manager   The application that provides the NeXT system with a graphical user interface.

WYSIWYG   Acronym for "what you see is what you get"; refers to the correlation between how a document appears on the computer screen and how it appears when printed.

ANNOTATED BIBLIOGRAPHY

This book, of course, barely scratches the surface of all the topics involved in the NeXT computer system. And there are other surfaces to be scratched. Here are some books to guide you. They don't represent an exhaustive list—far from it!—nor an exclusive one; they just happen to be the books that the author has owned and can recommend. Also note that this list does not include the technical documentation from NeXT, Adobe, and numerous other sources. Feel free to do additional research at your nearest bookstore.

THE HARDWARE

Obviously, there aren't a lot of books specifically about the NeXT hardware—the one you're reading right now is about it. However, there are a few manuals that give technical details about the processors used on the NeXT motherboard. Here they are.

MC68030 Enhanced 32-Bit Microprocessor User's Guide.
    Englewood Cliffs, N.J.: Prentice-Hall, 1989.
MC68881/MC68882 Floating-Point Coprocessor User's Guide.
    Englewood Cliffs, N.J.: Prentice-Hall, 1987.
DSP56000 Digital Signal Processor User's Manual. Motorola,
    Inc. , 1986.
These are typical hardware manuals, describing architecture, instruction sets, and timing signals in extensive detail. Not for the faint hearted.

UNIX

Since the UNIX operating system is widely known and used, there are many books dealing with a number of aspects of it. Most of these will be of some help to you, provided you want or need to learn more about the operating system on the NeXT computer.

Don Libes and Sandy Ressler, *Life with UNIX: A Guide for Everyone.* Englewood Cliffs, N.J.: Prentice Hall, 1989.
If there's just one book you get about UNIX, this should be it. It will teach you the basics of what you want and need to know; you can then pick and choose among the books below to figure out everything else. Its greatest assets are an intelligent, light-hearted (but not condescending) tone and a sense of history, explaining how the various aspects and attributes of UNIX came to be.

Paul Wang, *An Introduction to Berkeley UNIX.* Belmont, Calif.: Wadsworth Publishing Company, 1988.
The UNIX-compatible operating system sitting on top of Mach is compatible with BSD (Berkeley Standard Distribution) 4.3 UNIX, so this introduction to using BSD UNIX is the most appropriate. Its size and scope can be a bit overwhelming, though.

P. J. Brown, *Starting with UNIX.* Reading, Mass.: Addison-Wesley, 1984.
This tome, by contrast, is rather slim and very friendly in tone. It's a good volume for those of you who don't want to be told more about UNIX than you care to know.

Eric Foley, *UNIX for Super-Users.* Reading, Mass.: Addison-Wesley, 1985.
A good companion volume to *Starting with UNIX.* It tells you more of the advanced features of UNIX, but still doesn't get into excruciating detail. On the other hand, becoming a superuser often means learning to deal with those excruciating details.

David Fielder and Bruce H. Hunter, *UNIX System Administration*. Indianapolis, Ind.: Hayden Books, 1986.
A must if you're going to be a system administrator for a NeXT computer; in other words, if you've got your very own system, or if you're in charge of a system that several people will use. Large sections of the book don't apply much to the NeXT system but are still worth browsing through to understand why things are set up a certain way.

Bart Anderson, Bryan Costales, and Harry Henderson, *UNIX Communications*. Indianapolis, Ind.: The Waite Group/ Howard W. Sams & Company, 1987.
All you need to know about mail, USENET, news, and uucp. Again, not for the faint-hearted, but definitely a necessity if you're training yourself to be a NeXT system administrator.

PROGRAMMING

Here's where you can find the most books applicable to your tasks. If you don't know the C programming language, there are a host of books to teach it to you; the ones listed here are some of the better ones. Likewise, there are several books dealing with programming in a UNIX environment. However, at print time there is only one book dealing specifically with Objective C and none dealing with programming on the NeXT computer system. Not yet, anyway.

THE C PROGRAMMING LANGUAGE

As mentioned, there are a lot of books here. Unfortunately, not all of them are helpful or worth the price. These three books make a good basic library.

Stephen G. Kochan, *Programming in ANSI C*. Belmont, Calif.: Hayden Books, 1988.
A good introduction to programming in C. The Objective C compiler on the NeXT system is ANSI-compatible; you should be able to type in and run all the examples in this book.

Rex Jaeschke, *Portability and the C Language*. Belmont, Calif.: Hayden Books, 1989.

Anyone contemplating doing serious C development should read this book, as should anyone who is learning C. It does much to explain both the strengths and weaknesses of C.

Samuel P. Harbison and Guy L. Steele, Jr., *C: A Reference Manual, 2nd ed.* Englewood Cliffs, N.J.: Prentice-Hall, 1984.

Another must for any serious or would-be C programmer. This explains the syntax and semantics of the C programming language, based on the draft reports of the ANSI standard. A third edition of this book will undoubtedly be out soon; if it's available, get it instead.

OBJECTIVE C

This book about Objective C was published prior to the introduction of the NeXT system; several are now in the works (including the author's own).

Brad J. Cox, *Object-Oriented Programming: An Evolutionary Approach*. Reading, Mass.: Addison-Wesley, 1987.

Brad Cox is one of the original designers of Objective C; this book explains, step by step, the concepts behind Objective C and object-oriented programming in general. Be warned, though, that some of the Objective C syntax has changed since this book was written, and that this book has no information *per se* about programming on the NeXT system.

PROGRAMMING UNDER UNIX

As you write more complex programs, you'll want to know how to take advantage of UNIX system calls and facilities. Here's a trio of books, each with its own strengths, that should help you out.

Brian W. Kernighan and Rob Pike, *The UNIX Programming Environment.* Englewood Cliffs, N.J.: Prentice Hall, 1984.
The standard reference work about programming under a UNIX environment. Like the classic "K&R" (Kernighan and Ritchie) work on C, this book is terse and understated, sometimes telling you just a little less than you want to know. Still, it's worth having.

Stephen Prata, *Advanced UNIX: A Programmer's Guide.* Indianapolis, Ind.: Howard W. Sams & Company, 1987.
This volume is excellent for the programmer who wants to know more about UNIX but has no intentions of rewriting the kernel. It actually spends a good deal of time covering shell script programming, and then gets into making UNIX system calls from C. A more light-hearted and readable approach than the other two books in this section.

Keith Haviland and Ben Salama, *UNIX System Programming.* Reading, Mass.: Addison-Wesley, 1987.
A meaty, no-nonsense guide to interfacing C to UNIX. Don't let the volume's slim appearance fool you; this book has more hard information about UNIX system programming than anything I've found.

POSTSCRIPT

Chapter 8 mentioned three standard references on the PostScript imaging language. Here they are:

Adobe Systems Incorporated, *PostScript Language Reference Manual* ("The Red Book"). Reading, Mass.: Addison-Wesley, 1985.
This volume documents the syntax, semantics, and commands of the PostScript language. Note that this does not include the various extensions added for Display PostScript; nevertheless, it's a valuable book to have.

Adobe Systems Incorporated, *PostScript Language Tutorial and Cookbook* ("The Blue Book"). Reading, Mass.: Addison-Wesley, 1985.
An excellent step-by-step tutorial in using PostScript. It has lots of sample programs to type in, which you can test out using utilities such as Yap (found in /NextDeveloper/Demos).

Glenn C. Reid and Adobe Systems Incorporated, *PostScript Language Program Design* ("The Green Book"). Reading, Mass.: Addison-Wesley, 1985.
A more advanced book talking about issues in PostScript program design.

INDEX